ARRESTING DESTRUCTION

RECOVERY FROM ALCOHOLISM

MARTIN NOEL-BUXTON

Order this book online at www.trafford.com/
or email orders@trafford.com

Most Trafford titles are also available at major online book retailers.

Art Work by: Tim Walters.

Printed in Victoria, BC, Canada.

ISBN: 978-1-4251-8894-8

*Our mission is to efficiently provide the world's finest, most comprehensive
book publishing service, enabling every author to experience success.
To find out how to publish your book, your way, and have it available
worldwide, visit us online at www.trafford.com*

Trafford rev. 4/7/2010

www.trafford.com
North America & International
toll-free: 1 888 232 4444 (USA & Canada)
phone: 250 383 6864 ♦ fax: 812 355 4082

TABLE OF CONTENTS

FOREWORD

Most of us have shelves of biographies, in amongst which are the autobiographies. Increasingly they consist of the turgid reminiscences of politicians who have achieved high office not on account of their great ability or intellect, but, rather, because of their ability to stay out of trouble: their blandness. Alternatively, we are fed page after page of tabloid-style memoirs of "celebrities" yet to celebrate their thirtieth birthdays! Coincidentally, they often contain anecdotes of the authors' intake of alcohol or drugs, but there is seldom anything to be learned from them.

I suppose they are mostly written for financial gain or because of vanity but, either way, one rarely thinks more of the subject at the end of the book than one did at the beginning. Often, a great deal less.

Martin Noel-Buxton's autobiography – if that is what it is – is rather different. Martin has no vanity, and it certainly wasn't financial gain that caused him to put pen to paper. His is a book and a tale of unusual and raw honesty in an age of excuse and prevarication.

It is also far more than a tale of one man's journey through alcoholism to sobriety. The insights, observations and conclusions are those one would expect from an academic work, but without extensive research and experimentation this cannot be an academic work. It is, however, what used to be called a scholarly work, and should find its place not amongst the self-help or therapy books that are now so popular, but perhaps closer to the spiritual and theological works so beloved by our Victorian ancestors.

The study of alcoholism is relatively new, and debate still ranges between scientists, psychiatrists, doctors and others about its causes, and how to treat it.

With great courage and honesty and with extraordinary intellectual vigour Martin has dived into that debate, using his own life as an example of the illness and the misery it causes, as well as his recovery from it and the contentment he has now found.

To put it more simply, this is one of those rare autobiographical books that enhances both the respect and the affection in which the author is already held. It is also a significant contribution to the study of alcoholism.

Mancroft
London
October 2008

ACKNOWLEDGEMENTS

Many have contributed to the writing and publication of this book.

It all started when my longstanding friend Nick Walters said that there was a book in what I had experienced. It did not occur to me that I would be writing one, after all, how on earth did one write a book? However with Nick's invaluable support from start to finish I have produced this book. Without his help and advice it would never have been started let alone published.

Nick's brother, Tim Walters has produced the artwork for the front cover and I would like to thank him very much.

Among my family members who made the book's publication possible, I would like, in particular, to mention my brother, Simon Buxton, who spent many hours editing a late draft of the book and whose efforts and suggestions enabled me to produce a book hopefully fit for publication.

I would like to thank the members of my family who contributed to the publishing costs: Peter Adam, Sarah Adam, my brother Richard Buxton, Simon Buxton, my sister Clare Inskip and my children Charlie and Lucy Noel-Buxton. Without them my book would never have seen the light of day.

I am also very grateful to Benjamin, Lord Mancroft for agreeing to write the Foreword. We were for some twelve years colleagues on the Board of the Addiction Recovery Foundation.

1

MY EXPERIENCE AND HISTORY

MY HISTORY

I was born in Surrey into a titled English family in December 1940. My father was an alcoholic but my mother was not. My full brother was born in 1943. It was wartime and I suspect that my parents did not spend much time together before or after my brother's conception. I remember living only with my Scottish mother and my brother in Scotland until she died of cancer in the summer of 1949. Despite my mother's arrangements to the contrary, on her death my father successfully claimed custody of my brother and me. We left Scotland and we came to live with our father and his new wife in England. I was immediately sent away to boarding preparatory school.

These latter events in particular were no doubt traumatic for me and I remember very little of my life before my mother's death. I was reasonably happy at my prep school after the initial shock had worn off but the arrival of my brother resulted in my dropping from top of the class to nearly bottom. I showed little, if any, responsibility and I was passed over for head of set. It was, I believe, a good school and I had instilled in me the basic skills and attributes characteristic of what in the 1950s would no doubt have been referred to as the "English gentleman". I passed the common entrance exam with no difficulty and went on to public boarding school.

My public school was neither of the two well known ones to which the males (including my father) of my family traditionally go. That my father did not send me to his famous public school was to be a lasting and deep resentment of mine until I realized that he had sent me to the public school he did out of love – he loathed his time at his public school.

In my first year or so in junior house I was clearly somewhat disturbed playing the part of the P. G. Wodehouse character Bertie Wooster. Again I demonstrated no responsibility failing even to become a deputy house monitor (the lowest monitor or prefect rank) until the very end of my time at the school. I believe that my first alcoholic drink was at school at the age of sixteen or seventeen. It was a bottle of brown ale which I did not like and I did not finish it. I do not remember having another alcoholic drink until I was up at Oxford University.

I did well at school academically taking science "A" levels. I passed the entrance exam to my father's Oxford College with a year to spare and with the option of reading science or Modern Greats (philosophy, politics, and economics). I chose Modern Greats. Going up to Oxford presented a problem. I was not quite nineteen and everybody else seemed to be so much older mostly having done National Service in the armed forces. I sought to grow up rapidly by smoking a pipe but I could not handle the technicalities involved. However I found that alcohol provided the required confidence.

In my day, provided you passed an exam called "Prelims" at the end of your second term, you were virtually certain of staying up for the full three years of the Bachelor of Arts degree course. I made sure I passed Prelims and, once I had, I ceased to take any real interest in academe, doing as little work as possible and devoting myself to the pursuit of pleasure. I took to drinking wholeheartedly as an effective enhancement to my hedonistic lifestyle, mistaking pleasure for happiness. Alcohol soon started adversely to affect my life. I did virtually no work for most of my time at Oxford. I did not even revise for Schools (the final examinations). I came down with a third.

On coming down, having inherited quite a lot of money from my mother, I did nothing in particular until my father took issue with me and said that I had to do something. "What" presented a challenge. My father, being of independent means, had had no real work experience. He did recall, though, that we had a cousin who was a lawyer. He had been called to the Bar but had become a solicitor. In the event, I took Articles with his firm in the City of London in about 1963.

In 1964 I married my first wife. Her mother and father had divorced and her mother had married a close cousin of mine. A great deal of drinking went on at his house in the country and I drank a great deal there most weekends. I also drank heavily at home and in wine lodges at lunch time in the City during the week. My first marriage did not last long. We separated after 18 months or so and we were divorced in 1968 when I was twenty-seven.

I believe that my alcoholism took on a life of its own in my twenties. After my first wife and I separated my full brother and I had bought a weekend cottage together in Suffolk and we regularly drank together in the local pub. I remember him telling me that my drinking had qualitatively changed some time in my late twenties. I did not understand what he meant nor did I begin to comprehend what was happening to me until I began my recovery many years later with the help of members of Alcoholics Anonymous (AA).

I qualified as a solicitor in 1966 and started work as an assistant solicitor. The senior partner in my first firm after qualification wisely discerned that all was not well with me and he advised counselling. I attended regular counselling sessions for various periods over a number of years but to little, if any, effect. That I might be an alcoholic was never addressed. I became a partner with a firm in the City in 1971. By this time it had occurred to me that it might be a good idea if I stopped drinking so much alcohol.

I would regularly drink a considerable amount in the evening waking up with a bad hangover but still making it into work. I would resolve not to drink so much again yet I knew that I would soon resume drinking at the same level. Sometimes I would have to have a quarter or half bottle of vodka before I went into my office. Often I would have to have a drink as soon as the pubs opened. I would normally drink at lunch time. I really wanted to stop the vicious cycle of drinking, hangover and more drinking. I wanted to stop drinking as much as I did, in the way that I did, but somehow I was compelled to drink the amount I did in the way I did – once I had started I could not control how much I drank. Nevertheless, I could not contemplate living without drinking.

I met the woman who was to become my second wife and we married in 1972. In 1973 a doctor specialising in the field of alcoholism and other dependence advised me that I was an alcoholic. My wife also recognised that I had a drink problem and we went to see our doctor. He recommended that I go to AA. My then wife has since reminded me that I did indeed go to one AA meeting but returned vowing never to go again. I did nonetheless agree to take Antabuse pills. Antabuse is the trade name for the medication disulfiram which produces a highly unpleasant reaction when even a small amount of alcohol is ingested. It was, however, far too easy not to take the pills and I became an erratic binge drinker. In about 1978, I eventually agreed to Antabuse implants and these kept me from drinking alcohol for some three years.

My father died in 1980 and I succeeded to his title, becoming Lord Noel-Buxton. I did not drink. By this time we had two children and I had become a full equity partner in my firm specialising in company, commercial and intellectual property law. When my second wife and I separated in 1981 I drank again but quickly went voluntarily into a treatment centre in Somerset. I was soon "sectioned" out of the treatment centre under the Mental Health Act and locked up in a secure hospital wing. I was diagnosed as manic-depressive and, after being discharged, I was taken straight to another treatment centre in Chelsea where I was treated both as an alcoholic and as a manic depressive. After a while I went back to work.

I survived for about two years without drinking alcohol during which time (in 1982) my second wife and I were divorced. One Friday, in late 1983, I decided I would take a week off. I also decided to have a gin and tonic. As a result I was in blackout for at least a week ending up back in the Chelsea treatment centre I had been in before with a broken arm. After I came out of my alcohol induced coma I was taken to hospital to have my arm operated on accompanied by a twenty-four hour minder. Apparently, I had crashed my car and I was to appear before the Horseferry Road Magistrates for drunken driving.

After my operation I returned to the treatment centre and in due course

I attended Horseferry Road Magistrates Court where I was banned from driving for two and a half years and fined. My case was reported in the national press and my senior partner visited me in the treatment centre to say that if I did not resign my partnership, my partners would remove me under the terms of our Partnership Deed. I resigned. On being discharged I went home to live with my relatively new girl friend. She was to become my third wife in 1986. I soon found another position but I did not fit in and I was asked to leave after about eighteen months.

I thought I was special and different with unique problems incomprehensible to anybody else to which I could see no solution. It was only when, soon after leaving the Chelsea treatment centre in 1983, I spoke to another alcoholic from my own background, who said that he attended a particular AA meeting at lunch time in the City every week and would I like to join him, that I decided to attend that AA group and to try it out. It was only when I spoke to other alcoholics in the group that I realized that others had been through what I had and that I did not need to be entirely alone.

I continued not to drink and I attended that particular group each week. The group was for AA members who worked in the City. It lasted for two hours and members came and went as they pleased or as their work permitted. In order to facilitate this, the group was informal. It adopted none of the formalities of other AA groups in London and elsewhere. The only rule was one conversation at a time. We talked about alcoholism. I did not read any AA literature, I did not address its Twelve Steps and I did not become involved in mainstream AA at all.

With my remaining reserves of money running out, I eventually found another position in Norfolk in 1987 and my wife and I moved there. I went to a few conventional AA meetings in Norwich but soon stopped attending them. I continued not to drink alcohol except for one short lapse of an hour or so when I had at least one very large gin and tonic. With no signs of manic depression and with my doctor's consent I ceased my medication. We had a child.

In 1989 the firm I was with did not exercise its option to make me an equity partner and my engagement came to an end. I drank again. With no real prospect of work in Norfolk and with our house repossessed, we moved to Brighton where members of my wife's family lived. I managed to stop drinking again on my own. I was now insolvent and I entered into an Individual Voluntary Arrangement (IVA) which took care of my debts for the time being. I found work as a consultant with one and then another firm until after about four years my arrangement with the second firm came to an end by mutual consent. There was not the work for me viably to do. I drank again and my IVA failed. My third wife and I separated in August or September 1994. By willingly leaving all the possessions I had left except for some clothes and a few personal items with her I had effectively lost absolutely everything.

Deeply depressed, all I could think of was drink and death but one day early in October 1994 I experienced something which resulted in my ringing AA and attending an AA meeting instead of continuing to contemplate suicide. Some sort of distinct turning point had occurred. In hindsight I see this as my conversion. I had received a letter stating that I would have to vacate the flat in which I was lodging and I had nowhere else to go. This news caused me to buy and drink spirits rather than beer or wine for the first time since my last relapse. I became extremely drunk. That evening, by coincidence, my wife came round with her younger son by her first marriage to see how I was.

When I did not answer the door bell, her son climbed through a window into the flat and he let his mother into it. They found me in bed in a drunken stupor. I shouted at them to go away, which they eventually did, but I continued to shout at the wall in desperation at my situation. In not dissimilar circumstances Bill Wilson (1895-1971), who was AA's co-founder and leading proponent, in a deep depression which he later described as his "deflation at depth", had cried: "if there be a God, let Him show Himself". I cannot remember what I shouted, mostly profanities I suspect.

Wilson's cry, by his own account, was followed by his room being "blazed with an indescribably white light" and a conversion resembling the conversion of St. Paul to Christianity on the road to Damascus as described in the Bible. Wilson later referred to this experience as his "white flash" or "hot flash". After it he never again doubted the existence of God and he never again took an alcoholic drink. I did not experience such a conversion; I just passed out.

However, when I came to in the morning it was as if my brain had, in computer terms, crashed and re-booted with a distinctly different configuration. Before my "flash" I believed that nothing, except death, could stop me drinking again; after it I believed that I could stop with the help of AA. As a consequence, I decided to attend AA meetings again and, indeed, I attended an AA meeting in the evening albeit drunk. During the course of the meeting, I made a decision to attend another AA meeting, not having had a drink that day, one day soon.

I did indeed, without having drunk alcohol that day, attend another AA meeting on the 10th October 1994. From that day to this I have not had a drink. I went out to coffee with AA members after the meeting and it was suggested that I attended another meeting the following day. This I did not do, attending a local branch of the Department of Social Security (as the Department for Work and Pensions was then called) instead, to claim benefit. But I did attend a meeting the day after that and I soon found myself attending at least one meeting a day for several months. At coffee, I spoke to one man in particular who made a great deal of sense. For the first few meetings which we both attended, he continued helpfully to talk to me before and after the meeting itself.

My conversion had resulted in a change of mind set. This reconfigured mindset contemplated the possibility of a sober future achievable by AA attendance. I felt reasonable confident that AA could show me how to live without drinking. In the weeks and months which followed my first few meetings, I started substantially to do what was suggested.

I soon moved back to London from Brighton. After a while, I asked someone seven years into recovery to be my sponsor and he agreed to help me in my recovery on an ongoing basis. I substantially followed his specific suggestions. He led by example which, as Albert Schweitzer (1875-1965) wrote, "is not the main thing in influencing others. It is the only thing." He took me through the Twelve Steps included in the AA programme, and I continue to practise my interpretation and understanding of them as they have developed to this day while regularly attending and involving myself in AA meetings and maintaining close friendships with other AA members.

While it was an alcoholic from my own background who effectively introduced me to AA in 1983, my first AA sponsor, eleven years later in 1994, was an alcoholic from a completely different background to mine. As well as taking me through the Twelve Steps, he supported me on my journey into recovery for the first few years of it. I now have someone, with over twenty-five years of recovery, from my own background who although he is technically my sponsor, I suppose, is more like a particular friend. He does not play the role traditionally played by a sponsor of an alcoholic in the first few years of his recovery which involves taking the newcomer through the Twelve Steps, explaining the AA programme and giving substantial support to him. Rather my sponsor is the man with whom I discuss matters of particular concern to me from time to time.

After eighteen months or so back in London, I managed to obtain a Housing Association flat. Until a couple of years or so ago, I was able from time to time to find some gainful employment. I have rebuilt my life albeit on a small scale re-establishing relationships with my children, relatives and friends. Many AA members are my new found friends and supporters.

Since my last drink, I have maintained increasingly contented sobriety. I had not experienced this contentment while not drinking before. Eventually espousing AA has worked and is working for me. Being aware of my real alcoholism and what that entails, I do not dare substantially to desist from my current practices lest I return again to the hell for me of drinking alcohol. By attending AA, I am constantly reminded, particularly by those who return to AA after a relapse (which can be after a day or any number of days, months or years of abstinence), how vital it is to maintain vigilance in recovery. Alcoholism is cunning, baffling and powerful – and infinitely patient.

CHANGE

I hear in the AA rooms many other alcoholics describe their conversions where each had reached a point of desperation. I have read about others. The detail of their experiences may be different but their effect is the same, what I have called conversion amounting to qualitatively changed attitudes and actions. These qualitative changes have enabled the alcoholic to learn how to address life differently – in a way which makes it possible for them to live effectively without alcohol. In AA terms, the alcoholic adopts its Steps as a result of which he has a spiritual awakening and he recovers accordingly. In general therapeutic terms, because of the mindset change caused by his conversion, the alcoholic begins to adopt the altered attitudes and to learn and apply the skills conducive to sobriety, resulting in recovery.

This profound change can come about for any number of reasons and in any number of circumstances. In some cases the circumstances are like the circumstances surrounding my giving up smoking some years ago. I had accepted that it would be a good idea to stop but not yet. With a very bad chesty cough and wanting antibiotics I made an appointment with my doctor. He explained in some detail the likely consequences of my continuing to smoke. While I listened to him, I had no intention of stopping for the foreseeable future. Yet ten days later on the 9th February 2001, in the afternoon I ran out of cigarettes and I did not go out to buy more. I have not smoked since. Echoing another recovering alcoholic's words as regards his stopping drinking, I have no words to explain why my stopping smoking happened or how it happened when it did; it just did. Sometimes the alcoholic just knows, as he finishes a drink, that it is his last one.

In other cases an individual who really wants to stop drinking, perhaps one who feels that, having tried practically everything else, he has no other option, starts to attend AA meetings regularly. The AA message that recovery is possible can penetrate the individual's mindset sometimes slowly sometimes quickly. The alcoholic can find himself willing and, after a period of just turning up, beginning to believe that the AA programme could work for him. The kindly peer pressure of recovering alcoholics in the rooms of AA together with their contact outside the rooms can help the newcomer not to drink, or at least to keep attending meetings, until such time as his recovery begins. The other alcoholics can also support his continuing recovery once it starts. Many alcoholics cannot find recovery alone or amongst either their family or their friends but they can find it in the company of recovering alcoholics. A few months with alcoholics who enjoy living a sober life can make another alcoholic want sobriety more than another drink.

Marty Mann, the first woman eventually to achieve long term sobriety through AA, had a conversion not unlike mine. She like me ran into a personal crisis which filled her with a raging and righteous anger. As she fumed helplessly and planned to "get good and drunk and show them" her eye caught a sentence in the book lying open on her bed, which happened to be an early copy of *Alcoholics Anonymous* (AA's original text book), which read "We cannot live with anger". Her rage collapsed and in a moment of clarity she realized that she was not trapped. She saw that she was not helpless. She was free and she did not have to drink to "show them". As with me, her clarity had nothing to do with religion and everything to do with freedom. In the morning after my conversion I, too, felt that I was at last free to stop drinking.

For some alcoholics the conversion can be very low key. In one case, the last hangover of an alcoholic, who had previously attended AA to no real effect, had been on a Friday before a long weekend. After surviving the working day, the first difference between that late afternoon and all the others like it, was that he did not immediately go to a bar or home to have a drink. Instead he went to his club for a swim where strangely he did not have a drink. He was still so hung-over that he had to give up trying to swim. Instead he wrapped himself in a bathrobe and sat in a dark corner of the locker room feeling sorry for himself for two hours.

He does not know what happened during those two hours. All he knows is that after that time had passed he got dressed and made his way to an AA meeting that he had had no intention of attending. Everything about the group seemed different from the last time he had attended a meeting. Even the literature on display looked interesting. He bought a copy of *Alcoholics Anonymous*, listened intently and then, for the first time, he went for coffee with some members and continued to listen. The next morning he knew he did not have to drink.

My own story, which is not that unusual amongst real alcoholics who eventually manage to recover, illustrates the numerous difficulties attendant upon trying to answer such questions as to whether treatment or AA works and when an alcoholic enters recovery. For me it could be said that AA did not work in 1973 or really in the 1980s; but did in 1994 and thereafter. Formal residential treatment in one sense did not work for me at all, yet it kept me without a drink for two years or so and it re-introduced me to AA. Antabuse pills kept me without a drink from time to time and Antabuse implants for some three years. Having had treatment and with marginal AA help, I stayed without a drink, with only one very brief lapse, for about seven years up to 1989, but only to relapse.

Had I entered recovery before 1994, which was when I had my last drink? I would say not because my periods of abstinence were neither comfortable nor secure. Recovery is change and, essentially, I had not changed. Action should not be confused with change. I am now in "my teenage years" without a drink and I feel reasonably comfortable and secure in my sobriety. I believe that I have changed and that I may have truly entered into recovery at last.

I never found any of the formal one-to-one therapy sessions I had attended over the years before coming to AA particularly interesting or helpful. I was only too pleased when the practitioner thought that my sessions could end. It never occurred to me that they should continue indefinitely even when I could readily pay for them. In contrast I find AA meetings constantly interesting and I enjoy them and I look forward to attending them to my dying day. Alcoholics in recovery are fascinating people to be with, certainly for another alcoholic. I also communicate regularly with other recovering alcoholics by telephone and email.

Søren Kierkegaard (1813-1855) observed that "life can only be understood backwards, but it must be lived forwards". Accordingly, what I write now is written with the benefit of hindsight. I suspect that no particular thoughts about whether or not to drink alcohol crossed my mind until well into my twenties. Drinking was part of my lifestyle and that of my family and friends. Alcohol seemed to oil the wheels of life and the only substantial downside to begin with, seemed to be the hangover. But after falling down a stairwell amongst other incidents and with vague memories of bizarre behaviour in blackout, it must have occurred to me that it would be a good idea to drink less at least. Indeed in my late twenties I started to try to limit my consumption to, for example, one bottle of wine with dinner when I dined alone.

I had made efforts to stop drinking alcohol from the early 1970s. But my appreciation of the situation was totally unfocused. I suspect that if I had been pressed on the matter, I would have said that giving up alcohol was simply something the individual decided to do and that it was up to others (particularly members of the medical profession) to put in place appropriate outside factors that ensured that he adhered to his decision. I accordingly put myself into the hands of the medical profession. I sought to take the medication they prescribed and do what they suggested particularly when advised to go into treatment. But I kept on drinking again from time to time.

Until my conversion I appeared to have no effective long term way of combating my alcoholism. I felt defeated by it. I was conscious of it running continually in the background. I felt that something was very wrong with me. I thought I must be in some sense insane. I could not really cope with the difficulties of life and for years an abiding thought was that of suicide and how best to commit it. By late 1994 I felt that I could not live with or without alcohol.

However, by joining and engaging in AA, I have effectively arrested my alcoholism. Alcohol is no longer part of my life. After October 1994, I have experienced a number of crises which, before then, would almost certainly have triggered my drinking again. I now have a reasonably secure, stable and contented sobriety. I am coping with life well enough both in terms of dealing effectively with difficulties and in terms of my responses to life's strains and vicissitudes serving to prevent, avoid or control emotional distress.

The alcoholic can lose, as I have lost, his tense, aggressive, demanding, conscience-ridden self that feels isolated and at odds with the world. He can eventually, and I have, become a more relaxed, natural and realistic individual who can dwell in the world substantially on a "live and let live" basis. Conversions can supply an emotional tone to all subsequent thinking and feeling that can facilitate healthy adjustment.

SEEDS OF MY UNDERSTANDING

My study of science at school left me with a lasting fascination with science. My reading of philosophy at university left me with an enduring interest in philosophy. My practice of the law reinforced the enquiring nature of my mind which from school days had wondered about the origin of man in scientific terms and from university days his meaning in philosophical terms as well.

As I began to feel better my enquiring mind began to re-assert itself and I wanted to understand why I had been unable effectively to control my drinking before my conversion, what happened then and why I have been able to cope with life without alcohol since then. I started to study the literature relating to AA together with the scientific literature on alcoholism and to read a great deal more besides which I thought might assist me in my quest to understand my alcoholism and my recovery from it. Perhaps aspects of philosophy, religion and science would prove relevant to my enquiry.

I began to understand that, as a real alcoholic, I had not been able to, nor could I, consistently predict on any drinking occasion how long I would drink or how much alcohol I would consume. I now appreciate that, if I was again to take an alcoholic drink, I would sooner or later lose control and cause great damage. I had tried to drink normally, that is to say, largely conforming to standard, usual, typical or expected patterns, countless times without success and with more or less disastrous results. I had readily admitted well over thirty years ago that I was an alcoholic when a doctor said I was one but with the grandiosity typical of an alcoholic I quipped that it was the flaw that proved my genius. Not understanding alcoholism, or how to counter it, I had continued to lose more and more until I had effectively lost everything.

Before my conversion I felt that sooner or later I would drink again, while after it, I felt I had a good chance of not drinking again for the foreseeable future. This is what a substantial part of recovery involves for me. So what happened on that day in early October 1994?

MY CONVERSION

It is difficult for me to describe my conversion exactly as I was drunk at the time and I find it even more difficult to explain it. I have attempted a description of it above and I attempt an explanation of it below.

It may well be that the cumulative trauma which I had experienced and suffered as a consequence of being an alcoholic and drinking alcohol came to a head that day and that some neurological or psychological phenomenon occurred in my brain which triggered my conversion and the recovery process for me. The phenomenon was a pretty extreme experiential episode perhaps amounting to what has been called a "limit situation", a situation which has grown just about as bad as it can. The phrase was used by the German philosopher Karl Jaspers (1893-1969) and was elaborated by him in the context of situations involving chance, suffering, struggle, guilt and death. Limit situations cannot be resolved straightforwardly through objective, rational thought. A radical change of attitude is required to cope with them.

The phenomenon may well have taken place by virtue of the cumulative effects of alcohol on my brain combined with the particular additional trauma of that day. My reading of the relevant science suggested that it could well be that the normal neuronal communication within my brain between cortical and other brain areas was temporarily disrupted resulting in an intense experience. My new troubles relating to accommodation were heaped on the old and finally their weight perhaps proved more than my nervous system could take and a change in mindset occurred. Other alcoholics, who have experienced the phenomenon, have described it as their "moment of clarity".

There is nothing more profound for an alcoholic than to change from a hopeless suffering alcoholic to a hopeful one with recovery in mind. In respect of such a profound event it would be easy to assert some ineffable experience akin to a religious conversion. Some would say such experiences can be borne witness to only; they cannot be put into words. They defy explanation; they can only be experienced. I suspect that this is not, in fact, the case although their explanation is not easy or straightforward. I suspect that such experiences are, or will be, capable of scientific explanation.

However, the scientific knowledge is not yet available to give a fully fledged explanation. There has been an assumption that alcoholism is a relatively stable condition, but that may not be correct. Nonlinear elements in the processes of the development of alcoholism and recovery from it have been recognised yet only linear causal models have been developed. Further, neuroscientists still have little idea of how the brain works. While they are beginning to build up a picture of the physical and chemical bases of different subjective mental states, their work so far has not yet thrown much light on causality.

My reading of AA literature revealed more details of the conversion which Bill Wilson said he had had together with more details of what he called his white or hot flash as well as the details of what Marty Mann described as "the miracle happening to me". Further I found that Harry Tiebout (1896-1966), a psychiatrist who had studied AA and the profound change which many alcoholics experience at the beginning of their recovery, had briefly treated Wilson and he had also treated Mann. He described the profound change as a surrender and conversion experience followed by a conversion state. Tiebout published a series of papers between 1944 and 1961 describing the therapeutic process that he had observed in AA members.

Tiebout observed alcoholics recover from alcoholism through membership of AA and he sought to apply his psychiatric knowledge of alcoholism to this phenomenon. He became a strong supporter of AA. In view of the fact that my recovery has been in the AA context, it is hardly surprising that his expositions make sense to me. It may well be, though, that his explanations apply equally, or at least substantially, to real alcoholics who recover from alcoholism other than through AA participation.

His expositions could well apply particularly to all those alcoholics who can discern conversion in their lives, howsoever caused or arising, after which recovery starts. The conversion can occur for no obvious reason, by virtue of a particular occurrence, through trauma or as a consequence of treatment. It can occur as a result of a moment of clarity, by catching sight of a sentence in a book, as a result of what someone says or howsoever. Tiebout's explanations also seem essentially to be consistent with my understanding of modern behavioural change theory and may also have relevance to those many recovering alcoholics who cannot identify a particular conversion in their lives after which their recovery definitely started.

In any event, the best psychological insight into my attempts to stop drinking and to stay stopped and into my conversion that I have come across is, even today, that expounded by Tiebout in his papers, particularly *The Act of Surrender in the Therapeutic Process* written in 1949 as expanded in his later papers especially *Surrender versus Compliance in Therapy* (1953) and *The Ego Factors in Surrender in Alcoholism* (1954). His explanations make sense to me and help in elucidating my struggles to stop drinking.

Tiebout's papers may not fully explain others' experience. For example, his exposition may not necessarily adequately explain other possibilities such as an alcoholic who simply takes a grip on himself, learns about dependence and takes the action necessary to bring about his own recovery. The papers may not relate so much to an alcoholic in treatment who gradually learns with professional psychotherapeutic and other help how to attain and maintain sobriety. They may not explain so definitively the alcoholic who recovers in AA without a distinguishable conversion, only a date established in hindsight alone when he last drank alcohol. Even so Tiebout's model may well be helpful in furthering understanding of recovery in many cases.

Some recent empirical studies seeking to evaluate Tiebout's explanation have been conducted but they have been largely exploratory. Nonetheless they indicate that Tiebout's concept has relevance to at least a section of alcoholics. In particular Duane Reinert and colleagues decided to put Tiebout's idea of surrender leading inexorably to conversion to the test. They developed a surrender scale (the "Reinert S Scale" (1993)) based on Tiebout description of the concept. The results of trials using the scale suggest that Tiebout's concept may indeed identify key factors in the dynamics of recovery. Reinhart asserts that the role of surrender in treatment deserves additional research and clinical attention with a view to fostering greater effectiveness in treatment.

William Silkworth (1873-1951), a doctor who specialised in treating alcoholics and who had been Bill Wilson's doctor, used the phrases "conversion experience" and "psychic upheaval", to describe Wilson's white or hot flash after which he did not drink alcohol again. "Conversion" would certainly be the apposite word for me in describing my experience. Like Wilson, I underwent a psychic upheaval eventually resulting in my conversion from a practising to a recovering alcoholic.

However, the use of the word "surrender" needs to be addressed in the context of its use by Tiebout but also in the context of its use in the context of recovery from alcoholism more generally. In the context of AA it can be seen as having a religious connotation with the suggestion of surrender to God as he is understood by the alcoholic and conversion to a belief in God as the power greater than the alcoholic which can arrest his alcoholism as set out on the face of AA's Twelve Steps.

It seems to me that the word "surrender" can indeed be used to describe the key to my recovery, and the recovery of other real alcoholics, but in my case without any religious connotation. My surrender has been to my alcoholism and others to theirs. Because I and they cannot drink alcohol asymptomatically, I and they have stopped drinking alcohol. I and they have accordingly surrendered and stopped the fight to drink normally. For some other alcoholics in recovery who have always had a religious belief or who have come to believe in religious terms, using the word "surrender" with a religious connotation could well be equally apposite, even more apposite, in reflecting their understanding of the key to their recovery. Other suitable words in this connection might be "capitulation" by an alcoholic to his alcoholism and to "concede", that is, for the alcoholic finally to admit to the truth that he is one.

Tiebout emphasizes that the surrender as understood by him is an unconscious event, not willed by the alcoholic even if he should desire it. It can occur only when an individual with certain traits in his unconscious mind becomes involved in a certain set of circumstances. The abject and utter misery generated by alcoholic intake in the alcoholic can, before insanity, a wet brain or death intervenes, finally beat the alcoholic into surrender. In my case, the loss, pain and misery involved in my struggle to stop drinking and my continuing relapses over the thirty odd years before my conversion played their part in it. The mental and physical traumas and emotional shocks which abusing alcohol can bring about can be a great persuader. If the resultant disruptive emotions increase suggestibility sufficiently, it can, in some alcoholics, trigger conversion which can enable them to start taking the steps which can instigate the recovery process.

The conversion involves the individual's unconscious somatic state which colours everything with varieties of urgency and calm rendering some thoughts relatively unthinkable while presenting others to his conscious attention. The effect on the individual of his conversion according to Tiebout can be summed up by saying that "after trying to run his own case to his own ruination, he gives up the battle and surrenders to the need for help, after which he enters a new state of mind that enables him to remain sober".

According to Tiebout a further development in the unconscious mind is required, though, before the conversion becomes a settled state in which the alcoholic mindset no longer raises havoc with adjustment, serenity, and the capacity to function as a reasonable human being. The initial conversion can slowly or quickly be supplanted by the old or a new crop of resistances or negative feelings or it can slowly become more established. It can, in time, become a settled state of sobriety.

It seems to me that conversion is better described as a process rather than an event for many alcoholics. For some conversion is sudden, even instant, for others it takes some time. Sometimes quickly, sometimes slowly, some alcoholics get it, so to speak. I believe that, listening to alcoholics sharing (the oral contributions of members during meetings and outside them) in AA, I have a fair idea of who seems to have got it and those who have not or not yet. The latter seem still to be engaged in the fight against alcoholism and the former seem effectively to have given up the fight.

Reflecting this, Tiebout suggested that a distinction should be made between submission and surrender. In submission, Tiebout argued, an individual accepts reality consciously, but not unconsciously. There is a mental conflict between the conscious mind's intellectual recognition of the alcoholic's drinking problems and the unconscious mind's duplicitous compliance. The alcoholic can accept, in practice as a matter of fact for the time being, that he cannot beat the reality of the consequences of his drinking, but, lurking in the unconscious, is the conviction, however ill founded, that there will come a day when the situation will change. This implies no real acceptance and demonstrates that the struggle will continue. With submission, which at best is a superficial yielding, tension continues. But when an individual surrenders, the ability to accept the reality of the consequences of his drinking functions on the unconscious level of his mind and there is no residual battle. Substantial relaxation with freedom from strain and conflict can ensue.

I can relate my own experience to Tiebout's distinction between submission and surrender. From the time when I first took some action to address my drinking until my conversion I submitted to the fact of my problem drinking. I yielded from time to by complying with the pressures not to drink. But, while I stopped drinking for periods of time, some a number of years, a residual battle remained. I was far from relaxed and my life continued to be a strain with much internal conflict. When abstinent, I knew that one day I would drink again and it was a struggle trying continuously to postpone that day. After my conversion there has been little, if any, residual battle for me; my life has become increasingly relaxed with substantial freedom from strain and conflict.

MY BELIEF

I believe that I am a real alcoholic. I no longer believe that I have any effective control over my drinking. I have come to believe that for me AA involvement was crucial in my recovery and that, if I continue to attend

AA meetings and keep in touch with other recovering alcoholics, I have a reasonable chance of maintaining and sustaining my sobriety.

I have come to believe that as a real alcoholic I am, in a very real, practical sense, powerless over alcohol – I am powerless over the affect that drinking alcohol has on me. On any drinking occasion the duration of the episode or the quantity that I will consume is unpredictable. I have accordingly accepted that alcohol is, in a sense, a higher power than I am. I have experimented with extrapolating this idea of powerlessness and the belief in a higher power to my life generally. The idea can be useful, particularly in early recovery, as a cognitive gadget. I have come to believe it worth maintaining some sort of inchoate idea of a secular higher power in practice and acting as if there was such a power as my *modus operandi*, at least for some purposes. I certainly accept that I am not God and that I should not act as if I was.

It seems to me that such a higher power can be understood through experience, through what happens to me and how I deal with what happens to me, and through reason without my being able necessarily to conjure up something from my imagination which would correspond to it. However, the relevant power at any time and from time to time can be seen as having some content but only in the sense that it can be said to comprise one or other or many of the myriad and different forces of the external world, particularly those generated by other people, and of the internal forces within my body, brain and mind. I have some conception of some of these forces. My belief or confidence in them is based, not on faith, but on evidence, evidence gleaned from my own experience.

I am definitely not omnipotent, far from it. The less I try to control that over which I have no control the better. To a large extent, even an overwhelming extent, it is best just to move out of the way and allow decisions, in effect, to make themselves. Let the force or forces, whatever it or they may be that control that which I cannot, have sway, as it would seem it or they inevitably will. Shakespeare put it as follows in *Hamlet*. "There's a divinity that shapes our ends, Rough-hew them how we will. Our wills and fates do so contrary run That our devices still are overthrown; Our thoughts are ours, their ends none of our own."

Let me attend to my business, the business over which I appear to have some control, as best I can and hand the rest over to that or those force or forces which bear on matters from time to time and over which I have no control. From my experience I have reason to believe in such a force or forces, in higher powers, collectively a higher power, if you will, relevant to the way I seek to conduct my life.

The realization that not everything that is so in the world can be understood and controlled by me is liberating. The thought that I am powerless over so much can be therapeutic. If I act as if there is a higher power, which can simply be described as that which I do not understand, let alone control, and which I cannot necessarily visualise, and go with its flow, rather than fight it or flee from it, my experience is that I am happier and more joyous and free. It has brought me a great sense of freedom to leave many matters alone. So many things, perhaps virtually all things, work themselves out without any help from me or despite my attempts at active resistance. The more my mind, my self, is discounted, it appears, the more spontaneous and appropriate action is possible. No aspect of a higher power seems to me necessarily to require the existence or influence of God.

I disbelieve in God. Although I was brought up in an Anglican tradition and I was confirmed into the Church of England as a teenager, I do not now believe in God. Studying science in the sixth form, I soon ceased to believe in any meaningful God. I have had no religious beliefs since then and my recovery has not rekindled any despite my recovering in the AA context.

The traditional AA approach to recovery maintains that surrender to God, as the individual alcoholic understands him, is required together with a decision to turn his will and his life over to the care of God. In my early recovery, the implication seemed to me to be that, if I did not believe in a God of my understanding, I was unlikely to recover. This focused my mind on whether or not I could come to believe in God. I tried very hard to believe. For some time I acted as if God existed in the hope that I would come to believe as was advocated in AA's text book *Alcoholics Anonymous* but to no effect.

I find it difficult not to view religious faith as an excuse to evade the need to think and to evaluate evidence. A core sense of the word "faith" is belief in something based on conviction rather than proof. Nothing that I have experienced in AA has convinced me of God's existence. I have, however, developed during my recovery a belief in a secular higher power and in process spirituality as I have sought to explain in this book.

Either God exists or he does not. It is a scientific question which one day might be definitively answered. In the meantime, only the probability of his existence can be addressed. That God's non-existence is incapable of proof is inconsequential; there is never absolute proof of the non-existence of anything. As demonstrated by Bertrand Russell (1872-1970) in *Is There A God?* (1952), the burden of proof rests with the believers, not the disbelievers. The evidence supporting the existence of God is not equal to the evidence against. It seems to me that the evidence against far outweighs the evidence for his existence. Richard Dawkins in *The God Delusion* (2006) argues that believers have failed to make their case. He asserts that the factual premise of theistic religion is untenable. I agree with Dawkins's conclusion that God's existence is highly improbable.

However, while science has explained many things it has not answered the most fundamental existential questions. Such questions may simply be qualitatively different to those relating to the physical world in which science has proved so powerful. Science may one day be able fully to explain the fabric of the cosmos but may never answer such questions as why does the cosmos exist or what purpose does it serve. In the final analysis, asking why there is something rather than nothing using the essentially mathematical methods of modern cosmology may make no more sense than asking whether a convex mirror is happy or a concave one sad. Further, it may well be that philosophy can no more answer the questions than science can.

2

THE BOOK'S PURPOSE, TERMINOLOGY AND KEY REFERENCES

THE BOOK'S PURPOSE

I believe that describing my experiences of alcoholism and recovery, and addressing the processes of change and other factors involved, can be helpful to others. Many people are faced with confronting alcohol problems. Some individuals will be worried about their drinking. Others will have admitted that they are alcoholics but have not managed to stop drinking for very long. Some are in recovery from alcoholism. Some have relatives, friends or work colleagues who are heavy drinkers and who may be alcoholic whether in recovery or not. There are those health care professionals who are faced with patients or clients who are heavy drinkers and who have suffered and caused harm. There are those responsible for health care provision and policies for alcohol harm reduction.

Those who have had experience of alcoholism know what a destructive experience it can be both for the individual alcoholic and for those around him. Those who have been close to an alcoholic while drinking and, later, when in recovery, have observed in him the profound differences between the drinking individual and the recovering one. This book seeks to cast some light on the process of transformation from a drinking to a recovering alcoholic.

I hope that the individual who is worried about his drinking will find in these pages information helpful to him in deciding his best course of action. Hopefully, individuals who do not themselves have any sort of drink problem, but who are faced with dealing with those who have, will find explanations and descriptions helpful to them. I hope that alcoholics in recovery, health care professionals and policy makers will find that reading this book will enhance their understanding of alcoholism and recovery from it. I also hope that the book will be helpful, or will be of interest, to a wider audience interested in addiction in general and in alcoholism in particular. There seems to be a dearth of literature on recovery and on the processes of change and the other factors involved, such as spirituality and talk therapy.

TERMINOLOGY

An individual can, of course, be male or female. Rather than continually referring to "he or she", "his or her" and so on I have used only the masculine form. Please forgive any apparent sexism. This is not my intention; rather my purpose is to avoid tedious repetition.

There is much confusion concerning the use of the terms "alcoholism" and "alcohol abuse" or "alcohol misuse". In general, the term "alcohol abuse (or misuse)" is not well understood. When pressed, though, people tend to define alcohol abuse in terms of inappropriate heavy drinking. "Alcoholism" is probably the most widely used term and it is associated with the most extreme forms of alcohol abuse involving loss of control over significant aspects of daily life and with alcohol "addiction", "dependency" or "dependence".

Again there is confusion over the meaning of the terms "addiction", "dependency" and "dependence". Some would say that they are effectively interchangeable; alcoholism is an addiction to alcohol; alcoholics are dependent on alcohol. Others would say that "addiction" is broader than "dependency" or "dependence" and that "alcoholism" is an "addiction" and accordingly is broader than just dependence on alcohol. Some speak of addiction, and alcoholism as an addiction, in terms of concurrent disorder, alcohol dependence and mental illness or disorder at the same time. However the words "addiction", "dependency" and "dependence" for my purposes seem to me to be effectively interchangeable.

That there is confusion concerning terms is hardly surprising. Not only does harmful drinking reveal itself in so many guises and in so many stages of development that definition is problematic, but also those practising and researching in the field have failed to agree terminology. However, the World Health Organisation (WHO) in its publication *International Statistical Classification of Diseases and Related Health Problems* (Tenth Revision Version, 2003) (ICD-10) which includes alcohol related conditions uses the word "dependence" rather than "addiction" or "dependency" and the word "alcoholism" to mean dependence on alcohol. It uses the phrase "alcohol abuse" rather than "alcohol misuse" (the term usually used in England) to mean the harmful use of alcohol not amounting to dependence on it. I will use the WHO terminology. "Dependence" is also the word used in the American Psychiatric Association *Diagnostic and Statistical Manual of Mental Disorders, Fourth Edition, Text Revision* (2000) (DSM-IV).

A new description of alcoholism, the alcohol "dependence syndrome", has come to be used. A syndrome is a group of symptoms which consistently occur together, or a condition characterized by a set of associated symptoms. ICD-10 defines the dependence syndrome as follows. "A cluster of physiological, behavioural, and cognitive phenomena in which the use of a substance or a class of substances takes on a much higher priority for a given individual than other behaviours that once had greater value. A central descriptive characteristic of the dependence syndrome is the desire (often strong, sometimes overpowering) to take the psychoactive drugs (which may or not have been medically prescribed), alcohol, or tobacco. There may be evidence that return to substance use after a period of abstinence leads to a more rapid reappearance of other features of the syndrome than occurs with nondependent individuals."

In ICD-10 and DSM-IV alcoholism is accordingly conceived as an integration of physiological and psychological processes leading to heavy drinking that is increasingly unresponsive to external circumstances or adverse consequences. The dependence process involved in alcoholism is differentiated from social, legal and other consequences of heavy drinking.

In ICD-10 alcohol dependence is clinically defined by at least three of the following having been experienced or exhibited at some time during the previous year

- a strong desire or sense of compulsion to drink
- difficulties in controlling drinking behaviour in terms of its onset, termination or levels of use
- a physiological state of withdrawal, the occurrence of unpleasant physical and psychological symptoms, when drinking has stopped or been reduced
- evidence of tolerance, such that increased drinking is required to achieve effects originally produced by a lesser amount of alcohol
- progressive neglect of alternative pleasures or interests and increased amount of time drinking and recovering from drinking
- persistent use despite clear evidence of overtly harmful consequences, such as harm to the liver, depressive mood states consequent on drinking or alcohol related impairment of cognitive function.

The two criteria most easily measured biologically are withdrawal and tolerance. The other four criteria include elements of cognition, which are less accessible to biological measurement, but are becoming measurable using improved neuroimaging techniques.

The criteria for dependence of DSM-IV are similar to those of ICD-10. The concepts and definitions of ICD and DSM diagnoses form a unifying framework that underlies research and discussion of alcoholism in many countries. There are, however, continuing difficulties with regard to these criteria from the point of view of the neuroscientist which stem from the "positive on at least three" aspect of the criteria because some of the criteria are not measurable in biological terms. Nevertheless neuroscientists have made substantial advances in the understanding of dependence generally and of alcoholism in particular in recent years.

Alcohol abuse has been defined as consumption that leads an individual to experience social, psychological, physical or legal problems causing harm to himself, his family and friend or the wider community. Alcohol abuse differs from alcoholism in that it does not include an extremely strong craving for alcohol, loss of control or physical dependence. While alcohol abusers' ability to exert personal control over their drinking is more or less impaired, like normal drinkers they are ultimately able to control their drinking. Further, alcohol abuse is less likely than alcoholism to include tolerance (the need for increasing amounts of alcohol to achieve the same effect). It is not progressive in the way that alcoholism is. But while alcohol abuse is basically different from alcoholism, many effects of alcohol abuse are also experienced by alcoholics.

Alcohol abuse is primarily driven by environmental factors while alcoholism is driven by brain changes consequent upon its use often involving genetic factors with environmental factors playing a secondary part. The DSM-IV definition of substance abuse is a maladaptive pattern of alcohol use leading to clinically significant impairment or distress, as manifested by one (or more) of the following over a twelve month period

  ☐ failure to fulfil major role obligations at home, school or work
  ☐ drinking in situations in which it is physically hazardous
  ☐ recurrent drink related legal problems
  ☐ continued drinking despite having persistent or recurrent social or interpersonal problems exacerbated by the effects of alcohol.

In a departure from the DSM, ICD-10 does not include the category "alcohol abuse" but includes the concept "harmful use". "Harmful use" implies alcohol use that causes some physical, psychological or social problems caused by excessive alcohol intake in the absence of dependence.

I use the term "real alcoholic" to mean an alcoholic whose dependence on alcohol is severe and who cannot ever drink alcohol again without presenting symptoms of alcoholism. This is the rule not the exception. A real alcoholic should be differentiated not only from an individual who only abuses alcohol but also from any individual who, while he might meet the ICD-10 or DSM-IV criteria for being dependent on alcohol, could return to asymptomatic drinking. There may be a number of these, but it is with the real alcoholic that this book is particularly concerned and, in the final analysis, it is for the individual to decide whether he is or is not a real alcoholic, or indeed an alcoholic at all.

In the context of recovery from real alcoholism I use the term "recovery" to mean the process whereby the real alcoholic, being aware of his alcoholism, stops drinking alcohol and experiences a behaviour and attitude change as a result of his efforts. The change can amount to sobriety by which I mean the secure maintenance of stable, contented abstinence from alcohol and other relevant psychoactive substances and the growth of concomitant emotional sobriety. By relevant psychoactive substances I mean psychoactive substances excluding nicotine and caffeine and those legitimately prescribed by a doctor. Sobriety encompasses a contented, healthy, well adjusted sober life and lifestyle.

On the basis of ICD-10 and with a good understanding of its criteria, the alcoholic (particularly the real alcoholic) can usually be clearly distinguished from the alcohol abuser. To assist diagnosis, tests and tools are available: the Substance Use Disorders Diagnostic Schedule (SUDDS-IV), an objective event orientated 30-45 minute structured diagnostic interview, is one example.

I use the phrase "heavy drinker". This phrase has no standard definition. I use it to mean an individual who answers in the affirmative three or four out of the four questions in the CAGE test. This test is an internationally used assessment instrument for identifying problems with alcohol developed by John Ewing at the University of North Carolina in the United States of America (US). ("CAGE" is the acronym formed from the first letters of the words in italics in the questionnaire.)

The four questions are
1. Have you ever felt you should *cut* down on your drinking?
2. Have people *annoyed* you by criticizing your drinking?
3. Have you ever felt bad or *guilty* about your drinking?
4. Have you ever had a drink first thing in the morning to steady your nerves or get rid of a hangover (*eye*-opener)?

I use the word "harm". I use it in the sense used in the United Kingdom (UK) Prime Minister's Strategy Unit Report; *Alcohol Harm Reduction Strategy for England*, 2004 to include harm to the health of individuals, crime, anti-social behaviour, domestic violence, drink driving and its impact on victims, loss of productivity and profitability and social harms including problems within families. This use is consistent with the ICD-10 concept of "harmful use".

KEY REFERENCES

The Twelve Steps were set out in *Alcoholics Anonymous* which was published in 1939 and is known by AA members as the Big Book. The Steps disclose a basis upon which an alcoholic can cope with life without drinking. Despite the use of such phrases as "Power greater than ourselves", "God as we understood Him" and "spiritual awakening", AA does not demand that a member believes in anything in particular.

AA arose from a synthesis of principles and attitudes which came to its founders from religion and medicine. Its tenets have profound origins in the Oxford Group evangelical Christian fellowship of the 1930s which focused on a changed life attained by passing through stages involving a number of procedures and practices. Bill Wilson and Bob Smith (1879-1950), who founded what was to become AA in 1935, were members of the Oxford Group together with a number of early AA members. Wilson was AA's leading proponent until his death in 1971. Wilson described AA as "a synthetic gadget, as it were, drawing upon the resources of medicine, psychiatry, religion, and our own experience of drinking and recovery". AA, he wrote, "merely streamlined old and proved principles of psychiatry and religion into such forms that the alcoholic will accept them".

Bill Wilson, who wrote the main text of the Big Book, recalled the events which led to the formulation of the Twelve Steps in an article in the *Grapevine*, AA's international journal, of July 1953. The three main sources of inspiration, he wrote, were the medical opinions of William Silkworth, the tenets of the Oxford Group particularly as expounded by Samuel Shoemaker (1893-1963) and the writings of William James (1842-

1910). Silkworth was physician-in-chief of the Charles B. Towns Hospital in New York City where Wilson had been treated. Shoemaker was the Episcopal rector of the Calvary Church in New York City and a leading figure in the Oxford Group. James, as well as developing the philosophy of pragmatism, sought to develop psychology as a science. He went on to apply his methods to the study of religion, writing *The Varieties of Religious Experience* (1902).

Wilson confirmed in another article in the *Grapevine* in 1960 that the basic ideas embodied in the Twelve Steps were not new; those ideas could have been found elsewhere. They were, however, written by an alcoholic for alcoholics and put in a deliberate numbered sequence. As it was, Step One was drawn from Silkworth and reinforced by James who supplied the spiritual essence of Step Twelve in turn reinforced by Oxford Group tenets. The other ten Steps were drawn from Shoemaker and the Oxford Group.

Important for Wilson, Smith and the other alcoholics who contacted the Oxford Group was that its members laid great stress on one-to-one personal contact, honesty, unselfishness, making amends and meditation seeking God's guidance and that special care was taken not to interfere with the individual's personal religious views. The Oxford Group, like AA later on, saw the need to be strictly nondenominational.

AA's Twelve Steps are as follows.
1. We admitted we were powerless over alcohol – that our lives have become unmanageable.
2. Came to believe a Power greater than ourselves could restore us to sanity.
3. Made a decision to turn our will and our lives over to the care of God as we understand Him.
4. Made a fearless and searching moral inventory of ourselves.
5. Admitted to God, to ourselves, and to another human being the exact nature of our wrongs.
6. Were entirely ready to have God remove all these defects of character.

7. Humbly asked Him to remove our shortcomings.

8. Made a list of all persons we had harmed, and became willing to make amends to them all.

9. Made direct amends to such people wherever possible, except when to do so would injure them or others.

10. Continued to take personal inventory and when we were wrong promptly admitted it.

11. Sought through prayer and meditation to improve our conscious contact with God as we understand Him, praying only for knowledge of His will and the power to carry that out.

12. Having had a spiritual awakening as the result of these steps, we tried to carry the message to alcoholics, and to practise these principles in all our affairs.[1]

There is, classically, a downward trend of increasing alcoholism which bottoms out and turns into an upward trend of increasing recovery. When the trend changes from being downwards to being upwards is when conversion takes place as illustrated by Max Glatt's *Jellinek Chart of Alcoholism and Recovery* (1958). After conversion the alcoholic by adopting new attitudes and exercising new skills can begin his recovery. In AA terms he can have a spiritual awakening.

The chart was prepared by Max Glatt (1912-2002), a pioneer in the field of treatment for alcoholism, and named by him after E. M. Jellinek who wrote *The Disease Concept of Alcoholism* (1960). Glatt charted Jellinek's stages of gamma alcoholism and added the stages of recovery seeking to describe what to expect in the case of a real alcoholic, with no significant mental disorder or illness in addition to his alcoholism, as recovery progresses on the assumption that he successfully seeks help through group therapy (particularly AA) involving other alcoholics.

Recovery starts with an honest desire for help. The alcoholic becomes involved with a group of people discussing the issues of recovery. It may

---

[1] Reprinted with the permission of the General Service Board of Alcoholics Anonymous (Great Britain) Limited.

be a professionally facilitated group, AA or both. He learns that alcohol-ism is a disease, that he is an alcoholic and that recovery from alcoholism is possible. He finds out that there is a way that can arrest the disease and he meets people who are recovering from it. He becomes hopeful. He learns the relationship between alcohol and life problems. He begins to evaluate his life in terms of establishing priorities and begins taking an inventory of personal traits that can be utilized, modified or eliminated in the recovery process.

With the elimination of alcohol and with the help of others, he is able to begin making appropriate decisions about how to conduct his life. He improves physically and any physical illness is identified and appropri-ate treatment is initiated. As he feels better and thinks better, his sense of hope becomes stronger. He starts eating a balanced diet and feeling better physically. Worry is diminished as confidence increases because of new hope, new relationships and improved health. Taking things one day at a time promotes confidence. Realistic thinking replaces wishful think-ing and fantasy. He begins identifying true cause and effect relationships and recognizing personal alibi structures. Because of new feelings of control over life, self-esteem is reborn.

He begins to realize that self-esteem is directly proportional to the level of control people feel over their own lives and that, paradoxically, self-control comes by turning over unsolvable problems to a higher power and focusing on what is solvable here and now. Sleep pattern disturbances begin going away. Sleep becomes more natural and worries about sleep patterns are diminished. The desire to escape decreases as reality be-comes less frightening and as control, self-esteem, and self-confidence are restored. He again becomes involved with his family and he becomes aware of and more responsive to the needs of other family members.

His family begins to give positive feedback as family members begin to believe that this time the alcoholic is going to succeed. Life is no lon-ger focused on drinking. New interests and lifestyle change enable him to establish new relationships involving activities other than drinking. Value systems are established. There is less need to run from reality. He can see things as they are and he becomes capable of taking hard and serious looks at himself and his attitudes. He learns to control his own responses to feeling, anxiety, and stress. Mood swings become less extreme. He begins to appreciate that he can have some pride, some courage, and some dignity. He develops an awareness of people and relationships. He becomes able to initiate financial planning and to take responsibility for his own financial situation.

A new sense of pride and dignity brings about a change in appearance. The compulsion to drink has gone and he finds a pleasure in activities unrelated to drinking alcohol. He has a sense of satisfaction in sobriety. He is able to catch himself in denial and rationalization before they begin to cause problems. The group help process becomes an important part of his lifestyle. Relating to other recovering alcoholics enables him to be more accepting of self and more comfortable in his own situation. He becomes more accepting of others, less judgmental of family, less critical of friends. Old resentments are released and appreciation of other people increases. An enlightened and interesting way of life opens up with a road ahead to higher levels than ever before.

In reality, though, the process is often not smooth and simplistic; it is often not linear. Typically the chart of the alcoholic's actual progress would be a more complicated nonlinear pattern as the individual struggles to attain, sustain and maintain his recovery. Most individuals, who initiate recovery, or a semblance of it, relapse at some point returning to a previous stage before renewing their efforts (if in fact they do). The cycle can be repeated any number of times.

MAX GLATT'S JELLINEK CHART OF ALCOHOLISM AND RECOVERY

Descent (left side, downward):

Occasional relief drinking

Increase in alcohol tolerance

Surreptitious drinking

Urgency of first drinks

Unable to discuss problems

Drinking bolstered with excuses

Persistent remorse

Promises and resolutions fail

Loss of other interests

Work and money troubles

Neglect of food

Tremors and early morning drinks

Physical deterioration

Moral deterioration

Drinking with inferiors

Unable to initiate action

Vague spiritual desires

Complete defeat admitted

Middle descent column:

Constant relief drinking commences

Onset of memory blackouts

Increasing dependence on alcohol

Feelings of guilt

Memory blackouts increase

Decrease of ability to stop drinking when others do so

Grandiose and aggressive behaviour

Efforts to control fail repeatedly

Tries geographical escapes

Family and friends avoided

Unreasonable resentments

Loss of ordinary will power

Decrease in alcohol tolerance

Onset of lengthy intoxications

Impaired thinking

Indefinable fears

Obsession with drinking

All alibis exhausted

Recovery (ascent, upward):

Learns alcoholism is an illness

Stops taking alcohol

Assisted in making personal stocktaking

Spiritual needs examined

Onset of new hope

Appreciation of possibilities of new way of life

Regular nourishment taken

Realistic thinking

Natural rest and sleep

Family and friends appreciate efforts

New circle of stable friends

Facts faced with courage

Increase of emotional control

First step towards economic stability

Care of personal appearance

Rationalisations recognised

Group therapy and mutual help continues

Enlightened and interesting way of life opens up with road ahead to higher levels than ever before

Right side (ascent, upward):

Honest desire for help

Told addiction can be arrested

Meets former addicts normal and happy

Right thinking begins

Physical overhaul by doctor

Start of group therapy

Diminishing fears of the unknown future

Return of self-esteem

Desire to escape goes

Adjustment to family needs

New interests develop

Rebirth of ideals

Appreciation of real values

Confidence of employment

Contentment in sobriety

Increasing tolerance

3

ALCOHOL USE AND ABUSE

DRINKING ALCOHOL

Drinking alcohol, alcohol abuse, alcoholism and real alcoholism is a continuum. A continuum is a continuous sequence in which adjacent elements are not perceptibly different from each other, but the extremes are quite distinct. An individual's position on the continuum depends on many factors.

A normal drinker's consumption and choice of drinks varies from day to day and week to week. The dependent individual's drinking is more regular usually involving daily consumption. As dependence increases, the alcoholic drinks to maintain high alcohol levels and to avoid withdrawal. With more severe dependence an ever greater priority is given to drinking over competing needs and responsibilities. A subjective awareness of a compulsion to drink can also develop. There is a steep decline in the quality of life that accompanies increasing dependence. Thus the proper question can become not so much whether the individual is dependent but how far along the dependence path has he progressed.

On the surface, alcohol is seen in a positive light, primarily related to social activity. It is widely associated with pleasure, relaxation and "having a good time". The parts of the brain which drinking affects are those which are affected by many other human activities including eating, sexual intercourse and gambling. Most adults drink alcohol moderately and on a social basis and derive considerable enjoyment from doing so, but it has its problems. As Griffith Edwards puts it in *Alcohol the Ambiguous Molecule* (2000) "alcohol is fun, the wine of the Eucharist, a profitable and taxable commodity, but a drug among drugs and highly ambiguous in its costs and benefits".

Government statistics for 2004 suggest that, in the UK, about a quarter of the population had drunk alcohol on at least three days a week in the last twelve months. While ten per cent had had a drink almost every day in the last year, slightly more, fifteen per cent, had not drunk any alcohol at all in the last year. Many people gain social benefits from moderate drinking levels and alcohol plays an important role in the success of the leisure and tourist industries. However, alcohol abuse, particularly patterns of heavy drinking, lead to an increasing number of premature deaths and health problems and alcohol related disorder and injuries. Alcohol is causally related to more than sixty different medical conditions, in most detrimentally. The UK Office for National Statistics confirms that alcohol-related deaths in England and Wales have continued to rise throughout the last thirty years.

Alcoholic drinks in the UK have become more and more affordable since 1978 with consumption increasing in step with affordability. A range of factors are influential in determining when and why an individual starts drinking alcohol. Common factors initiating drinking are experimentation and peer pressure. Factors involved in continuing to drink include the psychoactive effects which alcohol has on the individual's consciousness, mood and thinking processes, peer pressure, pleasure and enjoyment, easy availability as well as affordability. Another factor in the initial and continuing use of alcohol is commonly a response to various negative feelings such as stress, loneliness, depression, boredom and insecurity in the belief that drinking is an effective antidote. Life problems such as bereavement, relationship problems and work stress can also be factors, drinking being viewed as an effective coping mechanism.

There are also many individuals who simply decide to go out and get drunk. They take the view that they can only "have a good time" if they drink heavily. These include the so-called "binge drinkers" particularly prevalent in the UK. These heavy drinkers take the view that as they work hard they are entitled to drink hard. They care not whether they are causing damage to themselves or others. They take no notice of anybody, particularly authority figures, who tell them that what they are doing is alcohol abuse and dangerous. For these drinkers, drinking is not about violent crime, facial scars and anti-social behaviour; it is about a "good night out", and nothing else. The great majority of these individuals are not alcoholics and will not become alcoholic. They do not have any independent major mental illnesses or disorders either.

Individual characteristics such as age, sex, gender, personality, genetic makeup and family background influence drinking behaviour and hence the risk of harm. External factors like background culture, peer pressure, environment, surroundings and advertising also influence drinking behaviour and risk of harm. Thrill seeking, rebellion, boredom, desperation and self-medication can play their part. Background factors such as difficulties experienced in childhood, including abuse, the death of a parent and parental alcoholism, have their effect but are usually considered more as contributing factors rather than actual reasons for drinking.

The interaction of these myriad factors and characteristics is crucial. While there is no such individual as one typical of a particular group of drinkers defined in terms of amount consumed, groups at greater risk of harm can be identified. Social risk factors are more important as regards experimenting with and use of alcohol while genetics, personality and certain mental illnesses are more important determinants of vulnerability to alcoholism. Once an individual becomes dependent on alcohol it is his dependence which effectively drives his drinking. Severely dependent alcoholics drink to function normally and to avoid or reduce withdrawal effects.

There are genetic contributions on several levels. Multiple genes are involved. Important examples of the genes involved are those controlling the metabolic pathways that affect the rate at which alcohol enters the body and the genes that affect neurochemical processes in the brain. There are countless cultural contributions attributable to innumerable behavioural concepts and ideas which are passed on or learnt from family members, through peer pressure, from the media and from society generally. There are many environmental contributions including poverty and domestic and workplace stress.

Alcohol is commonly abused by people seeking to self-medicate and reduce tension during, or in the aftermath of, trauma whether a deeply distressing experience or an emotional shock following a stressful event. A working memory and ongoing rules and assumptions kept in mind can develop which puts alcohol consumption high up on, if not at the top of, the heavy drinker's mental action list. Memory in general is the mental capacity to store and later recognise or recall events that were previously experienced. Working memory in particular is the ability to access certain rules and patterns for addressing ongoing tasks.

For some, the transition from drinking alcohol to developing a problem with it can be clearly marked by a traumatic event like the death of a person with whom the individual has an established romantic or sexual relationship (his "partner"). In others, a more gradual descent into alcoholism through prolonged regular use is the case. In any event, alcohol problems can affect anyone, regardless of age, sex or social background. Some see childhood issues, including genetic factors, as the most significant risk factors. Others see loneliness and boredom as central risk factors particularly for groups such as the homeless, unemployed and divorced or widowed people. Many are concerned that young people in the UK are particularly at risk of having alcohol problems in the future because of alcohol marketing strategies and their perception that drunkenness is acceptable. It was disclosed in the answer to a Parliamentary Question in 2005 that admissions to hospital for alcohol related conditions among those aged under eighteen had increased by eleven per cent since the mid 1990s.

HARM CAUSED BY DRINKING

The relationship between drinking and harm is not straightforward. Drinking certainly increases the risk of various physical sorts of harm and the risk grows with the amount drunk. Alcohol related harm is not limited to health problems, adverse incidents and accidents suffered by the individual drinker but also extends to family and friends, employers and society more broadly. The relationship between drinking and harm is shaped by the interaction of a range of risk factors relating to the individual, their family, their life events and experiences, culture and social norms and market factors.

Market factors include price and affordability, availability and setting and promotion and product innovation like "alcopops", "ready to drinks" and "shots". Price is an important factor particularly with supermarkets selling alcoholic drinks below cost, offering half price deals and so on. The interaction of the factors is as important as the factors themselves.

For most drinkers the main drawbacks are seen as hangovers and argumentative behaviour. But for those who are severely dependent on alcohol and their families and friends, the negative aspects are seen more broadly. They are seen in terms of the adverse impact on personal relationships. The negative aspects include aggression, violence, financial problems and ill-health.

Alcoholism involves immoderate, self-injurious, and socially damaging drinking and alcoholics invoke sufficient troubles for themselves, their families and friends, their employers, their occupational or social associates, and their communities and society generally so that alcohol problems and issues are major causes of disorder and suffering, as well as costly focuses of study and responses. One or more of the chronic nutritional deficiency diseases may develop. The classical physical disease associated with alcoholism is cirrhosis of the liver. Many of those who survive long years of alcoholism show a generalized deterioration involving the brain, muscles, endocrine system and vital organs, giving an impression of premature old age. Alcohol is linked to a high proportion of car accidents, deaths by drowning, falls, poisonings, self-inflicted injuries, murders and suicides.

There is much complacency, particularly in government, concerning alcohol and its adverse effects. There is also a general disavowal of the true state of affairs, a general denial, as regards the harm caused by alcohol abuse and dependence. A reason for complacency and denial is that alcohol is the nation's favourite drug. Most people drink it including politicians, journalists, judges, doctors, and policy pundits. For politicians there are the important issues of a million jobs, tax revenues and exports. There are few votes in being serious about alcohol problems. The votes that there are, are largely to do with such matters as disorder in town

centres and in the vicinity of pubs and clubs while the political power of
the drinks industry lobby is huge.

A report by the Academy of Medical Sciences *Calling Time, The
Nation's drinking as a major health issue* (2004) asserted that the UK
"has reached a point where it is necessary and urgent to call time on
runaway alcohol consumption". Internationally, an article in the *Lancet*
entitled *Alcohol and Public Health* (February 2005) reported that researchers had found that, overall, four per cent of the global burden of
disease is attributable to alcohol consumption. Thus alcohol accounts
for about as much of the burden of disease globally as smoking tobacco
(4.1%) and it is only surpassed by the burdens caused by being under-
weight (9.5%), unsafe sex (6.3%) and abnormally high blood pressure
(hypertension) (4.4%). In high income counties with very low mortality
like Western Europe, the US, Japan and Australia, more than half of the
alcohol related burden of disease is accounted for by alcohol abuse and
alcoholism.

The harm caused by alcohol abuse and alcoholism has been considerable and it is increasing. Even by 1736 the Grand Jury of Middlesex,
having declared of gin drinking that "much the greater part of the poverty, the murders, the robberies of London, might be traced to this single
cause", petitioned Parliament on the harm being done. Parliament's inten-
tions found immediate expression in the Gin Act 1736 imposing a licence
for retailers of gin together with a tax on the product. The persistent im-
ages of the nineteenth century were of the gin palace, seething crowds,
bodies on pavements, violence, the shame of women, hurt to children and
men ruined by drink. At the onset of the First World War David Lloyd
George was said to have remarked that the UK faced two enemies, the
Kaiser and alcohol, and that of the two he feared alcohol the more.

At least six and a half million people in the UK drink at harmful
levels and *per capita* consumption of alcohol increased by one hundred
and twenty-one per cent between 1951 and 2001. The *Psychiatric morbidity among adults living in households* report of a survey carried out
on behalf of the Department of Health in 2000 found that one quarter
of informants were assessed as having a hazardous pattern of drinking

during the year before interview. The prevalence of alcoholism in the six months before interview was 74 per 1,000 among the overall population, 119 among men and 29 per 1,000 among women. According to the UK government's own figures, drinkers under the age of 16 are drinking twice as much as they did ten years before, with one in five 13 year olds, and nearly half of 15 year olds drinking in the last week.

Of all psychoactive substances available in the UK, alcohol is responsible for more damage and death than all the other psychoactive substances put together. Alcohol is involved in half of all crime. Thirty per cent of offenders on probation and fifty eight per cent of prisoners have severe alcohol problems with alcohol being a significant factor in their offence or pattern of offending. Binge drinking alone is linked to some 22,000 premature deaths each year. Alcohol abuse and alcoholism is estimated to cost the UK National Health Service at least £3 billion per annum. The UK government puts the additional costs at £7.3 billion for crime, £4.7 billion for additional human and social costs of crime and at least £6.4 billion for lost productivity per annum. This all adds up to over £21 billion each year and the government admits that it does not have the data to quantify costs in human suffering, not only for drinkers but also for their families and friends.

Such a serious and widespread problem as alcoholism demands to be studied but, even today, despite the substantial advances in the understanding of dependence generally and of alcoholism in particular in recent years, the lack of general knowledge about alcoholism is deeply worrying. Even the professional literature on alcohol often abounds in controversy and lack of clarity, which, if unresolved, may add to uncertainty and may actually detract from knowledge. Many of the basic questions about alcoholism and alcoholics remain unanswered.

In the UK there is currently no requirement for medical schools to provide properly structured educational programmes on alcoholism. The General Medical Council has made no specific recommendation about the inclusion of education on alcoholism in the undergraduate curriculum. In addition to the lack of undergraduate education and training, there is currently no provision of postgraduate training and certification for doctors and nurses wishing to take a special interest in the management of patients with alcohol problems. However the Royal College of General Practitioners, the largest membership organization in the UK solely for general practitioners, does offer a National Drug Misuse Training Programme with two different certificate level training packages.

THE MORAL AND MEDICAL NOTIONS OF ALCOHOLISM

The concept of inveterate drunkenness as a disease is rooted in antiquity. The Roman philosopher Seneca (Lucius Annaeus Seneca c4BC-65AD) classified it as a form of insanity. Sir Walter Ralegh (or Raleigh) (c1552-1618) was perhaps the first person in England who came close to the identification of alcohol as a drug of dependence. He referred to its "potential fixity of habit". In contrast, leaders of the temperance and total abstinence movements of the nineteenth century saw inveterate drunkenness as an immoral habit which could be addressed effectively with spiritual guidance by God's grace. To them consumption of alcohol and especially heavy drinking was a sin, a moral weakness. Any suggestion that inveterate drunkenness was some sort of disease would improperly eliminate personal responsibility.

Before the mid nineteenth century a range of terms was used to describe the heavy consumption of alcohol. In 1849, a Swedish physician, Magnus Huss, in *Alcoholismus Chronicus*, coined the term "alcoholism" to denote both the action of alcohol on the human system and what he saw as the diseased disorder or dependence produced by alcohol. In 1884, the first British professional society devoted to investigating alcohol behaviour called The Society for the Study and Cure of Inebriety was formed based on the founder's theory that alcoholism was a hereditary physical disease. During the First World War, however, the Society, under new leadership, began favouring the term "addiction" over "inebriety" because it wanted to advance a new theory that heavy consumption of alcohol was a problem more psychological than physiological, a "disease of the will". Only then did the word "addiction" begin to designate a pathological relationship with a psychoactive substance like alcohol rather than just a devotion to, or the enthusiastic pursuit of, something.

The question of whether or not addiction, now referred to as "dependence" by the World Health Organisation, and alcoholism as one psychoactive substance dependence, was a moral or a medical phenomenon has persisted to the present day. The history of dependence illuminates at least two notions that the early twenty-first century has in common with the nineteenth. The first (the moral notion) is the belief that alcoholism is a bad habit and that alcoholics can accordingly recover from alcoholism with spiritual guidance. The second (the medical notion) is the belief that only medical science can unlock the mysteries of the body and mind and effect recovery from alcoholism.

The notion that drives the moral approach to alcoholism is that it is essentially a moral weakness and that, even if by overindulgence the individual has become dependent on alcohol, remission is the product of a transformation. It is believed that the individual cannot bring about his recovery. It is believed that no doctor, psychiatrist, psychologist or therapist can either. Only a higher power can by bringing about a transformation in the alcoholic. The fundamentalist moral notion is that heavy alcohol consumption is a sin. The only true higher power is God. The Bible puts it as follows. "Do not get drunk on wine, which leads to debauchery. Instead, be filled with the Spirit." *(Ephesians 5:18)*

The notion that drives the medical approach is that alcoholism is essentially an illness which can only be reliably treated with medication and therapy. Such treatment can bring about an effective cure if the patient substantially adheres to the health care professionals' regimen. Alcoholism should be studied and treated by them and not by priests. Psychiatrists and psychologists in particular and doctors and therapists in general have been notoriously uninterested, if not downright hostile, towards religion and spiritual matters.

Medical practitioners can be critical, in particular, of AA's unscientific approach to alcoholism and recovery from it. Many see alcoholism as a matter exclusively for science and the scientific approach. When faced with the need for effective treatment those holding this view often find themselves at odds with those in recovery who insist that their recovery would not have been possible without a spiritual element.

Both notions address alcoholism rather than the alcoholic who is seen as playing little, if any, constructive part. The alcoholic either surrenders to God's will (often expressed in AA to be that the individual be happy, joyous and free) or he surrenders to the health professional's regimen and the need to follow it conscientiously.

However, the dominant role that the individual plays, as contrasted with the kind of treatment deployed, needs to be recognised both as regards his persistence in treatment and the eventual outcome of treatment. It is important for those seeking to provide treatment that they accept that the alcoholic is absolutely central to his recovery because it is his personality change and his change of lifestyle which is involved in his recovery.

The approach which the founders of AA took did not focus on alcoholism but on the alcoholic. After a few years its leading proponent, Bill Wilson, reviewed the steps which the relatively small number of alcoholics who had then entered recovery had taken.

Wilson recognised that the budding AA programme of recovery included elements from both the moral and the medical approaches. The first of AA's Twelve Steps adopts the medical approach. The alcoholic needs to admit that he has a medical disease whereby he is powerless over the effect that drinking alcohol has on him and as a consequence his life has become unmanageable. The following ten Steps set out the outline of how the alcoholic can recover from the medical disease adopting the moral approach. The Twelfth Step speaks of having had a spiritual awakening as the result of taking the Steps.

These two notions often came (and, indeed, still come) into conflict. Nevertheless, the theory that if a bad behaviour was again and again repeated, it would become habit-forming and might ultimately lie beyond the individual's power to control it, enabled some accommodation of the competing notions. Even so the polarity between them may help to explain how controversy about the treatment of alcoholics has at times escalated into bitter warfare. A universally accepted reconciliation of the different elements in the two notions remains to be effected.

A simple reconciliation of the moral and medical notions of alcoholism may simply be that the nearer an individual is to the normal drinking end of the continuum of drinking alcohol, alcohol abuse, alcoholism and real alcoholism, the more the moral notion has relevance and the nearer he is to the other end, the more the medical notion has relevance.

The idea that people suffering from a habit (in the sense of a habitual practice not involving any dependence) could with spiritual guidance help themselves, was a mainstay of two influential movements, the temperance and total abstinence movements. On the other hand, some maintained that drinking alcohol in excess amounted to more than just a bad habit. The earliest British medical writing that characterized heavy drinking as a disease was Thomas Trotter's *An Essay, Medical, Philosophical, and Chemical, on Drunkenness, and its Effects on the Human Body* (1804). Trotter's notion remained undeveloped for a century, but by the end of the nineteenth century, as medical knowledge grew, drinking to excess entered the fields of psychology and physiology alike. That certain types of heavy drinking constituted disease was again declared by E. M. Jellinek in *The Disease Concept of Alcoholism* (1960).

Nonetheless some in the field could not see heavy drinking as a disease properly so called but saw it as a disorder, the germ of which reached far back into childhood. They placed the blame for subsequent alcoholism on the child's distance from the father, on marital conflict and on disrupted families in childhood. They saw alcoholics as suffering from unresolved feelings of grief and loss and feelings of guilt and rejection coming from childhood experiences, maintaining that drinking alcohol in itself did not create their problem. Rather it was their neurotic insecurity resulting in mental illness or disorder which brought about their alcoholism: it created a tendency in the individual to "self-medicate", that is, to reach for a drink to anesthetize his intolerable feelings. Some still believe that alcoholism is rooted in unresolved childhood issues. Research shows that a large majority of alcoholics have had physically or mentally abusive childhoods.

However while this self-medication of a mental illness or disorder can indeed be a cause of alcoholism so can alcoholism be a cause of a mental illness or disorder. It is now being increasingly recognised that alcoholism can usefully be considered as a distinct condition with a life of its own and it can have antecedents unrelated to childhood experience. Family studies have confirmed a hereditary as well as an environmental element association between parental and child alcoholism. Today it is recognized that mental illness, mental disorder, alcoholism and other psychoactive substance dependence are closely linked and health care professionals (medical practitioners, nurses, therapists, counsellors, treatment centre proprietors, social workers and the many others who deliver treatment services to those who abuse or who are dependent on alcohol) talk in terms of concurrent disorder. An individual's alcoholism and his concurrent mental illness or disorder may need separate treatment.

In 1981 John Mack, a psychoanalyst, wrote to a young client of his about drinking becoming a vicious cycle

"The drinking becomes a vicious cycle; hence your feelings of self disgust. You feel you are not living up to what you want to be, which brings much pain and guilt. But only drink can anesthetise these awful feelings, which in turn bring a further violation of one's sense of self. You fear the boredom, the depression and loneliness that will come in the wake of giving up the drinking. Yet, strange as it may seem, I am persuaded that these feelings are the *result* of the drink, that is, they are brought about by drinking itself. Thus, the drink is more the cause of the isolation and the feelings of boredom ... after all, you were not such a lonely adolescence once.

You like to think you can control the drinking, that you can make a decision when to drink and when not to and how much. Every rational man likes to think that he is in control of his decision making. But once you are addicted to alcohol – and make no mistake about it, you have a true addiction – it is not within your powers to make this decision. The alcohol has an uncanny capacity to stimulate all sorts of rationalisations, but all of these rationalisations are in the service of not giving up. It is as if the alcohol had a life of its own and took over the personality and brought about attitudes and reactions which will further drinking."

ALCOHOL ABUSE AND ALCOHOLISM

Alcohol is a psychoactive substance. Psychoactive substances have the ability to change an individual's consciousness, mood and thinking processes. Alcohol abuse and alcoholism are complex phenomena that defy simple description or explanation. Regardless of the mix of contributory factors, it is important to address how alcohol affects the brain in order to begin to understand alcohol abuse and alcoholism.

Real alcoholism is being increasingly seen as an irreversible chronic condition in biological terms where the loss in brain volume and impairment of function can only be partially reversed. The World Health Organisation's *Report on the Neuroscience of psychoactive substance use and dependence* (2004) states that "with recent advances in neuroscience, it is clear that substance dependence is as much a disorder of the brain as any other neurological or psychiatric illness". The report states that it is important to recognize that psychiatric disorders and psychoactive substance dependence like alcoholism are "diseases stemming from underlying neuropathologies".

Most health care professionals accept that real alcoholism is currently incapable of cure. Accordingly, its treatment entails total abstinence. To this end the alcoholic can benefit from and may need formal treatment by way of psychotherapy or pharmacotherapy. In addition to, or instead of formal treatment, he can attend a mutual self-help group like AA. In contrast, alcohol abuse is a disorder not involving dependence and not requiring abstinence.

ALCOHOLISM AS PERCEIVED TODAY

It is now generally agreed that two major general factors can be distinguished as contributing to alcoholism. The first factor is the biological effect that alcohol exerts on the individual and the second is the biological status of the individual drinking alcohol. The first factor relates to the short term acute effects which alcohol has on the central nervous system, particularly the brain, and the peripheral nervous system and to the long term effects on them that occur after chronic exposure. The second relates to the individual's biological constitution, particularly any inherited pre-disposition to dependence, which affects his response to drinking alcohol.

I have referred to the long-standing conceptual difference between the moral notion and the medical notion of alcoholism. Differences in the two notions can still lead to conflict as to the nature of alcoholism and the appropriate treatment for it. The moral approach sees alcoholism largely as a voluntary behaviour in which individuals freely engage. The medical approach, in contrast, recognizes that, while many individuals abuse alcohol without developing alcoholism, a small proportion do become alcoholics. The individuals whose drinking has become involuntary should accordingly be qualitatively distinguished.

Recent research suggests that most alcohol abusers do not progress to alcoholism. In one study only three and a half per cent of subjects meeting the criteria for alcohol abuse met the criteria for alcoholism after a five year period. For the small proportion that do become alcoholic, some become dependent very quickly but for most it takes from five to thirty years to develop alcoholism. Further recent research suggests that twelve to thirteen per cent of drinkers become alcoholic within ten years of picking up their first drink. The US Institute of Medicine puts the percentage of drinkers who become alcoholic at fifteen per cent. With a good understanding of the events and behaviour that define alcoholism, the alcoholic can be clearly distinguished from the alcohol abuser in most cases.

Alcoholism is increasingly seen as a condition essentially of the brain. Alcohol causes profound activation of certain areas of the brain through its direct effect on them and by virtue of alcohol related cues and environments. Through associated learning processes, these can eventually lead to dependence following repeated exposure. The pleasure or other desirable effect caused by drinking reinforces its continuance and eventually can result in anticipatory desire and motivation triggered by places, people, objects, situations, emotions or other reminders of drink and drinking. The alcoholic can find it virtually impossible to ignore these cues and reminders. The reason for drinking may no longer be the reasons which caused the habit in the first place but the occurrence of an overpowering cue or reminder. An alcoholic can drink not because he wants to but because he has to.

Just as different people drink for different reasons, it may be that the brain systems involved in alcoholism differ from one individual to another. Personal differences in biology (including genetic makeup) and environment will influence the neurobiological effects of drinking alcohol in any particular individual. Nevertheless, the alcohol dependence syndrome lays down a generally applicable medical model of impaired control characteristics.

Neuroscientists have established that alcohol primarily affects the regions of the brain that manage the deep-seated autonomic nervous system, which carries out the vital biological regulatory processes concerned with the individual's interaction with his environment. The autonomic nervous system controls vital bodily functions, like heartbeat and digestion, which keep the individual alive and it operates independently of conscious intervention. Accordingly, the effects which alcohol has on this system, which can include a coercive drive to consume alcohol, are not under conscious control. This mechanism is thought to account for the alcoholic's drinking notwithstanding that he objectively knows that he should not go on drinking with the potentially disastrous, even fatal, consequences of so doing.

The action of alcohol on the autonomic nervous system explains the physical dependence but does not fully explain the compulsive behaviour associated with alcoholism. It has also been established that alcohol affects the regions of the brain that manage the limbic system, particularly the mesolimbic dopamine system, which is thought to be involved in producing pleasurable feeling and is associated with feelings of desire and reward. The limbic system controls emotional response and motivation and plays a key role in the learning, memory and motivational processes of the brain. The action of alcohol on the limbic system can support and strengthen the compulsion to drink. This action is a further explanation for the alcoholic's compulsive behaviour. Alcohol changes the way the brain functions, the mind works and the individual behaves.

The biological systems that have evolved to guide and direct behaviour towards stimuli that are critical to survival can be recruited and abnormally strengthened by repeated use of psychoactive substances like alcohol leading to the behaviour patterns characteristic of dependence. Alcohol alters brain receptors and neurotransmitters. It changes the individual's consciousness, mood and thinking processes by causing defective neurotransmitter functioning. Abnormal proteins (which can be the product of abnormal genes) result in abnormal transmitter synthesizing and breakdown enzymes and abnormal receptors resulting in difficulties in controlling drinking behaviour and in progressive neglect of alternative pleasures or interests.

So the alcoholic's inability to control drinking is not just lack of will power. Alcoholics do not lack will power as the successful acquisition of alcohol by them in the most adverse of circumstances bears witness. Rather the lack of control over, and the inability to stop, drinking is the product of a pathological impairment of executive brain function. In a sense, the problem with alcoholism is not in the bottle but in the brain structure and chemistry of the individual.

Alcoholism is now seen in terms of an integration of physiological and psychological processes leading to heavy drinking that becomes increasingly unresponsive to external circumstances or adverse consequences. Attention has been focused particularly on how alcohol interacts with psychological expectations.

Scientists use the term "neuroadaptation" to refer to the process whereby the brain adapts and changes its circuitry, function and chemistry and consequent mental activity as a result of alcohol and other psychoactive substance use and abuse. Beyond its immediate rewarding properties, drinking alcohol can cause alterations that may take hours or days or, when drinking is heavy, months or even years to reverse after drinking alcohol ceases. In addition, drinking alcohol on a chronic long term basis can cause permanent changes in the brain.

The process of neuroadaptation is vitally linked with another process which scientists call "reinforcement". The reinforcing effects of alcohol create an environment which, if perpetuated, can trigger the neuronal adaptations that result in dependence. An individual will repeat an action which brings pleasure or other desirable result. For most, drinking alcohol brings pleasure and desirable results. The desirable results include release of tension and loss of inhibition. Accordingly, drinking alcohol becomes regular for many. This is called "positive reinforcement".

For some, regular drinking causes significant neuroadaptation which results in withdrawal symptoms. Withdrawal symptoms include severe shaking, sweating, headache, nausea and vomiting, agitation and rapid heart rate, anxiety, insomnia, tremor, seizures, disorientation, outbursts of irrational behaviour and sometimes hallucinations. The symptoms generate cravings for alcohol. This is called "negative reinforcement".

It is generally accepted that the development of alcoholism, as with other dependence, is complex and progressive, is influenced by multiple genes, by nature and nurture, and effectively takes place in the brain and in the mind being the brain operating in an individual as uniquely configured in him by his individual history and that of the society in which he grows up.

COMBATING HEAVY DRINKING

Before the 1930s substantial attempts to combat the adverse effects of alcoholism largely involved temperance and total abstinence societies, predicated on the moral notion of alcoholism, some of which were started early in the nineteenth century. The medical response to the alcoholic centred on the establishment of special residential institutions, relatively pleasant for those who could afford the private ones and unpleasant for those who could not. By the early years of the twentieth century confidence in and support of the special residential institutions had declined but with the decline no new consensus emerged on the remedy for alcoholism. Up to the end of the 1960s, in the absence of any proper scientific research into the effectiveness of treatment approaches, individual practitioners championed any one from the ever-widening range of physical treatments which were being offered as a cure for alcoholism.

The late 1930s saw the development of AA, a movement which adopted elements largely from the moral approach but also from the medical approach, in a practical way. It emerged as a voluntary fellowship of men and women whose primary purpose was to stay sober and help other alcoholics achieve sobriety. Modern pharmacotherapy has its origins in the early 1950s. Starting in the late 1960s many of what were thought, on a medical basis, to be the effective elements of treatment were combined into the Community Reinforcement Approach which continues to be developed.

The moral notion of personal responsibility and agency embodied in the temperance and total abstinence movements still inheres in AA. Although alcoholics have the medical disease of alcoholism they may yet recover by following a spiritual path. In AA spirituality is differentiated from formal religion. One of AA's innovations is its emancipation of spirituality from its explicit roots in traditional religion. For AA members, no medication, no treatment, no doctor, no clergyman can substitute for the alcoholic's own personal responsibility for the decision to stay sober just for today and not to take the first drink for it is the first drink which triggers, immediately or some time later, the alcoholic's compulsion to continue to drink.

AA addresses the alcoholic and not alcoholism. It leaves medical issues to the medical profession and religious issues to the clergyman, rabbi, guru or religious scholar or official. It proceeds on the basis that the alcoholic has a disease which can be addressed by a practice of its programme of meetings and complimentary activities underpinned by its Twelve Steps. It has no theoretical views as to the nature of alcoholism and it has no particular theological dogma as to the spiritual basis of its programme.

Just because participation in AA, which essentially involves mutual self-help, can be effective does not mean that alcoholism is after all a will power or poor judgement condition. Alcoholism is increasingly being accepted as a chronic relapsing condition which is not primarily under conscious control. Such approaches as AA and psychotherapy work to the extent that they effectively address the largely subconscious dysfunctional brain function and the conscious and unconscious dysfunctional mental activity of the individual, that is to say, the brain and mental chemistry which is not operating normally or properly in the alcoholic. AA and effective psychotherapy, like cognitive behavioural therapy, work by virtue of their effecting a change of mindset (the established set of attitudes held by an individual by virtue of his current neuronal circuitry) through re-evaluation and self-education – by learning.

Learning is a process that results in a relatively permanent change in behaviour or behavioural potential based on experience. Experience is not the mere internal sensing of external occurrences. Myriad external occurrences present themselves to an individual's senses which never properly enter into his experience because they are of no interest. Those items of which notice is taken particularly, can have an influence on shaping the mind. Further, experience is not so much what happens to the individual as what he does about what happens to him.

The cognitive behavioural mechanisms embodied in various therapies and treatment programmes can facilitate the change from a drinking alcoholic to a recovering one. A primary agent of change is group affiliation and virtually all effective treatment programmes, particularly Community Reinforcement Approach programmes, have at their core group therapy. The personal mix of AA meetings, rendering service, regular contact in person, by telephone and email with other AA members, reading and writing and practice of the Twelve Steps in some manner which is the AA programme also has the group at its core.

HISTORICAL RESPONSES TO ALCOHOL ABUSE

Examples of the moral approach to recovery from alcoholism prior to the 1930s date back at least to the first Native American recovery circles as early as the second half of the eighteenth century. Individual Native Americans started to turn their own negative experiences with alcohol into a social movement of mutual support. Outside the Native American movement, total abstinence societies composed of alcoholics began to appear as early as 1831. Alcoholics also found support in seeking and maintaining abstinence in the myriad total abstinence societies which developed throughout the US, Europe and elsewhere from the early nineteenth century as well as in the many fraternal abstinence societies and clubs which developed later some linked to nineteenth and twentieth century treatment institutions.

For instance, the Washingtonian Movement (originally styled the "Washington Total Abstinence Society"), formed in 1840, was particularly, if briefly, successful in helping alcoholics to achieve sobriety. While it had at least 600,000 members at its peak in 1843, by 1845 its energy was spent and only the Boston Societies continued until 1860. It was the first widely available mutual self-help fellowship organised by and for alcoholics in recovery and there are threads linking the Washingtonian Movement with AA emerging a century later. Bill Wilson was well aware of it and he learnt vital lessons from it and its rather speedy decline.

Mutual self-help was carried on by many of the fraternal temperance societies and reform clubs which grew and declined between 1840 and 1940. Many had as members individuals who had been members of the Washingtonian Movement. The patient clubs and aftercare associations linked to treatment programmes link the fraternal temperance societies and reform clubs with the alcoholics involved in the Oxford Group and the emergence of AA.

An example of a fraternal abstinence society or club linked to a treatment institution was the Keeley League. The first of the Keeley Leagues was formed in 1891. They were mutual self-help associations of patients who had received treatment at Keeley Institutes the first of which was opened in 1879 and the last of which stopped accepting patients for treatment in 1966. During the 1940s representatives of AA approached the Keeley Institute about integrating AA into the Keeley treatment and AA meetings were sometimes held on Keeley premises.

From the 1830s, particularly in the US, some alcoholics became active in total abstinence work often using their personal stories on the lecture circuits to underline the need for complete abstinence. Clergymen also carried the same message in the US, Europe and in many other territories. For example, the temperance crusade of Father Theobald Mathew (1790–1856) in pre-famine Ireland was very successful. As a result of his advocacy in the years 1838 to 1845, the number of those who took the pledge of abstinence reached some three to four million out of a population of eight million. By the outbreak of the First World War there were well over three hundred temperance and total abstinence bodies in the UK alone. In addition to passing the message of abstinence, Salvation Army Hostels, Gospel Halls, Mission Halls and other groups inspired by their particular religions tried to help alcoholics.

The medical approach to recovery from alcoholism such as it was prior to the 1930s lacked appropriate methods and techniques to combat alcoholism and to bring about recovery. For the most part only incarceration and various types of banal physical treatment were offered. A text published in 1893 by the American Association for the Study and Cure of Inebriety included the following. "Prolonged hot baths are of the utmost service in the treatment of inebriety ... The preparation of hyposcyamus, conium, stramonium, camphor, hops, aconite, ether and chloroform are all of great service if given with judgement ... Milk heated to boiling is very valuable ... If there are decided signs of cerebral congestion the occasional application of a leech behind the ear is good practice..."

It was not until the 1930s that endeavours to develop a scientifically based treatment plan or therapy for those seeking help for acute alcohol problems was started inspired by Francis Chambers at the Institute of the Pennsylvania Hospital in the US. Before the 1930s, generally speaking, the emphasis of the medical approach was on sobering the alcoholic up, after which he was discharged with little or no understanding of the alcoholic or alcoholism. However, effective long term combating of alcoholism on a sizeable scale received a large boost with the start of what was to become AA in 1935. AA's survival takes on an added historical significance in the light of the demise of the large number of fraternal total abstinence societies and clubs which preceded it, particularly in the US, and which also focused on recovery.

Although some doctors had realized that some form of cognitive psychology was of urgent importance to alcoholics, it was generally accepted that its application presented difficulties beyond their conception. Even today alcoholism can be treated as if it were an acute illness rather than a chronic condition. When alcoholics relapse, as they so often do and often soon after treatment, some argued right up to the 1990s and beyond, that this showed that treatment did not work rather than that it stopped working when it was withdrawn as is the case with chronic diseases.

COUNTER MEASURES

Those seeking to put in place successful, appropriate and cost effective counter measures against alcoholism and alcohol abuse need to keep in mind the distinction between alcoholism and alcohol abuse. Alcoholism is at one extreme end of the alcohol use, abuse and dependence continuum. By ICD-10 definition alcoholism involves dependence on alcohol. Alcohol dependence involves unconscious conditioning and involuntary behaviour and it needs to be treated differently in many vital respects to alcohol abuse which does not involve dependence. Unlike alcohol dependence, alcohol abuse is essentially wilful. Alcohol abusers can be susceptible to pressure to stop and punishment but these factors *per se* have no effect on alcoholics. The majority of heavy drinkers are alcohol abusers who can, in the final analysis, control their drinking and not alcoholics who cannot, in the final analysis, control theirs.

Education and campaigns to encourage sensible drinking will have no effect on the drinking behaviour of alcoholics. Indeed, education will have little, if any, effect on the drinking habits of the alcohol abusers unless combined with other measures. Education and public information approaches can, though, mobilise public support for prevention measures. The long running drink-drive campaign, for example, has been successful because it has worked in tandem with policies on identification of offenders, tough enforcement and penalties which focus on preventing reoffending.

In the authoritative article in the February 2005 issue of the *Lancet*, Robin Room of the Centre for Social Research on Alcohol and Drugs, Sweden, Thomas Babor of the Department of Community Medicine and Health Care, University of Connecticut School of Medicine, US and Jürgen Rehm of the Addiction Research Institute, Switzerland and the Centre for addiction and Mental Health, Canada, as well as addressing the global burden of disease attributable to alcohol, assert that despite the scientific advances, alcohol problems continue to present a major challenge to medicine and public health. This is, in part, they say because population-based public health approaches have been neglected in favour of approaches to the individual that tend to be more palliative than preventative.

Until governments accept that evidence-based prevention measures are available at both the individual and population levels and are prepared to implement them, harm reduction countermeasures will achieve little. A case in point is the UK Prime Minister's Strategy Unit's *Alcohol Harm Reduction Strategy for England* (2004), which emphasises cooperation with the alcohol drinks industry and eschews effective strategies. The evidence is that increasing alcohol prices and reducing the licensing hours during which alcoholic drinks can be sold effectively reduces alcohol related harm. Yet the UK government does not currently see either of them as part of a harm reduction strategy.

The World Health Organisation has recognised excise tax policy as one of the most effective alcohol policy tools in reducing alcohol related harm because of its effect on price. Although the UK Chancellor raised alcohol duties and prices in the 2008 Budget, this was for revenue raising purposes in order to provide additional support for families and lift more children out of poverty. The increases were unrelated to alcohol harm reduction. Recent UK legislation has allowed increases in licensing hours up to twenty-four hours permitting pubs and clubs which successfully apply, to remain open all day and all night. A stark discrepancy exists between research findings about the effectiveness of alcohol control measures and the policy options adopted by government, particularly the UK government. In many instances the interests of the drinks industries have effectively exercised a veto over effective policies.

4

ALCOHOLISM AND TREATMENT

ALCOHOLISM, ALCOHOLICS AND THEIR TREATMENT

Alcoholism is extremely powerful in nature. The condition is usually progressive and often fatal. It is characterized by impaired control over drinking, preoccupation with alcohol, continuation of drinking despite adverse consequences and distortions in thinking, particularly denial. Even when recognised as a problem, alcoholics commonly view their alcoholism as being out of control, as trapping them or taking hold of them.

Typically for the real alcoholic, after a relatively gradual progression from the individual's first alcoholic drink, driven initially by choice rather than by compulsion, he eventually becomes completely preoccupied with drinking. A whole range of negative effects result and they become out of control. Despite the experience of negative effects, a wide range of factors, including physical dependence, compulsion and increasing tolerance levels, drive continued drinking often in increasing quantities. As his alcoholism develops, the individual can develop a realisation of his problem with alcohol and the need to change by doing something about his drinking. As the uncontrolled negative effects of drinking increase they can occasionally be influential in tipping the balance in favour of behavioural change, rather than continuing drinking, as they increasingly outweigh the opposing factors influencing continuing drinking.

All alcoholics in recovery have suffered a fortuitous build up of crises in many areas of their lives caused by their drinking which eventually for some, in some way, seems to force them into recognition of their condition or to precipitate such recognition. Very little is known about the cognitive processes through which the alcoholic recognises his condition and makes the decision to stop drinking. Most alcoholics, particularly real alcoholics, never recognise their condition and never take an effective decision to stop and they go on drinking to the bitter end of death or insanity seeing no solution to their condition except death. Some seek suicide accordingly and some successfully commit suicide.

Recovery depends on the severity of the alcoholism and on the individual encountering the right kind of life experience, the right configuration of crises, which can amount, in the individual's circumstances, to a recovery experience, that is to say, to a surrender and conversion experience and a maintained conversion state, to conversion. Paradoxically, in cases of very severe alcoholism, the severity itself and its consequences can eventually be favourable to recovery. The consequences of severe alcoholism are disruptive human emotions, particularly fear and anger, and trauma. Trauma and powerful emotion can trigger recovery. Overwhelmingly powerful trauma, or trauma sustained long and hard enough to increase suggestibility, can cause effective mechanisms of change to come into play and bring about recovery.

Specific life experiences, which amount to conversions because of the individual's particular circumstances at the time, appear often to be the critical factors in initiating recovery. Such general factors as growing older, treatment or having a stable pre-morbid personality, for example, do not seem to be particularly significant in initiating it. Conversion can occur at any time in the life cycle of alcoholism depending on the severity of dependence, the nature of the life experience and the circumstances of, and the configuration of the various crises experienced by, the alcoholic. Where an individual is only mildly dependent on alcohol which has lasted only a short time, a simple change in life conditions can bring about conversion. Very severe dependence can create profound trauma which can also effect conversion.

The fortuitous occurrence of life experiences which can disrupt entrenched habits and minimise relapse can take place at any time. The fortuitous experiences can include taking on an activity that competes with drinking alcohol, enforced abstinence, a marvellous new occupation, a new romantic attachment, attending AA or undergoing treatment but more often they include traumatic experiences including the built up of adverse circumstances causing a traumatic incident. They usually occur outside any therapeutic setting.

However, treatment as a factor in recovery can play an important, sometimes crucial, role. Treatment of different kinds can produce various benefits and many years later individuals can remember particular treatment episodes as being particularly significant in their eventual recovery. Since the available research suggests that a range of competently applied treatments with different theoretical underpinnings are likely to give roughly the same outcomes, it is somewhat difficult to establish what aspects of treatment are effective. Even though the positive components of treatment remain unclear, effective treatments probably have in common the capacity to catalyse and support natural processes of recovery.

No particular treatment is necessarily particularly effective. The circumstances of the alcoholic are more important than the amount or nature of treatment undergone. As regards initiating recovery the focus should be on the alcoholic's circumstances rather than on treatment components. It is the recognition by the alcoholic of his condition and the decision to stop drinking which is critical and treatment can help the individual to remain faithful to his decision. It is the decision to stop drinking and the commitment to abstinence which is vital rather than the factors which happen to bring about conversion.

Notwithstanding the fact that some alcoholics can recover without the aid of treatment or participation in a self-help group, the vast majority of alcoholics, particularly real alcoholics, can benefit from treatment. Many alcoholics engage in lengthy and extensive contact with treatment agencies before achieving recovery and their exposure to treatment could well have been crucial. Further, many alcoholics have found attending AA and practising its programme has been an essential factor in their recovery. Treatment and AA attendance can be helpful in many ways. For example, treatment or AA attendance can be helpful in nudging an alcoholic towards a more constructive way of seeing things and can help enhance self-efficacy.

Alcoholics, if they are to recover, need to believe that change is possible and skilled therapists and counsellors can be helpful in convincing alcoholics of this as can other alcoholics in self-help groups. Alcoholics need to be motivated and again therapists, counsellors and others in self-help groups can enhance motivation and, change being required, they can be helpful in clarifying appropriate goals. Successful recovery involves avoiding relapse. Avoiding relapse can be achieved by learning practical skills through counselling, therapy or self-help group participation. The chances of continuing abstinence can be increased with the building of supportive networks, particularly through self-help group attendance. Change needs to feel good for it to be maintained and positive affirmations of progress by therapists, counsellors and self-help group members can help alcoholics feel good in their recovery.

The great majority of real alcoholics do not achieve recovery. They go on to the bitter end, blotting out the consciousness of their intolerable situation as best they can. They do not ask for nor do they accept help. They seek not how to learn to live a contented sober life. There is no material change in them, no capitulation, no conversion and therefore no recovery. However, results from the US National Epidemiologic Survey on Alcohol and Related Conditions (NESARC) analysis (2001-2005) strengthen previous reports that many persons can and do recover from alcoholism. The analysis, the largest and most ambitious co-morbidity study ever conducted, revealed that there are considerable levels of recovery from alcohol and other psychoactive substance dependence.

Within the field of alcoholism and recovery from it there remain in general terms two distinct notions about alcoholism, one moral and one medical, which have their respective historical origins. The moral notion approaches alcoholism as a moral issue it being essentially a bad habit and accordingly alcoholics can recover from alcoholism by themselves albeit, many would say, only with the espousal of spiritual principles. The medical notion approaches alcoholism as a chronic illness and accordingly only medical science can effectively address it and bring about recovery from it. However doctors are increasingly recognizing the effectiveness of self-help groups like AA.

Treatment approaches still reflect the differences between the two notions. The Community Reinforcement Approach aims to achieve abstinence by eliminating positive reinforcement for drinking and enhancing positive reinforcement for sobriety. This approach is based on the latest neuroscientific understanding of alcoholism as a condition essentially of the brain and mind. SMART offers free scientifically based mutual help groups (including groups online) based on a Four-Point programme with a scientific foundation. AA offers a twelve-step based spiritual programme of recovery yet stresses that alcoholism is a disease. The Minnesota Model treatment is based on AA twelve-step facilitation therapy. SOS, while following the AA model to some extent, offer an alternative recovery approach for those alcoholics who are uncomfortable with the spiritual content of traditional twelve-step based programmes.

The treatment of alcoholism is a young science and the natural history of alcoholism over time is still far from being understood. Until fairly recently, alcoholism treatment research lagged behind standard medical and behavioural treatment research and randomized controlled trials, the most objective type of treatment research methodology, were rarely used by researchers. Many commonly used treatments have still not been adequately evaluated and need to undergo thorough controlled clinical trials. Far-reaching studies will be required to understand alcoholism and recovery from it and to diminish the current ineptitude in the field. Much more longitudinal research as to treatment effectiveness is needed. The still utterly mysterious way the brain's neuronal networking transforms the individual's subjective experience needs to be understood.

The processes by which alcoholics recover from alcoholism remain substantially unclear. Relatively little is known about them and about the contributions of treatment interventions and processes in facilitating recovery. Susan Greenfield, in *i.d. The Quest for Identity in the 21st Century* (2008), points out that while correlating biochemical processes with reports of how individuals feel can slowly begin to build up a picture of the physical and chemical bases of different subjective mental states, such correlations do not yet address causality.

She writes as follows. "Our current ineptitude is hardly surprising since neither the drugs, nor the transmitters they manipulate, have so-phisticated emotions locked away in the interstices of their molecular bonds! Rather, in some as yet still utterly mysterious way, the neuronal networking that can be so heavily influenced by drugs in turn transforms the holistic landscape of the brain, and with it your subjective experi-ence – like the well-known butterfly flapping its wings on one side of the world and, via a complex series of knock-on events, changing the climate on the other side of the planet."

However, there seems little doubt that key processes in recovery are those relating to the reversal, countering and compromising of the con-ditioning, reinforcement and neuroadaptation mechanisms which lead to alcoholism in the first place. But it remains unclear whether there is a spiritual component in these key processes and, if so, spiritual in what sense. Perhaps the neural mechanisms of placebo effects play a part. The spiritual component may amount to no more than the placebo effect or something akin to it. Recent studies have shown that the placebo effect based on expectation alone can be very powerful. Perhaps a crucial com-ponent in some alcoholics' recovery is that they expect or believe that their treatment, or their action in addressing their alcoholism, will work. It may be that, in some cases, the individual's very expectation concern-ing, and belief in, the efficacy of his action (whatever it may be) alone make it work for him.

UNCERTAINTIES

Some treat alcoholism as an acute illness rather than a relapsing condi-tion. Some maintain that alcoholics have an uncontrollable lifelong dis-ease that must be treated for the rest of their lives. Some say that because some alcoholics recover from alcoholism on their own without receiving any treatment, alcoholism cannot properly be described as a disease at all.

It is arguable that, without more longitudinal studies of both treated and untreated alcoholics, the current student of alcoholism can still go little further than to agree with Don Cahalan who in *Problem Drinkers: A National Survey* (1970) pointed out that with the passage of time "some alcoholics will die, some will become abstinent, some will return to social drinking and some will be unchanged". The proportion of alcoholics following any particular route is unknown. However, studies show that a minority of alcoholics remain sober one year after treatment while the majority have periods of sobriety alternating with relapses. Still others are unable to stop drinking for any length of time and others stop drinking for the rest of their lives. But, notwithstanding the difficulties, progress is being made. Many gaps remain to be filled in our knowledge of alcoholism but much is known about it that could be used to shape policy responses if properly correlated and evaluated.

APPROACHES TO TREATMENT

The 1930s saw the beginnings, in the US, of the AA movement and of modern psychotherapy. These two approaches to combating alcoholism together with pharmacotherapy, dominate the field of treatment for alcoholism at the beginning of the twenty-first century. The origin of modern pharmacotherapy, the treatment of diseases using medication, can be seen in the early 1950s when Antabuse, the first medication approved in the US for the treatment of alcoholism, was released.

By the beginning of 1939 AA membership had reached one hundred and the book *Alcoholics Anonymous* was published and the movement became known by that name. The book, the 4th edition of which was published in 2001, consisted of a basic text backed up by stories of individual alcoholics' experiences in the form of stories. Bill Wilson was the author of the basic text.

In writing it, Wilson drew heavily from the tenets of the Oxford Group particularly as expounded by Samuel Shoemaker with whom he was in constant close touch at the time. Growing out of the First Century Christian Fellowship started by Frank Buchman, an American Lutheran minister, in the US some years earlier, the Oxford Group emerged during the 1920s. Buchman believed that no one was beyond God's reach and anyone could make a new start. The Oxford Group attracted alcoholics desperate to make a new start by stopping drinking.

Shoemaker helped Wilson in his writing of the basic text of the Big

Book. The Twelve Steps of recovery, largely based on Oxford Group doctrine, are included in chapter 5, *How It Works*. Copies of Wilson's manuscript were distributed amongst selected members of the budding fellowship for evaluation and changes were made, mostly to the stories. In 1949 Wilson wrote to Shoemaker as follows. "So far as I am concerned, and Dr Smith too, the Oxford Group seeded AA. It was our spiritual wellspring at the beginning."

The book asserted that the real alcoholic was unable to control his drinking using his own uninformed devices. He had to find something which could enable him to cope, that is, deal effectively, with life without drinking alcohol. As he was effectively powerless over alcohol, the book argued, it had to be a power greater than himself. Accordingly, the book's main purpose was to enable the alcoholic to find such a power.

Twelve Steps and Twelve Traditions, written by Wilson helped by a couple of AA members, was published in 1953. Wilson described this book as follows. "This small volume is strictly textbook which explains AA's twenty-four basic principles and their application, in detail and with great care." Numerous other books and pamphlets have been published since then.

AA is a voluntary, worldwide fellowship of men and women from all walks of life who meet together to attain and maintain sobriety. Each group has the one primary purpose of carrying AA's message of recovery to the alcoholic who still suffers. The only requirement for membership is a desire to stop drinking alcohol. It contributes a great deal of help to countless alcohol abusers and alcoholics. AA has never attempted to keep any record of membership. However, based on reports to its US General Service Office in 1998, membership worldwide was then at least two million. Based on a Survey conducted by AA in the UK in 2005, membership was about 34,000. Both figures are probably underestimations.

The first AA meetings in the UK took place in London in 1947. Growth was slow at first, with only four or five groups and fifty members in London by 1953. AA had, however, spread to Manchester, Liverpool and other parts of the country. The first known meetings in the west of England and in Scotland were in 1948. The first UK AA Convention was held in Cheltenham in 1956. By 1974 England had over a hundred groups and by 1988 it had some four hundred. There are now well over six hundred weekly meetings in greater London alone.

In 1951 the American Public Health Association endorsed AA and it was presented with a Group Lasker Award "in recognition of its unique and highly successful approach to that age-old public health and social problem – alcoholism". The closing words of the citation declare that:

"Historians may one day point to Alcoholics Anonymous as a society which did far more than achieve a considerable measure of success with alcoholism as a stigma; they may recognise Alcoholics Anonymous to have been a great venture in social pioneering which forged a new instrument for social action, a new therapy based on the kinship of common suffering, one having vast potential for the myriad ills of mankind".

Francis Chambers, a lay therapist, joined the staff of the Institute of the Pennsylvania Hospital in the US in 1935. With the support of senior medical staff members at the Institute, he worked out a psychotherapeutic treatment plan intended to address the acute alcohol problems of those seeking help. Chambers, an alcoholic, had been treated unsuccessfully at eleven different treatment institutions before he received counselling from Richard Peabody as a result of which he stopped drinking. Peabody, also an alcoholic, was a client of Courtney Baylor who began work in 1913 as probably the first alcoholic to work professionally as a paid counsellor. Peabody, who established a private counselling practice in the early 1920s, trained Chambers to become a lay therapist.

Chambers' therapy, heavily influenced by Peabody's training, had the then rare characteristic of being a positive rather than a negative approach. By and large, at this period, most treatment consisted of the facilities offered by rest homes and cures, where the whole emphasis was placed on sobering a man up. Temporary sobriety having been achieved, he was then discharged with little or no understanding of himself or his problem. With Edward Strecker, who held the Chair of Psychiatry at the University of Pennsylvania, Chambers wrote the book *Alcohol: One Man's Meat*, published in 1938. This book, because it presented a positive treatment plan, had the effect of stimulating a more optimistic approach towards alcoholism.

There are two main therapeutic approaches to the formal treatment of alcoholism in treatment centres, which can be residential or day-care centres. One is the Minnesota AA Model (MAAM) and the other is the Community Reinforcement Approach (CRA). The MAAM based on AA philosophy and twelve-step facilitation therapy emerged in the early 1950s and remains very popular. The MAAM is based on AA philosophy and its aim is to facilitate attendance at AA meetings and involvement in AA by combining therapy with twelve-step practice. Individuals typically are guided through the first five Steps and they are actively encouraged to attend AA meetings, to become involved in the AA fellowship and to practise its programme.

The MAAM draws heavily on the experience of AA members in its concept of alcoholism as a primary, progressive disease whose management requires sustained abstinence and an active, continuing spiritual programme of recovery. However, many health care professionals, across Europe in particular, eschew this US disease concept of alcoholism and prefer the World Health Organisation's concept in accordance with its ICD-10 definition of the dependence syndrome quoted previously. In simple terms, the MAAM adopts the moral approach to alcoholism while the CRA adopts the medical approach.

Over thirty-five years ago in the US, many of the perceived active ingredients of alcohol treatment were combined in the CRA. The first study demonstrating the effectiveness of it appeared in the US in 1973. The approach is multifaceted and it has been continuously developed since its inception. It aims to achieve recovery by eliminating positive reinforcement for drinking and enhancing positive reinforcement for sobriety. In nearly every review of alcohol treatment outcome research in the US the CRA is listed among approaches with the strongest scientific evidence of efficacy.

The CRA is designed to make changes in the individual's daily environment. Several treatment components including group therapy are integrated into the approach. The aim is to build up the alcoholic's motivation to stop drinking, to initiate recovery and to learn new coping skills and behaviours. The CRA's underlying philosophy is simple. The alcoholic's life needs to be reorganized to make recovery more rewarding than drinking if recovery is to be brought about. The alcoholic, the health care professional and, as appropriate, his family members, work together to this end seeking to change the alcoholic's mindset and lifestyle, particularly his social support system and activities.

The focus of many of the treatment components is on increasing the alcoholic's sources of positive reinforcement that are unrelated to drinking. As individuals become increasingly dependent on alcohol, their range of non-drinking activities, such as hobbies, sport and social involvement narrows substantially, resulting in increasing isolation. Accordingly, an important component of recovery for the alcoholic is to reverse this isolation process by increasing the range of enjoyable activities that do not involve drinking and by becoming involved with other people in non-drinking situations.

Several treatment components can help in this process. For example, social and recreational counselling is used to help the client choose positive activities to fill time that was previously consumed by drinking and recuperating from its effects. Activities are preferred that bring the client into contact with other people in non-drinking contexts. Such activities might include participation in common interest clubs such as sports clubs, visits to alcohol free establishments or participation in volunteer activities. Other components of the CRA are designed to help clients organize not only their leisure activities but also, if necessary, their regular daily lives.

The CRA can take the form of structured day care programmes providing intensive community based support, treatment and rehabilitation with clear programmes of defined activities for a fixed period of time with specific attendance criteria, usually four or five days a week for a minimum of twelve weeks and an aftercare programme available for at least two years. CRA centres usually employ health care professionals with appropriate skills and ties within the community, including social services, general practitioners, borough councils and police enabling them to provide a structured day care service and to make referrals where necessary.

The CRA approach differs from MAAM's approach in its emphasis on self-efficacy and the practical ways of eliminating positive reinforcement for drinking at the same time as building support for sobriety, rather than on AA and its Twelve Steps. While clients are introduced to and are encouraged to use outside support groups, projects and activities, they are encouraged to look further than AA, Narcotics Anonymous or other Twelve Step based fellowships. The approach takes cognizance of the fact (often forgotten by health care professionals) that many individuals recover from alcoholism without going anywhere near a health care professional, treatment agency or AA. The view is taken that while some individuals may be able to recover on their own, a course of CRA treatment can facilitate and bring about natural recovery.

Many MAAM treatment centres have sought to incorporate in their treatment models elements of the CRA in order to enhance the traditional MAAM. CRA and enhanced MAAM facilities can provide similar treatment elements and components, any substantial distinction between them being with regard to the emphasis on AA tenets, twelve-step work and AA attendance. In particular, MAAM treatment centres place emphasis on such concepts as a power greater than the alcoholic, spiritual awakening and keeping it in the day as propounded in AA, none of which concepts CRA treatment centres and many other therapies would necessarily agree with, let alone espouse.

Modern pharmacotherapy, the third substantial approach to combating alcoholism today, had its origin in 1951 when Antabuse was approved by the US Food and Drug Administration (USFDA). It was introduced as "the drug that builds a 'chemical fence' around the alcoholic, now available for general prescription use in the fight against the Nation's number one emotional disease". It can act as a deterrent but only if it is ingested. The difficulty is that the alcoholic has the choice between drinking and taking it, and the urge to drink can easily win. There is very little research to support claims that use of Antabuse is an effective treatment by itself. However, other medications have continued to be developed.

Naltrexone (ReVia) (the second medication to obtain USFDA approval in 1986) interacts with brain chemistry and has shown promise. It is said to help alcoholics control the urge to drink by altering the effects of alcohol. Researchers believe that such opiate antagonists (substances which initiate a physiological response) when combined with a receptor (something which responds to a particular neurotransmitter) can help alcoholics change their behaviour when used in conjunction with psychotherapy. Another medication, acamprosate (Campral) (the third to obtain USFDA approval in 2004, although legal in Europe since 1989) has also shown encouraging results. It, too, alters the effects of alcohol although it is not an opiate antagonist. Effective medications do seem to be becoming available for treating alcoholism but in the context of wider treatment. No doubt other medications will be approved in due course.

TALK THERAPY

Alcoholism is one of the few conditions which can be effectively treated verbally. In therapy and counselling sessions, the client and his therapist or counsellor talk to each other. Treatment may simply comprise therapy or counselling sessions or it may be a Community Reinforcement Approach or Minnesota AA Model programme embodying such sessions. In AA meetings members share orally. They also talk to each other before and after meetings, at other times face to face and on the telephone. AA members also communicate by email and they read AA and other recovery related literature. They may attend AA literature study groups, particularly ones studying the Big Book.

Therapists and counsellors, as well as just talking, sometimes suggest that a client undertakes some written work like a life story or a comparison of the advantages and disadvantages of drinking or, in AA, a sponsor will suggest a written Step Four moral inventory and later a Step Eight list of persons harmed. An AA sponsor is one alcoholic who has made some progress in recovery who agrees with another, usually less experienced one, to help in his recovery on an ongoing basis. Recovery can be initiated, sustained and maintained by verbal communication orally and in writing.

In the AA context, the member goes to a meeting for his own sake, for help in attaining, maintaining and sustaining recovery by listening and talking. He shares his experiences by talking about them and listens to others talking about their experiences. He talks, and listens to others' talking, to help himself. Bill Wilson talked to Bob Smith (AA's other co-founder) not so much to help Smith but to stop himself, Wilson, taking a drink, although Wilson emphasised to Smith that he was speaking to him because, as Wilson saw it, they needed each other. Smith found talking to Wilson helpful because, as another alcoholic, Wilson was the first living human with whom Smith had ever talked who understood alcoholism from actual experience, not from reading or hearing about it.

Psychologists have only just begun fully to appreciate the usefulness of stories and of storytelling in the recovery process. Two forms of cognitive functioning have been distinguished which have been termed "argument" and "story". Both have the purpose of convincing, but where argument convinces the intellect of logical truth, story convinces the emotional mind of experiential truth. Experiential truth can be much more important than logical truth in recovery.

Purposeful storytelling, particularly mutual storytelling, can be a mechanism whereby alcoholics can begin to understand their lives and appreciate reality by listening to and taking notice of the feedback from others consequent upon their storytelling. Changes in the alcoholics' beliefs, attitudes and behaviour can be brought about from this experience. This is what happens in the rooms of AA and when recovering alcoholics talk to each other inside or outside the rooms about their alcoholism and how to cope with it. This mechanism can be seen as the crucial factor in AA's effectiveness rather than belief in God.

SPEECH ACTS

Because alcoholism can be effectively treated through oral communication, speech acts play a large part in recovery. They are some of those complex groups of things surrounding the use of words including those which are typically performed when speaking. There are all sorts of other things individuals can do with words in addition to simply making statements. Individuals by speaking can also perform acts. They can, for example, make requests, ask questions, give orders, make promises, give thanks, offer apologies, make affirmations, and express beliefs.

Almost any utterance is really the performance of several acts at once, distinguished by different aspects of the speaker's intention. There is the saying of something, what is done in saying it and the affect the saying has on the listener. In general, speech acts are acts of communication. However, some have the function not so much of communicating but of affecting states of affairs. Speech acts in the form of storytelling can convince an individual of experiential truth as well as logical truth in the form of argument.

The later Wittgenstein (Ludwig Wittgenstein, 1889-1951) came to think of language not primarily as a system of representation but as a vehicle for all sorts of social activity. "Don't ask for the meaning" he admonished "ask for the use". But it was J. L. Austin in *How to Do Things with Words* (1961) who presented the first systematic account of the use of language. While Wittgenstein could be charged with having conflating meaning and use, Austin was careful to separate the two. He distinguished the meaning of the words used from the speech acts performed by the speaker when using them. The distinction is between saying something and what is done in saying something. This broader distinction applies to both statements and other sorts of speech acts and takes into account the fact that the individual does not have to say "I suggest ..." to make a suggestion, "I apologize ..." to make an apology and so on.

Austin distinguished the simple act of saying something meaningful, the force of employing language for some purpose, and the further act of having an actual effect on those who hear the utterance. For example, by saying to a friend "that is a revolting shirt" in addition to communicating the speaker's evaluation of the shirt, he might also insult the friend or persuade him to dress differently. Certain effects can be achieved by saying things. Austin observed the effect that an utterance can have on the thoughts, feelings and attitudes of the listener. Many utterances not only describe reality but also have an effect on it. The attitudes and concepts that individuals acquire and transmit are in general the ones most likely to seem convincing to them in their circumstances. This is an aspect of human minds being organised as they are.

In the recovery context, most, if not all, start their recovery at a very low ebb, prey to great fear and uncertainty. They will usually want guidance and, in a therapeutic environment like a therapy session or an AA meeting, they are more likely to accept the assertions, claims and statements made by the therapist or other AA members respectively. In an AA meeting the frequent assertion of the role of God in recovery can be more readily accepted. AA advocates certain attitudes and concepts and by virtue of the meetings and other communication which are part of the AA programme and the AA fellowship generally, they can flourish and can pass from one member to the next facilitating, even bringing about, recovery.

Positive regular affirmations can change negative attitudes into more positive ones and affirmative word and speech usage can empower. These speech acts can encourage the individual to change and can, spreading as ideas, encourage others to change. The changes brought about by speech acts expressing therapeutic ideas can play a crucial role in initiating, maintaining and sustaining recovery.

In AA, for example, denial of alcoholism is transformed into an insistence upon the spoken admission "my name is so-and-so and I am an alcoholic" before saying anything else in an AA meeting. This is an important example of a speech act relevant to recovery. The person who utters these words is engaging in surrender and is giving up the claim that he is not an alcoholic. The alcoholic is also claiming a passport and bonding with a room full of listeners who feel safe in using the same formula as a password. It is a formulation of the problem, an explanation of past behaviour and the cornerstone for the building of recovery. It is a new definition of what is wrong and has been wrong probably for many stressful and perplexing years. When first spoken by an emotionally charged individual in an AA meeting, it can in itself amount to an effective conversion leading to the individual's recovery.

Fertile phrases and useful ideas imparted by doctors, counsellors, friends, family and other alcoholics in the context of addressing alcoholism can catch on in the mind and facilitate and drive the recovery process in the individual alcoholic. Useful ideas would also include those expressed in slogans such as "it is the first drink that counts", "nothing is so bad that a drink will not make it worse", "stick with the winners" and "pick up the telephone not the glass".

Storytelling is very useful in the recovery process. Story convinces the mind of the truth of experience. Belief by the alcoholic as he contemplates recovery that alcoholics are capable of recovery and that some have contentedly stopped drinking is important. Recovery is facilitated by mutual storytelling relating to how alcoholics drank, stopped drinking and entered into recovery. Listening to the stories can bring about beneficial changes in the alcoholic's beliefs, attitudes and behaviour.

ONE-TO-ONE AND GROUP THERAPY AND AA MEETINGS

In one-to-one therapy, the therapist can teach the alcoholic how to change enough and the alcoholic can learn sufficient skills to address recovery. Group therapy can be an even more potent way of doing this by virtue of more individuals taking part in the informative dialogue. Group therapy can be conducted formally in a treatment centre with a professional facilitator or informally in an AA meeting. AA meetings exemplify the elements which make up what can be for the individual an effective course of talk therapy embodying the speech acts which further recovery.

Today there is a wide variety of therapy and treatment available and a large number of schools of psychotherapy in particular. The efficacy of the practice of some of the individual disciplines is uncertain. The future for many schools of therapy and methods of treatment should depend on continuing research, not only into theory and practice, but also into clinical efficacy. Alcoholics may be less suited to psychotherapies like psychoanalysis which delve deeply into their past. They may be better helped by cognitive behavioural therapy or motivational enhancement therapy, for example. Many recovering alcoholics combine regular therapy sessions with regular AA attendance.

A typical Central London lunch time meeting lasts for an hour. The meeting opens with the Secretary introducing himself by stating his first name and that he is an alcoholic and asking for a few moments silence for members to remember why they are present and the still suffering alcoholic. He then asks another member to read AA's preamble, which reads as follows.

"Alcoholics Anonymous is a fellowship of men and women who share their experience, strength and hope with each other that they may solve their common problem and help others to recover from alcoholism. The only requirement for membership is a desire to stop drinking. There are no dues or fees for A.A. membership; we are self-supporting through our own contributions. A.A. is not allied with any sect, denomination, politics, organization or institution; does not wish to engage in any controversy; neither endorses nor opposes any causes. Our primary purpose is to stay sober and help other alcoholics to achieve sobriety.[2]"

Thus the scene is set. The Secretary has identified himself as an alcoholic and the basis and purpose of the meeting has been established. The Secretary then introduces another AA member, whom he has previously chosen, to speak for ten to fifteen minutes sharing his experience of aspects of his alcoholism and recovery. The meeting is then thrown open for either raised voice or raised hand general sharing. Members respond to the speaker by sharing their experience. The meeting is brought to a close by the Secretary when a collection is taken, those who made the meeting possible thanked and the Serenity Prayer chorused. The Serenity Prayer reads as follows. "God grant me the Serenity to accept the things I cannot change; Courage to change the things I can; and Wisdom to know the difference."

In such manner, with numerous variations, AA meetings bring into play the effective factors embodied in talk therapy. By virtue of a mixture of ritual and speech acts individual alcoholics can facilitate and enhance their recovery. By listening to alcoholics sharing their experiences regularly over time and by sharing their own, they can keep abreast of what they need to bear in mind and to do to maintain their sobriety.

In AA meetings in central London it is quite apparent, listening to the

---

[2] © AA Grapevine Inc. 1947 Reprinted with permission

sharing, that some members espouse the traditional AA quasi-religious approach and share in terms clearly based on the assumption that recovery can only be brought about by virtue of a spiritual experience involving belief in God as they understand him (usually the Christian God) while other members express their irreligion and share on the basis that God has not played any part in their recovery. Some members of AA believe in God and some do not, yet they meet together in harmony without any conflict between them and recover together notwithstanding their different beliefs.

This suggests that the crucial factor in AA that has the effect of maintaining long term sobriety, may not be so much the emphasis on God, as understood by the alcoholic as expressed in AA's Twelve Steps and literature, but rather the continuing participation in a support group of fellow alcoholics that promotes a lifestyle based on a practical programme which can enable alcoholics to cope with life without drinking alcohol. Certainly it suggests that neither belief in God as a supernatural power nor in spirituality in a religious content sense is an essential ingredient of successful recovery.

TREATMENT AND SOCIETY

Society's failure to treat alcoholism begins with a failure to diagnose people with alcohol problems early on. Heavy drinkers who are not yet dependent often respond well to medical advice but screening and advice is rarely conducted or given in doctors' surgeries or in emergency or other hospital units. Compared with chronic diseases, only a small fraction of alcoholics are identified and treated in the early stages of the condition. It is far easier to treat alcoholism early in its natural history, before the drinker evolves an elaborate denial system to alleviate his despair. The earlier the alcoholic can be engaged the better; early minimal interventions can be remarkably effective while treatment of long term alcoholics severely dependent on alcohol can be extremely problematic. The general approach to alcoholism is unlike that expected and demanded for the treatment of diabetes, hypertension, asthma or virtually any chronic disease.

In the UK today, while in the private sector treatment for alcoholism can be excellent, in the public sector, while much dedicated effort is made by health care professionals and others in the field, treatment is generally underfunded and haphazard and consequently ineffective. The various components as may be necessary from time to time, in an individual's case, to initiate and sustain his recovery are not usually substantially available or deployed at the appropriate time in a coordinated manner. The requisite components in addition to treatment itself include such services as housing, education, employment, child care, mental health, general practitioner and debt counselling. All these components cannot be provided by a single public agency resulting in their delivery being uncertain.

There is a growing recognition that the alcoholic's psychology needs to be treated as well as his physiology and that the treatment of alcoholism should emphasise ease of access, chronic rather than acute care and collaboration rather than confrontation. Alcoholics rarely receive the help that they need until they are in crisis. And even then, they are usually treated for a limited period of time and then left to their own devices, as if cured. It should also be recognised that the relationship between the alcoholic and the health care professional is usually far more important than the type of treatment practised. The alcoholic's view should not be discounted or marginalised during the treatment process. His view is vital to his recovery.

There is a qualitative distinction between the twelve-step and the psychotherapeutic approaches and the pharmacotherapeutic approach. The first two are effectively talk therapy while the third involves medication. The proponents of pharmacotherapy are recognising that medication alone is usually not enough: it should be combined with one or other or both of the other approaches. Further psychotherapists, even twelve-step facilitation therapists, are recognising the need for medication often in the detoxification stage and as a useful adjunct for some clients in later stages. Increasingly treatment programmes are combining pharmacotherapy and psychotherapy. However, notwithstanding the use of medication for detoxification purposes and its use in treatment as an adjunct to therapy, alcoholism is one of the few conditions which can be effectively treated through verbal communication alone.

Treatment needs to be tailored for each individual as he presents himself for treatment. While alcohol abuse and alcoholism is a continuum, at some stage an individual who becomes an alcoholic passes a point at which he becomes dependent on alcohol. Dependence commonly starts as mild dependence and can develop, sometimes slowly sometimes quickly, through moderate to severe dependence. At the mild end motivational enhancement therapy, other counselling or AA attendance may be sufficient to bring about recovery. But this will only be so if combined with the treatment of any medical or mental illness and with the addressing of any other issues affecting the individual's ability to address his recovery adequately such as housing, debt or personal relationship issues.

Individuals with moderate to severe dependence may require cognitive behaviour therapy, pharmacotherapy, and sustained attention by medical, psychiatric, social services, criminal justice and other service providers as required. Those with severe dependence unresponsive to repeated treatment attempts, especially when combined with chronic medical or psychiatric illness or disorder may require the sustained deployment of the full panoply of treatment and other services as appropriate as long as may be necessary. However, there are many alcoholics with very severe dependence and profound problems who find recovery through AA participation alone.

There are also countless alcoholics across the whole continuum of dependence who, because of no treatment, or because of inadequate or inappropriate treatment or in spite of excellent, timely and apparently adequate and appropriate treatment, never achieve recovery. Whether treatment works and whether an individual finds recovery appears to be something of a lottery. Perhaps scientists, in their attempts to address alcoholism and recovery from it, will, one day, establish a body of knowledge which will afford sufficient understanding of the condition so as to make effective treatment and recovery less uncertain.

Formal treatment is only one way of addressing alcoholism. Many individuals who change their drinking behaviour do so without engagement in any formal treatment and many achieve sobriety by their own efforts. Although formal treatment, particularly psychotherapy, can provide an excellent environment for change, there are fewer differences and many more similarities between those who change relying on treatment and those who change without any formal treatment. In effect it can be said that all change is an inside job, being in essence self-change, that formal treatment is but professionally coached or facilitated self-change and that AA is but mutual self-change.

While there is persuasive evidence to suggest that formal treatment of various kinds can produce benefit for alcohol abusers and alcoholics alike, one of the paradoxes of recovery from alcoholism is that the trigger which initiates the recovery process in the great majority of cases takes place outside any clinical interaction. Formal treatment should be seen usually as a reinforcement mechanism, occasionally as a starting point but never as the whole solution. Non-treatment factors associated with recovery and sobriety, like substitute dependence, behaviour modification, enhanced hope and self-esteem and social rehabilitation, should be given due weight.

Social services including access to housing, employment, child care and other benefits services, mental health services, education and vocational training, debt counselling and criminal justice may have to be accessed in order to prevent adverse factors bearing on the alcoholic's cognition and making him less likely to address his alcoholism. Inappropriate housing, in particular, is often one of the most destabilizing factors in the recovery process. Often a great deal of energy and resources are devoted to providing appropriate treatment but none to the matter of housing. Unemployment is another destabilizing factor; so is lack of child care particularly for women. Living with an unhelpful partner in a destructive relationship can be profoundly destabilizing. Relapse is frequently the consequence of failure to address destabilizing factors.

It is difficult to measure the efficacy of alcohol treatment for many reasons. Control groups made up of no-treatment individuals, of individuals attending formal treatment sessions only, of those just attending self-help groups such as AA and so on are inherently difficult, if not impossible, to form in practice. Alcoholism should be addressed as a chronic relapsing condition and not as an acute or temporary illness. It is difficult to distinguish between recovery due to treatment and to other causes. In the absence of adequate data, about all that is generally accepted is that treatment of some kind is usually better than no treatment at all.

Each approach, twelve-step, therapy and medication, was at first met with an optimistic welcome. The initial optimism has since, inevitably, been qualified by the realization that each approach has, along with successes, many failures. This does not mean, of course, that psychotherapy or pharmacotherapy cannot be useful or that the AA programme cannot be helpful.

AA continues to help countless alcoholics. Therapy, in one-to-one sessions and as developed in the Community Reinforcement Approach and the enhanced Minnesota AA Model treatment approach, continues to help numerous alcoholics in their quest for sobriety. Antabuse, despite some fatal failures and its inherent difficulties, can be helpful, either in pill form or as an implant, to some alcoholics in reinforcing their determination not to drink while attending AA or therapy sessions. It can be used as a component of the Community Reinforcement Approach. Naltrexone and acamprosate are being increasingly prescribed in order to enhance the effectiveness of other, non-pharmacotherapeutic treatments. Research into additional potentially useful medications continues.

The multifaceted nature of the Community Reinforcement Approach and the enhanced Minnesota AA Model approach exemplifies the variable, combination treatment approach to the treatment of alcoholism which is increasingly being accepted as best practice today.

5

TRANSFORMATION

THE IDEA OF TRANSFORMATION

A drinking real alcoholic who becomes contentedly abstinent can be described as transformed. In profound ways he becomes a different person. He can cope with life without drinking while before he could cope with little without a drink inside him.

In Harry Tiebout words, the alcoholic in recovery effectively maintains a conversion state following a surrender and conversion experience. Tiebout considered the surrender an unconscious event, not willed by the alcoholic. Surrender takes place only when an individual with certain traits in his unconscious mind experiences a particular set of circumstances. The conversion state in some cases amounts only to submission.

MAKING CHANGES AND NEUROADAPTATION

Whether there is indeed a useful distinction to be made between unconscious and conscious states of mind in conflict or between surrender and submission and whether it is useful to speak of an individual's surrender at any one time as more or less permanent may well be debateable. Modern cognitive therapy treats awareness as a continuum rather than as a dichotomy separating conscious from unconscious experience. What does seem to be the case, though, is that some alcoholics eventually do go through a process of transformation, a process of neuroadaptation in the brain. They accept their alcoholism, surrender to their condition and start to develop an increasingly stable contented sobriety as time passes provided that they do not pick up that first drink.

The new constellations of neural connections in the brain involved in conversion can develop through use and become more established. Neuronal connections are highly dynamic and they are changed by experience. As the alcoholic pursues his sober life, the neural connections involved in his sober experiences can strengthen and grow and lessen the likelihood of his taking a drink. In time they can build up an increasingly secure and contented sober mindset and lifestyle. At the same time the old constellations of neural connections relating to the drinking mindset and lifestyle can begin, and can continue, to atrophy, or at least become less potent, by virtue of disuse. Because of its plasticity, the brain is able to organise and re-organise in response to experience.

Alcohol affects brain functioning and mental activity by its capacity to interfere with the biological system of chemical messengers which all the time is regulating the balance between activity and inactivity in brain cells and brain circuitry. Once alcohol is no longer being ingested it can no longer interfere with, or in some way hijack, the functioning of extremely complicated brain and mind systems. Accordingly, the brain's functioning can begin to return to increasing degrees of normality as the damage caused by alcohol capable of repair is increasingly repaired over the weeks, months and years.

CONVERSION

An alcoholic whose alcoholic mindset remains totally dominant is going to continue to drink. The dominance of the alcoholic mindset needs to be compromised. Conversion initially reflects a state of personal desperation and helplessness. It is evidence that the alcoholic mindset has been compromised. An awareness of vulnerability has surfaced and the alcoholic has become more tractable. The more conversion involves a profound hopelessness or a deep desperation the better a predictor it is of a continuing recovery thereafter.

Harry Tiebout seems to me to have expressed exactly my own experience. From 1973 until 1994, I had a series of minor conversions and a number of unsustained conversion states which lasted for varying lengths of time. As I see it, I failed to take the action necessary to sustain any of my successive conversion states and therefore to achieve any lasting recovery. But I hope that my conversion in 1994 and my continuing AA involvement since then have established a lasting state of genuine recovery.

Nowadays Tiebout's expositions may seem somewhat dated and limited. His insistence on surrender, conversion and conversion state as he saw them and his emphasis on defiance and grandiosity may only have relevance to some alcoholics. Alcoholics may not necessarily have to surrender and be converted nor are they necessarily all defiant and grandiose quite in the way Tiebout describes them in *The Act of Surrender in the Therapeutic Process*. In *Surrender versus Compliance in Therapy* he expands on his distinction between surrender and submission and in *The Ego Factors in Surrender in Alcoholism* he expands on the relevant character traits involved.

Reading his papers as a whole, Tiebout's model of recovery seems to me to be consistent with modern models of change. Tiebout's model and modern models recognise that reality needs to be accepted and then addressed by doing something about it, that change does not usually proceed in a linear fashion and that there is a vital need for maintenance.

Tiebout speaks of conversion as a process that can take time and that the conversion can be major or minor. He expands on what he means by "defiance" and "grandiosity" and most alcoholics appear to exhibit, to a greater degree than non-alcoholics, the personality traits to which Tiebout refers in *The Ego Factors in Surrender in Alcoholism* as being those which need to be substantially surrendered or severely compromised if recovery is to be achieved and sustained.

In the process which Tiebout maintains the alcoholic must undergo before his alcoholism can be arrested, the personality traits which need to be addressed are immature traits which have been carried over from infancy into adulthood. He identifies them as "a feeling of omnipotence, inability readily to tolerate frustration, and excessive drive, exhibited in the need to do all things precipitously". The traits as they manifest themselves in adulthood can be characterised as immature character traits.

The alcoholic tends to harbour feelings of being special and different as a hangover from the infant's feeling of omnipotence. The alcoholic can find it difficult to function happily on an ordinary level. He takes for granted his ability to administer his affairs and those of others. He believes that he is a natural executive and he can see others as jealous people intent on blocking his progress. His difficulties in tolerating frustration stem from an inner imperiousness. Behind this lies the assumption that he should not be stopped. As an aspect of his excessive drive, the alcoholic tends to jump to conclusions and to act hastily without giving matters due consideration.

The immature alcoholic assumes that he should never be stopped. Accordingly he takes it for granted that it is right for him to go ahead. He has no real expectation of being stopped and hence has little capacity to adjust to that eventuality. An individual who cannot readily stop, when it is appropriate, is fundamentally immature. Stopping is essentially a matter of discipline. Discipline is thus involved in recovery; for the immature alcoholic it is a disciplinary experience. He must acquire the discipline to stop drinking; he needs to accept a disciplined way of life.

It makes sense to me that the immature character traits outlined by Tiebout are those which conversion needs to and can compromise. These are the traits which need to be addressed if recovery is to be sustained and maintained by exercising the discipline and skills requisite for success. However, Tiebout's and Glatt's concepts of the processes involved in recovery need to be considered in the light of more recent, general models of the stages and processes of change.

TRANSTHEORETICAL MODEL OF CHANGE

There are numerous models of change but one is generally accepted as being particularly useful in the context of recovery. It is the Transtheoretical Model of behavioural change (TM) developed in particular by James Prochaska, John Norcross and Carlo DiClemente in the US as outlined in *Changing for Good* (1994). The model focuses on the decision making of the individual. Other models focus on social influences or biological influences on behaviour. The TM seeks to explain why a change is or is not maintained. It is currently a very popular, perhaps the most popular, model in the addiction treatment field and can throw further light on the recovery process and its progression.

The model, based on more than fifteen years of research as to how people change on their own and with the help of others, is so called because it draws on the essential tenets of many diverse theories of psychotherapy. It emphasizes that change is a process which has stages and particular processes of change are particularly helpful at different stages. Change involves an experiential factor which is cognitive in nature and a behavioural factor which is action oriented. In most cases the experiential processes dominate in the earlier stages of change while the behavioural processes dominate in the later stages.

The TM identifies six well-defined stages of change
□ pre-contemplation
□ contemplation
□ preparation
□ action
□ maintenance
□ termination.

The way to foster successful change is to understand at what stage an individual is and then to identify what strategies and techniques facilitating which process or processes of change are appropriate to move the individual forward.

The TM identifies nine well-defined processes of change
□ consciousness raising
□ emotional arousal
□ commitment
□ countering
□ social liberalisation
□ self-re-evaluation
□ environmental control
□ reward

☐ helping relationships.

The conversion involved in recovery essentially embodies the processes and mechanisms which move the individual on from the precontemplation to the following stages in the TM. The alcoholic's surrender is the key which switches him from denying his alcoholism to contemplating how he can recover, preparing the action he needs to take to initiate and sustain his recovery, taking the action he needs to take to recover and doing what he has to do to maintain his recovery. The initial surrender mechanism involves the penetration of the alcoholic's denial system in a way which renders it substantially inoperative or ineffectual.

Denial, in the context of alcoholism, is more than a single psychological defence mechanism disavowing the significance of events. It also encompasses a range of psychological manoeuvres designed to reduce awareness of the fact that drinking alcohol is the cause of an individual's problems rather than a solution to those problems. Denial can become an integral part of alcoholism and a major obstacle to recovery. The alcoholic's denial system is the system of belief, used as a psychological defence mechanism, which enables him to function as a drinking alcoholic and which prevents him from admitting and accepting his alcoholism and from embarking on recovery.

The contemplation, preparation, action, maintenance and (to the extent that it may apply to some alcoholics) termination stages in the model reflect the stages of recovery which the alcoholic needs to go through to initiate and maintain sobriety. The processes of change in the model reflect the processes which the recovery alcoholic needs to take advantage of, or use, in his recovery.

The first mentioned process of change "consciousness raising" was first described by Sigmund Freud (1856-1939). It is an early stage change process and it would seem to be the basis of conversion. An early stage of change, and therefore of recovery, is the raising of the level of awareness thus increasing the quality of information available and improving the likelihood of making informed decisions. The process can be fast or slow.

The consciousness raising would seem often to involve a strong emotional state which substantially, sometimes dramatically, reconfigures the individual's brain and mind and this is what happened to me. This aspect would seem not only to be as described by Tiebout but also to equate with the process of "emotional arousal" in the TM which parallels consciousness raising but which works on a deeper emotional level and can be equally important in the early stages of change. The emotional arousal process is also known as "dramatic release" or "catharsis".

The new constellations of neural connections involved in conversion need to be used and developed or they atrophy. Once I chose to change, to stop drinking, I had to accept responsibility for my own change, for my own sobriety. I needed to realize that only I could respond, speak and act for me and, as it happened for me, to commit to AA. This vital step in the recovery process is called "commitment" in the TM. The first aspect of commitment is private, deciding to change, and the second is announcing the decision to others which, in my case, amounted to my continuing to attend AA meetings thus regularly stating that I was an alcoholic and asking other members for help.

Tiebout describes the components of the real alcoholic's mindset as he saw it, which so long resisted help and which were finally forced to give in, essentially as defiant individuality and grandiosity. He saw these components as the immature adult manifestation of infantile feelings of omnipotence, intolerance of frustration and excessive drive. They can express themselves in feelings of being special and different, in an inner imperiousness and in an impatience of delay. I would have characterised myself as being defiantly individualistic and grandiose. I certainly had feelings of being special and different and I exhibited a certain imperiousness and impatience of delay.

In recovery these immature traits need to be addressed if sobriety is to be sustained and maintained. This process is the TM's "countering" process. As a result of my commitment to AA, I became exposed to the countering process, which is, in effect, counter-conditioning. AA attendance and speaking to other alcoholics has for me become an effective countering technique in addressing my alcoholic mindset which so readily reverts to attitudes of defiance and grandiosity in particular and of arrogance in general. AA also exposed me to two other of the model's change processes, "social liberalisation" and "self-re-evaluation". It put me into a context of social liberalisation by attending its meetings and by seeking the company of other alcoholics. By listening to other alcoholics and by conversations with them I could begin my necessary "self-re-evaluation".

The remaining three change processes set out in the TM, "environmental control", "reward" and "helping relationships", also play their part in the recovery process. Like countering, "environmental control" is action orientated. I have, through AA, restructured my environment so that I am far less likely to drink alcohol. In AA, I give and receive praise and general reinforcement for progress in recovery and this would seem to equate to "reward". More formally, the "chips", which members can claim at some AA meetings for the first twenty-four hours, the first three, six and nine months and each successive twelve month period of continuous sobriety from another member while other members clap, amount to rewards. The "helping relationships" process of change is the essence of the AA mutual self-help group itself, providing as it can support, caring, understanding and acceptance.

6

RECOVERY

THE BEGINNING OF RECOVERY

One day, for some real alcoholics, their last prop, whatever that might be, is withdrawn or ceases to be effective for whatever reason. Someone or something, who or which had stood for their last iota of hope as regards their continuing to drink and who or which had actually become established as an ultimate resource when they were in difficulty, has gone. Accordingly, the way becomes open for the alcoholic's conversion once all support is withdrawn, when he has nothing to defy and he finds himself desperately needing help with no defiant ideas left about being able to drink like normal people. He can feel finally beaten, and he can both know it and feel it. Once he has surrendered the alcoholic can really want help. He can begin to accept, without inner reservation or conflict, the reality of his condition and the need for help. From then on, his mindset can change and his recovery can begin. Harry Tiebout calls this the "surrender reaction".

With some alcoholics the surrender reaction is the start of genuine growth and maturation. For some this may eventually mature into a conversion state that needs no specific relapse activity to sustain it. In terms of the Transtheoretical Model of change, the termination stage may possibly be reached. More likely, a conversion state equating to the maintenance stage in that model, is the only one ever reached. In those cases the individual never loses the need to practise some sort of relapse prevention programme more or less assiduously or continue some sort of relapse prevention activity. Many fearing relapse continue some sort of alcoholism related activity whether they are in the maintenance or termination stage to be on the safe side.

At the very beginning of recovery the consequences of a crisis can be profound. Numerous conversions are triggered by the trauma generated by crisis. The interaction between crisis and consequent behaviour can shed light not only on the story of the alcoholic which exemplifies the classic downward trend of increasing alcoholism which bottoms out and turns into an upward trend of increasing recovery. It can also illuminate the moment when the trend changes from being downwards to being upwards and such moment being described as conversion. It can also shed light on the alcoholic whose story is more complicated. Often the alcoholic's actual progress would be more of a nonlinear pattern as he struggles to attain, sustain and maintain his recovery. The interaction can also illuminate the story of the recovering alcoholic who maintains and sustains his sobriety by coping with successive crises which develop his ability better to cope with life and its difficulties.

On that evening early in October 1994, my perception was that my place to stay, in effect my last prop, the last of my resources, was to be taken from me. I had already lost my house, my job and my money. My third wife and I had separated. I had only a few clothes and other personal effects left. I was living in a small flat on a temporary basis. That day I thought I was going to be evicted with absolutely nowhere to go. I believe I finally surrendered to my alcoholism. My fighting and debating substantially diminished. Triggered by this surrender I entered a conversion state in which the changes initiating, sustaining and maintaining my recovery began effectively to occur.

Although I may have submitted, even surrendered, to my alcoholism on previous occasions on that occasion, for some reason, it amounted to a lasting conversion rather than to just a temporary surrender or submission. Perhaps something qualitative changed in the configuration of my brain and accordingly in my mind – I do not know. Perhaps I finally accepted my alcoholism. Acceptance itself is a major psychological step. Acceptance is a step beyond recognition; a further operation in the process of change. Perhaps, at last, I accepted the reality of my alcoholism not only consciously but also unconsciously. Perhaps my ability to accept reality at last began to function on the unconscious level of my mind. Whatever the case may be, I seem finally to have got the message, so to speak.

A profound realization, a substantial moment of clarity, a dramatic event involving trauma or emotional shock or against a background of traumatic events and amounting to a strong emotional state or shock, can all trigger conversion and initiate recovery. The alcoholic one day can suddenly realize that his drinking no longer has the desired effect and that something has to be done. The alcoholic's eldest son dies as a result of his drinking; her husband leaves her; he wakes up in hospital badly injured after a road traffic accident he can remember nothing about; his home is repossessed; he is sacked for his drinking; Social Services take the children into care. However, for some real alcoholics nothing dramatic or traumatic needs to happen for the recovery process to start. Practically anything, even nothing in particular, can initiate it if the circumstances surrounding the individual are sufficiently conducive.

According to Tiebout, surrender is the moment when the unconscious forces of defiance and grandiosity actually cease to function effectively. Many real alcoholics in recovery can identify that moment. When it happens, the individual is wide open to reality. He can listen and learn with comparatively little conflict and fighting back. The conversion switch can be thrown initiating his conversion to new attitudes and ways of feeling, to a new mindset and consequent behaviour. He can become receptive rather than antagonistic to life. Surrender can free the individual from the compulsion to drink. He can begin to accept life on life's terms including his alcoholism. Surrender, the accepting of reality and of his alcoholism, in particular, on the unconscious level, can be very positive and creative on the conscious level when maintained by virtue of accepting his drinking as beyond his control and asking for help accordingly. The individual in the conversion state after surrender can work in reality and with it.

But the change does not necessarily last and having had a conversion, the alcoholic can slowly, or not so slowly, revert to his former attitudes and ways of feeling. Resentment is often the cause of this. With some, though, including me, the conversion can be the start of genuine growth and maturation. In any event, Tiebout asserted that "the surrender experi-

ence is followed by a phase of positive thinking and feeling that under-
goes various vicissitudes before it becomes established in some form or
other in the psyche, or it is lost completely, becoming merely a memory
and a mirage".

    As I have already suggested, for many real alcoholics the mainte-
nance stage of recovery is the only one ever reached. In these cases the
individual usually needs to rely on some activity on a regular basis to
supply the necessary stimulus to maintain the conversion state in the face
of the difficulties of life in general and his resentments in particular, if
he is not to relapse. Such activity could be attendance at AA meetings
and significant practice of its programme, therapy, counselling, joining
a peer support project or the practice of a religion. I continue regularly
and frequently to attend AA meetings because I enjoy them and also as
a relapse prevention measure in case I am one of those who is still in the
maintenance stage.

    For a number of alcoholics it is only when one or more of their code-
pendents stop supporting their behaviour that they finally surrender and
start to face reality and take responsibility for it. In the context of alcoholism codependence refers to the process whereby an individual assists
or enables an alcoholic to continue to drink. The term emerged from
twelve-step treatment programmes. It is generally used to help individuals from alcoholic families understand the ingrained behaviour patterns
they may well have learned growing up in a dysfunctional family involving alcohol dependence or abuse. A codependent individual may exhibit an excessive desire to be helpful to others while neglecting his own
needs. Codependence is distinguishable by characteristic behaviour that
seeks to remove or take away the natural consequences of the alcoholic's
behaviour. Codependent behaviour can be driven by a need to continue
to feel needed by the alcoholic.

    But, while experiencing a crisis or something else may make the al-
coholic realize that something needs to be done, this does not necessarily
amount to any sort of effective surrender as far as recovery is concerned.
Far from initiating conversion or stimulating the alcoholic to seek help
from a doctor, therapist or counsellor or to join a treatment programme

or to attend AA, the realisation that something needs to be done often only results in attempts to cut back on alcohol consumption, mistakenly believing that it can be controlled.

JUST TRYING

Just trying to stop drinking alcohol or to cut back on drinking is not enough for the real alcoholic. Stopping drinking or substantially cutting back leaves a huge vacuum. Other dependences can replace alcohol dependence. Codependence on another (classically a partner) or others can take over the alcoholic's life. Alcoholic drinking takes up a great deal of time. The vacuum needs to be filled.

If the vacuum cannot be filled with healthy activity, a healthy dependence perhaps can suffice for the time being at least. Attending a day care programme, AA attendance, working out in the gym or practising a religion can amount to healthy dependencies. They can all help in the short term and they can provide long term recovery elements as well for a strong recovery foundation for the future. It can be argued that what the dependent individual is dependent on is much more important than being dependent *per se*, certainly in terms of harm reduction. Dependence on AA, Christianity or physical exercise is clearly less harmful than an active dependence on alcohol or other psychoactive substance.

Neither a drinking alcoholic nor one taking any relevant psychoactive substance can really be said to be in recovery. Personal resources like coping skills, self-sufficiency, risk perception, optimism, health-related behaviour and ability to resist social pressure are important. Setting boundaries and learning how to say "no" effectively can be critical in the recovery process.

EARLY RECOVERY DISTURBANCES

The alcoholic in early recovery usually suffers what can be called emotional growing disturbances. His cognitive function is often poor. Alcohol and the experiences surrounding its abuse will have resulted in his brain functioning abnormally. The ability of the alcoholic's brain to cope with raw experience and sensation will be compromised to a greater or lesser extent. In many cases the real alcoholic will not be in a mental state ably to cope with life without a drink, without help. In particular, new neuronal circuitry, flexible in its interactions with the senses and the outside world, needs to be established. There is a need to develop new skills and beneficial constraints of the mind. This takes time.

The alcoholic will at the very beginning put much emphasis on the immediate largely physical withdrawal from alcohol symptoms. He will usually have experienced these and knows how dreadful they are, but that many of them, for example shaking, sweating and nausea, usually only last a few days, although some, like anxiety and insomnia, can last for considerable periods. But he will have no understanding of, or preparation for, the secondary emotional withdrawal symptoms that he will encounter during the first year or two of abstinence.

By drinking, the alcoholic avoids the full impact of circumstances and the natural emotional consequences of them on him. As a result, he does not learn how to cope with much in life without drinking. When he tries for the first time to cope with situations with which non-alcoholics have long learned to cope, he can experience profound difficulty. He does not have the requisite skills and inbuilt sober coping mechanisms. The resultant secondary withdrawal symptoms can often take the form of insidiously disguised protests against reality and in bombardments of rationalisation urging him to return to drinking. He will need motivation and discipline to resist those urges and to maintain his recovery regime. He will need to learn how to cope with much in life without a drink for the first time.

Severely dependent on alcohol and attached to little else, the real alcoholic needs not only to break his dependence but also to learn how to have stable relationships with those around him. He needs to learn not only how to communicate honestly with others and to reveal his true self to them but also how to cope with their responses without relying on the one thing, alcohol, upon which he has relied for so long. The greater the intimacy between the alcoholic and the other person the more difficult this will be. The alcoholic needs also to become more flexible and open regarding the outcome of his actions. He needs to learn not to pursue inflexibly what he wants. As well as espousing the process of recovery, the recovering alcoholic needs to learn how to cope with life in all circumstances without picking up a drink. Recovery is not just a process; it is also something that requires knowledge, motivation, self-discipline and ability.

Release from stable bondage, however stressful, rarely, if ever, brings quick or instant relief. In early recovery depression and divorce are common and occupational stability is poor. Real alcoholics can return as virtual strangers to their families and to occupational responsibility from which they have been long separated by alcoholic haze and mutual discrimination. Re-entry into family responsibility and the occupational world is difficult and should be taken as slowly and gently as possible. The process can take years. The maintenance of abstinence is vital: continuing abstinence can achieve progressive social improvement, whereas continued alcohol use is associated with progressive deterioration of social, occupational and physical well-being.

At times the first few years of sobriety are stressful and disturbing, but decreasingly so. I am very grateful that I managed to live through them with the constant help of my first sponsor and other alcoholics in recovery without taking an alcoholic drink.

DEMANDING AT FIRST

Recovery at first, can, as I found out, be demanding and sometimes very stressful and disturbing. To begin with it takes determination, effort and discipline, and it does not come easily. Indeed recovery for the real alcoholic could be paradoxically described as unnatural for him. Like the experienced motorist who is totally unaware as he drives along of the numerous learned skills which enable him to do so, the alcoholic is totally unaware as he contemplates drinking or drinks of the numerous learned cues which keep him drinking. For the real alcoholic it has become his nature to drink.

To stop drinking the alcoholic needs to identify and counter the learned and conditioned cues which keep him drinking. He needs to bring them to mind. Using the motoring simile, a motorist who had always driven a car with a manual gearbox, buying a new car with an automatic one, would have to bring to mind his conditioned reflex of declutching in order to stop doing it. In like manner the alcoholic needs to recognise his conditioned drinking reflexes in order to stop drinking.

It is not easy to sustain and maintain the effort which the attitudes and actions essential to recovery require. The conditioned cues, once established, are difficult to extinguish and the original learning from which they are derived is not erased. It is much easier to drift back into old attitudes and inaction, back into his natural pattern of drinking. This requires little or no effort. Recovery requires substantial effort and discipline particularly in early recovery. As it progresses, though, recovery can become less onerous as the practice of recovery skills becomes habitual and deep seated. The actions and attitudes of recovery can become to an increasing extent second nature.

Recovery involves a change in the alcoholic's mindset by the rejection of much learned behaviour and by learning new behaviour and attitudes and practising a new way of living. Drinking alcohol needs to be removed from the action list of the brain's working memory. It involves learning a new discipline with all the concentration, effort and discipline which that entails.

If, for example, someone wants to learn the law and to practice it, he should appreciate that he is highly unlikely to achieve that alone and that he best learn from experienced lawyers. If he wants to practise as a barrister in England, he must arrange for one to be his pupil master. Lawyers learn law from other lawyers; they practise it with other lawyers and they learn from their continuing practise of it. The real alcoholic who wants to recover from alcoholism in like manner should appreciate that it is highly improbable that he can learn how by himself. He best find help from other alcoholics experienced in recovery and arrange for one to be his sponsor. As with lawyers, who are helped by and learn from other lawyers, recovering alcoholics can be helped by and can learn from other recovering alcoholics. By learning and practising the skills involved in achieving and maintaining recovery the alcoholic can sustain recovery.

The skills involved in learning how to recover from alcoholism, however, are more complex than those involved in an individual unversed in law learning a particular law. The skills are more like a senior French lawyer trying to learn English law which proceeds on a completely different basis to French law. He would have to discard his deeply conditioned principles of French law and substitute the often inconsistent, sometimes contradictory and, to him, novel principles of English law.

The fundamental difficulty for the alcoholic who wants to learn how to maintain sobriety is that his drinking is the product of automatic, unconscious behaviour patterns triggered by deeply conditioned unconscious cues developed from childhood of which he is totally unaware unless they are pointed out to him and he is prepared to recognise them. His action in picking up a drink is largely brought about without reference to the brain's rational thought and decision making processes which are substantially by-passed. The brain's executive function is taken over by conditioned, learned responses.

The real alcoholic first needs to become consciously aware of and to recognise the unconscious cues, which evoke automatic changes in organ systems and behavioural sensations and which drive his alcoholism. He needs to become aware of them by conscious effort informed by awareness and knowledge of dependence and how it works. He needs to make the effort to learn how to live without something which has been so much part of his lifestyle and to put something healthy in its place.

The alcoholic can find in another alcoholic someone who can be his tutor and mentor. He can learn recovery from other recovering alcoholics and he can practise it with them. He can also learn from others, such as doctors, counsellors and therapists. He can find sources of expert advice and can ask for and can take advice and act upon it even when it is difficult or when to do so forces a change in established ways of thinking and acting. Recovery from alcoholism must be actively pursued and practised if long term stable and contented abstinence and emotional sobriety is to result. Recovery and sobriety are not states, they are processes requiring action and sustained action at that.

Once alcoholism has taken on a life of its own in the alcoholic, and in the real alcoholic in particular, he has firmly implanted in his mind beliefs and consequent behavioural patterns. To rebut these beliefs and patterns by argument is problematic. However, beliefs and behavioural patterns countering the alcoholic mindset can be implanted in some alcoholics, depending on their temperament and circumstances, after brain function and mental activity have been sufficiently disturbed by circumstances resulting in induced fear, anger or excitement.

In recovery, what was once felt as an obligation can become a desire, even a pleasure. André Comte-Sponville in *A Short Treatise on the Great Values* (2002) writes as follows. "To act well at first means to do as is done ... ; then it means to do what ought to be done ... ; and finally, it is to do what one wants to do ... ." In recovery terms, the alcoholic can first act as he must, then as he ought to and in due course as he wants to, with his attitude changing accordingly. Bill Wilson in *Twelve Steps and Twelve Traditions* makes the point as follows. "So we of AA do obey spiritual principles, first because we must, and ultimately because we love the kind of life such obedience brings. Great suffering and great love are AA's disciplinarians; we need no others."

Although recovery from alcoholism can be taxing initially, so are most things really useful. It amounts to learning a new way of life. Learning anything new like a new skill or a new discipline is inevitably challenging. However, the effort required to maintain recovery diminishes and the discipline becomes less demanding as recovery matures. Sobriety can increasingly become a relatively effortless contented and enjoyable way of life.

FACTORS IN RECOVERY

There are many factors relating to dependence and recovery from it which apply whichever particular psychoactive substance on which the individual happens to be dependent. These include genetic predisposition, the involvement of the autonomic nervous and limbic systems and the reinforcement, conditioning and neuroadaptation processes. Nowadays many alcoholics are also dependent on other psychoactive substances.

No alcoholic can be said to be in recovery if he is still using or abusing any relevant psychoactive substance even if abstinent from alcohol.

Many individuals dependent on psychoactive substances other than alcohol attend twelve-step fellowships such as Narcotics Anonymous which are based on the AA model. Many treatment centres and therapists cater for those dependent on any psychoactive substance. Much of what is written about the alcoholic will apply substantially to other psychoactive substance dependent individuals, but I am addressing alcoholism in particular rather than dependence on other psychoactive substances which can have their own distinct characteristics.

In recovery the emotions play a far greater part to begin with than the intellect. The abdication of his control over alcohol, the initial surrender of the real alcoholic to his alcoholism, is commonly more a question of feeling sick and tired of feeling sick and tired rather than being intellectually convinced that giving up alcohol is the way forward. Increasingly, though, the intellect can contribute to the recovery process. Although reason was not the prime driver of the conversion which instigates recovery, reason can play its part in sustaining the conversion state and in driving recovery. The alcoholic needs to resurrect or acquire the ability and skills to recover. He needs the self-discipline to maintain his recovery.

Recovery is a behavioural change and the same kind of sequence is required for making all behavioural changes. The bases of the inappropriate thinking supporting the drinking alcoholic are deeply ingrained and largely subconscious. In order to recover, the first thing the alcoholic needs is to become aware of his thought processes. Secondly, he needs to recognise which thoughts and judgements are awry. Then he needs to substitute appropriate thoughts and judgements for inappropriate ones. Finally, he needs feedback to inform him whether his changes are appropriate. This sequence can be brought about in many ways including undergoing therapy or counselling, by attending a treatment centre or AA or by the efforts of the alcoholic himself.

Many, particularly in AA, see recovery as a never to be completed process rather than an achieved state of affairs. For some recovery is seen as lasting a lifetime. For some there is a need for continuing motivation and application. However, alcoholism and recovery are both continua and individuals differ widely. While for some recovery is a lifetime experience for others recovery takes a relatively short time and after a while maintaining sobriety requires little if any substantial effort and recovery is, for all intents and purposes, completed. As regards AA attendance some alcoholics recover with only a brief involvement with AA, others attend AA for a number of years and then stop and others continue to attend AA for the rest of their lives. A number of alcoholics recover by themselves and they are able to stay contentedly sober without ever attending AA or making use of any other form of recovery resource.

As for me, I expended a considerable amount of time and effort on my recovery to begin with but the amount of time and effort has diminished over the years and I now simply attend AA regularly which I enjoy doing. At first I attended an AA meeting virtually every day. I still usually attend two or three meetings a week. Attending offers me an opportunity to watch alcoholics recover, to see them help each other, to help others, to be helped by others and to enjoy the fellowship of a host of friends which has grown up about me. Frequent contact with this circle of friends, who are alcoholics like me, brightens my life.

For those who adopt the AA philosophy in particular, recovery from real alcoholism is commonly seen as a lifestyle change involving a process and not as an event. Recovery through AA can be seen in general terms as the alcoholic joining (or rejoining) the human race, so to speak, in three stages, by joining AA itself and relating to other AA members, by relating to and again becoming part of his family and circle of non-alcoholic friends and by participating in society more generally. Some AA members do not significantly move on from the first stage while others leave AA far behind and engage exclusively with family, friends and society.

Personality influences the processes of recovery and coping within the social context. Personality can be seen as the process whereby the individual's brain – that seething morass of cell circuitry which is being constantly reconfigured by personal experience as Susan Greenfield puts it in *The Private Life of the Brain* (2001) – is "personalised" into "mind" or "self" over time from birth, continually evolving throughout life. In recovery an individual's personality, identity, mind or self, call it what you will, is, like recovery, a dynamic process in constant reformulation. It is currently impossible to predict who will recover from alcoholism. As with alcoholism itself, recovery from it is progressive. Recovery is progressive in the sense that there can be a tendency while in recovery for the behavioural patterns of the alcoholic to improve cumulatively in effectively coping with the realities of life. Over time the alcoholic's ability in recovery to behave appropriately can gradually increase.

Recovery is a process of incremental change. Recovery includes two aspects one time dependent and the other experience dependent. The first is the spontaneous improvement which occurs simply by remaining abstinent. The second requires that the alcoholic is willing and able to change and that he takes the necessary action to effect and maintain change.

The changes which amount to recovery are rendered possible because Susan Greenfield's "seething morass of cell circuitry that has been configured by personal experience" which is the mind, is being constantly updated as time passes by virtue of the brain's plasticity. Physical changes in the degree and extent of connections between neurons in certain brain regions occur as a result of simple everyday experience, what happens to an individual and what the individual does about what happens to him. Change is accordingly possible but the processes and mechanisms by which lasting changes in character and modulation of impulses take place is extremely complex. It is very far from being understood.

However, the Transtheoretical Model of change has been tested in dozens of empirical studies. The model seems to set out how an individual's wish to change can be helped along the way. The model suggests that the most effective change is self-motivated, but that structured guidance greatly enhances the effectiveness of the individual's efforts.

The change requisite for recovery involves change within the individual, within his brain and mind but the process of change also benefits from engagement with other helping and supporting people. Because the human being is an evolved social animal, this is not surprising. AA maintains that most alcoholics cannot recover alone: for those alcoholics their best chance of recovery is with the help of other alcoholics. This is not inconsistent with the fact that some alcoholics recover without professional assistance and without AA. However, going it alone and declining care, support and other forms of assistance from others is unlikely to be effective. Most who change themselves do so with some help from others, directly or indirectly. Throughout the processes and cycles of change, the assistance or example of others can beneficially be enlisted, brought to bear or taken notice of whether formally or informally, professionally or casually.

There is no doubt that a major predictor of sobriety is an effective support network of some kind. The network need not specifically comprise other alcoholics although such a network can be particularly helpful. Recovery is an inside piece of work and responsibility requiring a change in mindset and in individual behaviour. It is this change which one-to-one cognitive behavioural therapy and motivational enhancement therapy, in particular, seek to facilitate. The change also requires ability and any requisite ability which is lacking in the individual usually requires engagement with other people in order to acquire it and in order to learn how to change. This ability is what group therapy and AA meetings seek to teach and foster. The individual must take responsibility for his own recovery but he usually needs to learn how from other people. Numerous treatment facilities provide both one-to-one therapy and group therapy accordingly.

The process of recovery in the real alcoholic does not amount to a cure but to an arrest of the condition. Once the alcoholic has stopped drinking for a significant period of time (three to four months appears to be a significant marker), has understood the basic facts about dependence, has accepted the fact of his alcoholism, has a reasonably clear idea of sobriety, is attempting some sort of personal recovery programme and the change in mindset and attendant belief system has significantly started accordingly, he can be said to have started recovery, to be "in recovery".

Many in recovery, particularly in AA, describe themselves as "recovering alcoholics", not "recovered". This reflects the view that, for the real alcoholic, recovery amounts only to an arrest not to a cure. In a sense, real alcoholics can never fully recover because they cannot return to asymptomatic, let alone social or care-free, drinking. For them the very best next thing is reasonably secure, stable and contented sobriety and to die sober, not having had a drink since the start of their recovery.

As regards my own recovery, I am happy to use the phrase "in recovery"; recovery seems to me to be a process which is on-going. On the other hand, as "recover" means a "return to a normal state of health, mind or strength", I would not object to being described as "recovered"!

ACHIEVABLE RECOVERY

Recovery is achievable for those who emotionally want it and not, as a rule, for those who, only intellectually, admit that they need it. A critical first step in recovery is the recognition by the alcoholic that there is a problem about which he alone rather than anybody else can do something. Nobody else, be it a partner, relation, employer, doctor, priest, therapist or counsellor, can resolve the drinking problem for the alcoholic. Without the recognition that it is an inside piece of work and that he is responsible for his recovery and without belief in his ability to recover, the alcoholic is unlikely to do anything useful towards changing his mindset and drinking behaviour.

Essentially, alcoholics recover not because they are treated but because they heal themselves in the sense that they willingly engage in the healing process trusting in their ability to change and exercising enough discipline to maintain change. Recovery is not simply detoxification but a lengthy process which can involve the work of several years, even the rest of their lives in the case of some real alcoholics. Maintaining and sustaining sobriety is seen by some, particularly in AA, as a never ending but rewarding process.

Until my conversion, it had never occurred to me that I could, in any real sense, be responsible for my own recovery. If pressed I would probably have said that recovery was dependent on the efficacy of appropriate outside treatment. I submitted to various treatments but I never really changed; I never really accepted my powerlessness over the effect which alcohol had on me or my need to change. But, as detailed earlier, something happened to me in October 1994, way outside any therapeutic setting or clinical interaction, which I can only take to be (hopefully) my definitive conversion upon which I have since built by my own efforts, albeit with the help of others particularly other alcoholics in AA.

Medical detoxification is only the first step and by itself does little, if anything, to change long term alcohol use. Detoxification only safely manages the acute physical symptoms of withdrawal associated with stopping drinking. It is rarely, if ever, sufficient in itself to trigger long term abstinence. It is but a prerequisite for it. Treatment should usually start immediately after detoxification if it is to serve any useful purpose and continue as long as required if long term sobriety is to be achieved.

For many alcoholics there is a need to appreciate that any life run on self-will can hardly be a success and that a radical reorientation is required away from a habitual preoccupation with self towards the wider community of human beings. There is a need for conduct which recognises others' interests alongside that of the individual himself and for the espousal of less self-centred principles accordingly.

Humans are by nature a social species. They are not individuals thrown together trying to cope with the resultant problems. Humans have sophisticated mental equipment in the form of evolved emotions and ways of thinking which are designed for social life. Accordingly, successful life in society depends on the reduction in the proportion of selfish individuals and on means whereby selfish individuals can be inhibited. The alcoholic must accept the need for a balance between the natural tendency to assert himself on the one hand and actions conducive to the public good on the other. His judgment as to what is good or bad, his moral code, needs to be on this basis which would seem to be in accordance with his evolved morality.

Carl Jung wrote "we cannot change anything until we accept it". Recovery involves change and acceptance plays a large part in recovery accordingly. It does not imply approval of something but rather an objective awareness of it. Only by being aware of things and accepting them as they are can reasoned action (or inaction) be addressed. Alcoholics need to accept their alcoholism. Following Jung, one alcoholic addressing acceptance in his personal story, *Doctor, Alcoholic, Addict*, in AA's book *Alcoholics Anonymous* wrote as follows. "Until I could accept my alcoholism, I could not stay sober; unless I accept life completely on life's terms, I cannot be happy. When I am disturbed it is because I find some person, place, thing, or situation – some fact of my life – unacceptable to me, and I can find no serenity until I accept that person, place, thing, or situation as being exactly the way it is supposed to be at the moment. … I need to concentrate not so much on what needs to be changed in the world as on what needs to be changed in me and in my attitudes."

Bill Wilson addressed acceptance and humility as follows. "Our very first problem is to accept our present circumstances as they are, ourselves as we are, and the people about us as they are. This is to adopt a realistic humility without which no genuine advance can even begin. Again and again, we shall need to return to that unflattering point of departure. This is an exercise in acceptance that we can profitably practice every day of our lives. Provided we strenuously avoid turning these realistic surveys of the facts of life into unrealistic alibis for apathy or defeatism, they can be the sure foundation upon which increased emotional health and therefore spiritual progress can be built."

Henry Ward Beecher (1813-1887) wrote the following. "God asks no man whether he will accept life. That is not his choice. You must take it. The only choice is how". In this connection the axiom, quoted in AA's *Twelve Steps and Twelve Traditions*, that "every time we are disturbed, no matter what the cause, there is something wrong with us" is empowering; by accessing inner mental resources individuals can think themselves out of uncomfortable emotion. On a basis of acceptance and humility, recovery takes place.

7

LIFE WITHOUT ALCOHOL

BEFORE AND AFTER

Recovery is the process whereby the aberrant, limited and negative mindset and attendant belief system of the drinking alcoholic changes. Alcoholics in recovery speak of how it was before, of not having felt part of anything and of feelings of resentment, uneasiness, isolation, dissatisfaction, insecurity and depression. They speak of having nothing, of having no belief to cling to, of having no trust in anything because by drinking they had lost trust in themselves. In sobriety, they say, words like "concern", "consideration" and "love" begin to have meaning when they had little meaning before. While they believed themselves capable of love, they recognise that the emotion before recovery was essentially a reflection of self-interest. They recognise in recovery that before recovery little, if anything, penetrated beyond their mind perceived self.

In early sobriety, if in the frequent company of other alcoholics through treatment, AA attendance or otherwise, individual alcoholics can begin to feel concern and consideration for those other alcoholics. This concern and consideration for other alcoholics can develop into concern and consideration for parents, partners, children and others accompanied later by genuine love. My experience reflects this.

TOWARDS SOBRIETY

Sobriety involves a profoundly felt release from the grip of alcoholism, particularly as regards the compulsion to drink. In time, the real alcoholic, with no substantial concurrent disorder, can realize that he does not, as I have realized that I do not, suffer from any mental illness like bi-polar disorder or schizophrenia. He realizes, as I have, that he does not have any grave emotional disorder. He realizes that alcoholism has been and is his problem. Alcohol virtually destroyed him and that it is the one thing that can needlessly destroy him again. In recovery positive attitudes gradually take root. The desire to live and to take part stirs, as do the alcoholic's hopes and desires. His perceptions and evaluations carry a new sureness. His capacity to stand his ground increases and he begins to feel for others.

The alcoholic finds himself able, however briefly at first, to put himself in others' shoes. He comes to feel his separate existence solidly enough both to enjoy being alone and to want to be close to others. Sobriety includes more enthusiasm for life and feeling more part of his social circle. It entails a sense of feeling more whole and of being able to accept and realise more of his potential and to reach out to more people and to more of life. It embraces accepting other people's differences and accepting them more as they really are. As a result many areas of the alcoholic's life expand and improve.

In sobriety, the individual moves beyond his former self-centred frame of reference towards espousing those qualities and factors which enable him to cope contentedly with life against the background of his essential nature as a social being with an evolved morality.

I see this as the essence of the spiritual awakening spoken about in AA and beyond by many of those who are substantially in recovery and many practitioners in the recovery field particularly in Minnesota AA Model treatment centres. The alcoholic begins to understand something of himself and of the world about him and new worlds open up. He begins to appreciate that he is not the centre of the universe but only a small part of it. He starts to realize that he should not play God. He starts to recognize that many things can never be fully or even substantially understood. He increasingly accepts his life as a minute part of the whole, accepting each day, each moment as but a small manageable segment of time in which difficulties need not be overwhelming. Many speak of their own understanding of some sort of spirituality and of a requirement for some concern for others.

The beneficial constraints of mind involved in a sober mindset, belief system and lifestyle become increasingly established. The individual's pre-occupation with self diminishes. This lessens the adverse impact of his physical world laden with his personal meaning and significance, with evaluation of his past and projection into his future. As Seneca wrote "true happiness is ... to enjoy the present, without anxious dependence upon the future" and, I would add, resentful contemplation of the past.

The emotional experiences of living soberly and other concomitant factors can enable the mind to perceive the world more realistically and hence more rational and positive meaning can be attached to raw sensation and to life itself. This may involve a trend towards the limitation of neuronal connections activated at any one moment to a band of activity neither too little nor too much, to appropriate, balanced mental activity. The beautiful sunset can be enjoyed without being eclipsed by worry about financial insecurity.

The escape from anxious projection of the future or resentment regarding the past is possible for the adult human brain but the escape does not usually last for very long. Emotion inevitably fades into thinking and by thinking pleasure can dissolve into fear. The brain and the mind are in a constant state of flux with mercurial assemblies of neurons determining how the individual feels at any one moment. The periods of balanced mental activity resulting in contentment may be transient but the experience of living in recovery tends to increase their duration and to make the oscillations about the balance point less extreme.

The individual's mindset and attitudes, his self, is far from immutable. Even in very old age, within the day, within the hour, the individual changes. All the time, his experiences, and how he deals with them, leave their marks on him. These in turn influences how he interprets and deals with new happenings. As the sober alcoholic's brain and mind evolve, as he understands his condition more deeply, he becomes more able to live contentedly.

In recovery, the alcoholic increasingly learns emotionally to live in the moment, to live one day at a time, to be grateful to be alive and, most of all, to be sober. As Susan Blackmore in *The Meme Machine* (1999) puts it, his consciousness can become more open, spacious and free. He becomes increasingly conscious of the tiny moment which he can appreciate and savour. He learns that the enjoyment of the moment need not be compromised by concerns about the past and for the future.

Alcohol once had the chemically induced effect, temporarily, of making the present dominant to the exclusion of the alcoholic's inner reality of resentment as to the past and anxiety as to the future. The alcoholic learns that the sober practice of keeping things in the moment can create a more permanent inner reality which is less resentful and less anxious. By keeping his emotions in the moment, resentment and anxiety can be kept more effectively at bay in a way drinking never could. His increasing experience of sober living builds up confidence. He finds pleasure in the moment, in the here and now, without the need to drink alcohol.

However, the living in the moment, one day at a time, essentially relates to the individual's feelings and emotions. In order to live a reasonably organised and fulfilling life due practical attention needs to be given to the future. The future needs to be addressed and planned at least to some extent and action taken to ensure that business, social, financial and other commitments are met.

Living one day at a time is an AA principle and it is far from being universally adopted in the treatment field. For example, while exponents of the Community Reinforcement Approach and other treatment approaches might consider the principle useful in the early stages of recovery, many see it as being of far more limited value later. The individual needs to move forward and plan for the future. Most alcoholics have been living in the moment concerned only with the next drink, one day at a time, for far too long. In contrast to the AA approach, the Community Reinforcement Approach and other approaches want the alcoholic to look to the future because that is where they are going and it is the future that they need to address.

Paradoxically the childlike traits which played their part in the development of the individual's alcoholism can emerge in recovery as factors in his increasing contentedness and awareness of the pleasurable sensuality of the present. These traits can derail the morose train of inner worries for longer and more effectively than drinking. The alcoholic begins to see that pleasure is, literally, a sensational moment of life. Pleasure is a function of taking the self, the mind, out of the living equation. He finds a true non-chemical and better substitute for alcohol and he can begin to address his other compulsions and obsessions.

The recovering alcoholic becomes part of the human race and he becomes more proactive. He begins to enjoy, rather than endure, mundane things and ordinary activities. He recognises more and more the need for the other people in his world and he appreciates them more. He learns incrementally to take his self more out of his living equation. He learns to love some other people and even himself. He can conceive of happiness; he increasingly experiences it.

Happiness is elusive but can perhaps be summed up as being essentially about contentment, a state of satisfaction and the recovering alcoholic increasingly experiences contentment and a degree of satisfaction. He begins to realize that happiness is a by-product of something else. Happiness is less about attaining what he wants, it is more about accepting what he has. He comes to realize that he will not be content if he is continuously searching for contentment *per se*. It is no good looking for happiness; he meets it by the way. It is not something readymade; it is a product of his attitude, thinking and action.

Democritus (Democritus of Abdera, c460-c370BC) suggested that happiness is a condition that can be achieved through "moderation, tranquillity and freedom from anxiety". John Stuart Mill (1806-1873) wrote that he had learned to seek his happiness by limiting his desires, rather than attempting to satisfy them and Epictetus (55-135) that "there is only one way to happiness and that is to cease worrying about things which are beyond the power of our will". "Only man" wrote John Dryden (1631-1700) "clogs his happiness with care, destroying what is with thoughts of what may be". True happiness can be characterized as enjoying the present without anxious dependence upon the future or painful contemplation of the past.

The recovering alcoholic learns not to dwell in the past, nor to regret it but to learn from it. He learns not to worry about the future so much;

he recognises that he has coped so far in sobriety and he develops confidence that he can continue to cope. He comes to believe that he will be given nothing which, with help, he cannot cope with sober, without drinking. He comes to experience substantial contentment and to enjoy it some, even most, of the time by the use of the skills and techniques learned about in recovery.

Whether the contentment expressed and experienced by an alcoholic in substantial recovery is something to which a mature, well adjusted non-alcoholic would relate is not within the cognisance of either. Whether the attributes of the recovering alcoholic's existence equate, qualitatively, or indeed quantitatively, with those of such a mature, well adjusted non-alcoholic must inevitably remain unclear. It is an individual matter and no one person can be both a real alcoholic in long term recovery and a well adjusted non-alcoholic.

Alcoholic drinking and subsequent sobriety each profoundly change the individual's personality. Some say that the change from the alcoholic identity to the sober identity involves the development of a new identity, others that it results in the development of the identity that the individual would have had if he had not drunk alcoholically in the first place. In view, though, of the profound traumas and emotional shocks that real alcoholics suffer during their drinking careers and the resultant physical and mental consequences, it may well be impossible for them fully, or indeed even substantially, to revert to the personality they had before the onset of alcoholic drinking. I feel that I am now a very different person from the one I was before I started drinking or would have become if I had not drunk alcoholically. But then I am very much older now and, if I had not drunk alcoholically, my life experience would have been profoundly different.

THE CHANGES INVOLVED

Alcoholics Anonymous expresses the changes involved in recovery and sobriety in the following passage, the word "we" referring to alcoholics in substantial recovery. "We are going to know a new freedom and a new happiness. We will not regret the past nor wish to shut the door on it. We will comprehend the word serenity and we will know peace. No matter how far down the scale we have gone, we will see how our experience can benefit others. That feeling of uselessness and self-pity will disappear. We will lose interest in selfish things and gain interest in our fellows. Self-seeking will slip away. Our whole attitude and outlook upon life will change. Fear of people and of economic insecurity will leave us. We will intuitively know how to handle situations which used to baffle us. We will suddenly realize that God is doing for us what we could not do for ourselves".

The recovering alcoholic experiences an onset of new hope and an appreciation of the possibilities of a new way of life. An enlightened and interesting way of life opens up. The alcoholic can cease to be a burden and he can become a useful member of society. Some describe sobriety in terms of the qualities of process spirituality, qualities which include love, compassion, patience, forgiveness, humility and tolerance. They presume some level of concern for others' well-being. They are generated by the spiritual factors, characteristics, beliefs, attitudes, coping mechanisms, actions and inactions involving both the individual and others, enabling a person to cope contentedly with life, embodied in process spirituality. The recovering alcoholic finds that the spiritual actions which he undertakes, and which are motivated not by narrow self-interest but by concern for others, actually benefit him too.

Recovery from real alcoholism is usually no ordinary success story. For most alcoholics the surrender to his alcoholism does not come easily; it can be distressingly slow. It can entail at first the hardest kind of work and the sharpest vigilance which no doubt explains, at least to some extent, why the proportion of alcoholics who achieve long term sobriety is so small. But for some, after an effective conversion, recovery starts. Although effort and discipline, often considerable effort and discipline, may be required to begin with, as recovery progresses the effort diminishes and the discipline becomes less demanding and life becomes increasingly contented and enjoyable without so much effort or hardship.

WIDER PERSPECTIVES

Some of the factors in the recovery process can perhaps have a wider application beyond alcoholism. Many, who appear to live successful and comfortable lives, apparently lacking nothing, certainly in material terms, experience unease, dissatisfaction and unhappiness below the surface. They often feel isolated and depressed. It might seem reasonable to think that wealth, position and prestige would have reduced suffering more than is actually the case. But wealth often makes people unhappy. It gives them too much control over what they experience, over what happens to them and how they deal with what happens to them. People try to translate their own fantasies into reality instead of tasting what reality itself can offer. In materialistic societies stress related disorders replace the water-borne diseases of primitive societies.

Human beings generally long for status. In societies where an individual's status is decreasingly fixed at birth by virtue of an inflexible social hierarchy, his position increasingly depends on what he can make of himself. Comparisons are increasingly made with others and dissatisfaction arises because of failure to keep up with peers in every particular. The individual tends to see his status as he perceives it to be seen by others. His quest for status urges the individual towards the satisfaction of successive goals, none of which can provide permanent satisfaction.

High status is thought by many (but freely admitted by few) to be one of the greatest benefits. For this reason, the individual worries whenever he is in danger of failing to conform to the ideals of success laid down by his society. He worries that he may be stripped of dignity and respect, he worries that he is currently occupying too modest a rung on his perceived ladder of life or is about to slip to a lower one. He might not worry so much if status was not so hard to achieve and even harder to maintain over a lifetime.

Recovery teaches the individual to be grateful for what he has and not to compare himself as he intimately knows himself with the outward appearances of others about whom he really knows little or nothing. Recovery teaches him to be himself and to be realistically indifferent to what goes on in the minds of other people. He learns that to attach too much value to the opinions of others cedes far too much power and influence to them.

In modern self-sufficient and individualistic societies it is harder and harder to show one another basic affection. The consequent stress related disorders related to self can only be addressed in terms of relationship, the indispensable interface between one individual's desire to be happy and the desire of others also to be happy. Happiness is inner peace, achieved by guarding against factors which obstruct it and cultivating those conducive to it, of which the most important is basic attitude. To desire something for no reason beyond sensual pleasure tends to bring problems as well as being transient.

Indulging the senses and drinking salt water are alike; the more the individual partakes, the more his desire and thirst grow. Effort and self-sacrifice are required if happiness is to be enjoyed. Happiness cannot effectively be pursued in itself. Both the short-term benefit to the individual's own and the long term benefit to others' happiness must be considered and sacrificing the former for the latter is often required. In the context of recovery from alcoholism a vital factor which needs to be addressed is the extreme dominance of self in the alcoholic. In society too it would seem to be the dominance of self which leads to difficulties.

RECOVERY FOR FAMILY MEMBERS AND FRIENDS

Drinking alcoholics pursue immoderate, self-injurious, and socially damaging drinking life-styles which invoke substantial troubles for themselves, their families, their friends, their employers or employees, their occupational or social associates, and their communities and society generally causing disorder and suffering. Family members often suffer violence, poverty, social isolation and other profound negative experiences. Alcoholism brings with it misunderstanding and fierce resentment. It results in emotional and financial insecurity. It causes deep distress in partners, children, parents and friends which can often be severe and long lasting. Breakdowns in family structures and systems, communication, social life, health and finances frequently occur.

Recovery for the family members and friends of alcoholics requires a firm commitment to make the family member's or friend's own well-being a priority and, as with the alcoholic, it involves effort and discipline. Prior to recovery many neglected themselves because they were waiting for someone else to take care of the situation, some were so concerned with the alcoholic that they failed to attend to themselves. They, too, must learn to take responsibility for tending to their own needs. The family member or friend must stand back and accept that the alcoholic cannot be changed; only the alcoholic can change himself. In both cases recovery is an inside piece of work; it is the individual's responsibility.

The family member or friend, just like the alcoholic, needs to concentrate not so much on what needs to be changed in the world (particularly in the case of the family member or friend, in the alcoholic) as on what needs to be changed in the family member or friend and in his attitudes. The family member or friend needs to abandon codependent activity which reinforces mutually harmful behaviour patterns and concentrate more on his own needs. He must preserve his own health and sanity and re-establish his own life if he is to be of use to himself and to others.

There are large numbers of families affected by drinking problems who often suffer in silence. There are positive ways of helping families that need not be intensive and could be used successfully irrespective of the alcoholic's behaviour. To date the needs of family members and friends and their potential contribution to the treatment process have been relatively neglected.

AL-ANON
After my conversion, I joined AA wholeheartedly and, with the help of my AA sponsor, I was able to start addressing all the then outstanding problems consequent upon my alcoholism. My professional and general background helped in dealing with most of these problems which, in early recovery, related to my creditors and my being homeless in particular. But my difficulties with personal relationships, particularly with women, needed to be addressed too. As a child of an alcoholic and with many other personal relationships with alcoholics I found Al-Anon, in addition to AA, invaluable.

Originally it was to help the wives of alcoholics that what was to become the Al-Anon Family Groups started. They now help those close to the alcoholic as well. At the beginning of what was to become AA and for some years thereafter, the members' wives were very much involved with their husbands (most members at that time being married). However the wives increasingly began discussing their problems without their husbands. They realized that they too needed help and they sought solutions following AA principles and the Twelve Steps in particular.

Al-Anon is, in effect, the mirror image of AA adopting AA's Twelve Steps and Traditions, its approach and much else. In Al-Anon family members and friends of alcoholics admit that they are powerless over alcohol; particularly over the affect alcohol has on the alcoholic and over the alcoholic himself. The family member or friend learns that he cannot cure the alcoholic and that if he continues to try or becomes or continues to become too bound up with the alcoholic, his life becomes unmanageable too.

Al-Anon recognises that in general alcoholics act and family members and friends react. To break the vicious spiral of action and reaction, Al-Anon teaches detachment for relatives and friends of alcoholics. Detachment in this context means that the family member or friend mentally separating himself from the condition of alcoholism. Al-Anon reminds members that they have choices; that they need not make their lives unmanageable along with the alcoholics by automatic reaction. Detachment is the freedom to own what is the individual's own and to allow others to own what is their own. This freedom allows an individual to keep his own identity and still love and care about others and identify with their feelings.

I had a relationship with another alcoholic in early recovery which I found very difficult and painful. A couple of friends in AA suggested that I join Al-Anon. I attended Al-Anon meetings frequently for about a year and I studied its literature. I still attend Al-Anon meetings from time to time and refer to its literature.

What I have learned and learn in Al-Anon (especially about detachment) has been, and is, to me invaluable. It has helped me to come to terms with past alcoholic relationships, particularly those with my father and first wife. It has also helped greatly with my relationships generally including those with the other alcoholics in my life. I find that learning about how the non-alcoholic members of Al-Anon practise the AA programme and apply AA's Twelve Steps very helpful in my own practice of the AA programme and how I apply AA's Twelve Steps.

Detachment as practised in Al-Anon can have general application. It can give the individual an inner calm, an acceptance of another's limits, and the freedom to live his own life with integrity. Detachment is a skill in living, and like other skills, can be learned and practised. Gradually, it can become a natural response. True detachment takes root and grows over a period of time as the individual's understanding of the recovery process deepens. Those who are both alcoholics and family members or friends of alcoholics can recover in both fellowships, AA and Al-Anon, in parallel: these people are sometimes called "double winners" or, more recently, "dual members".

Detachment and codependence are linked. Detachment also involves the individual depending less on others, on what they do, say or feel, to the detriment of his own well-being and of his decision making. As the Al-Anon literature says "detachment is not caring less; it is caring more for [the individual's] own serenity".

8

CHARACTERISTICS OF ALCOHOLICS

CHARACTERISTICS OF ALCOHOLICS BEFORE RECOVERY

Individuals prone to dependence spend more time feeling unhappy and are more likely to experience negative emotions such as dysphoria (a state of unease or generalised dissatisfaction with life), fear, anxiety, and feelings of depression. Most, if not all, real alcoholics have in common a mindset and a set of ways of behaving which deal inadequately with normal social relations and which interfere with, or simply take the joy out of, daily living. They often amount to something missed along the way in the growing up process of developing successful ways of coping with life.

Howsoever this mindset and set ways of behaving arise, the alcoholics who have it have an incomplete frame of reference for what is normal feeling and behaviour. They often have a problem with following a project through from beginning to end. Drinking alcoholics, in particular, are habitual liars. Lying can amount to an effective denial of unpleasant realities, cover-ups, broken promises and inconsistencies. The real alcoholic's judgement is commonly impaired with life being viewed in black and white terms with little grey gradation. Ordinary difficulties become more severe. Life for the real alcoholic, driven by his dependence, can become a very serious, angry, joyless and resentful business.

The ability of alcoholics to comfort or soothe themselves is commonly limited to a significant or substantial extent. They also usually have a greater sensitivity to emotional pain, in the sense of mental suffering or distress. Alcohol can counter this pain. Individuals prone to dependence often discover, usually in their teens, that certain substances, such as alcohol, marijuana, stimulants, sedatives, narcotic analgesics and nicotine make them feel better, even at one with their fellows. They can learn to see drinking as the solution to all their problems. Over time their brains adapt.

This adaptation is the neuroadaptation process, which changes the structure, function and chemistry of the brain. Over time anxiety and resentment, in particular, develop. Drinking becomes the way the alcoholic copes with his unhappiness, dysphoria, fear, anxiety, resentment, problems and difficulties. Drinking can also become the only way by which everyday things can be accomplished. Some alcoholics cannot get out of bed without a drink. While the alcoholic may have started drinking for its pleasurable or other desirable effects, drinking may continue to relieve the discomfort associated with withdrawal. Thus the primary motivation for drinking can become the alcoholic's need to drink to function normally or at all.

When the alcoholic tries to stop drinking, much more unhappiness, dysphoria, anxiety and depression is felt. Further he can find that he is incapable of performing certain actions without the prop of alcohol – until he is taught how to perform them without a drink. His brain has become trained to rely on a mood altered by alcohol in order to perform everyday tasks. For example, when one experienced fisherman, who had fished for years but never without drinking, first went fishing in recovery he had to be shown how to bait his hook. Before they enter into recovery most alcoholics believe that they cannot live their lives without drinking. If they are to recover, they need to come to believe that they can and to learn how.

Some of the neuroadaptation consequent upon drinking alcohol is reversible, but with prolonged heavy drinking some of it becomes permanent. The reversible neuroadaptation can take days, months or even years to reverse after abstinence starts. Part of the product of the permanent neuroadaptation in the brain and its function may well be the variable but persistent sense of discomfort which alcoholics can continue to feel and which can lead to relapse long after they have stopped drinking.

Pleasure and innate fear are generated by relatively small constellations of neurons. Learned fear and anxiety, by contrast, is a state of mind that is initiated and perpetuated with very little external assistance. They are generated by relatively large constellations of neurons. The alcoholic's mindset can be dominated by learned fear and anxiety. In terms of brain function the generation of learned fear and anxiety is different from the generation of pleasure and innate fear. Pleasure and innate instinctive fear are very much the product of the moment. Learned fear, worry and anxiety, on the other hand, depend on the ability to forsake the present moment and to contemplate an unsatisfactory past and to anticipate an uncomfortable future; this needs a large amount of neurons. Depression also involves a large number of neurons. Only by virtue of substantial circuitry built up over years of networked experiences can the individual dwell obsessively on the past and project fearfully into a future perceived to be full of danger and loss.

Many alcoholics are emotionally immature. The human infant has great self-esteem and believes in the omnipotence of his wishes, thoughts, gestures and words. But, in the well balanced adult, these infantile traits have been substantially modified by later experience. The mature adult has learned that a more modest self-evaluation is more realistic. This process of growing up can be painful. Many alcoholics have not engaged much in the process and remain substantially immature emotionally. This may be because they have adopted at an early age the tactic, when faced with difficulty, of the easy quick antidote, the quick fix, rather than the long term more demanding solution. Typically, such antidotes include childish behaviour and the use and abuse of alcohol and other psychoactive substances.

It is now increasingly accepted that the alcoholic's inability to stop drinking alcohol is not lack of will power. Alcoholics do not lack will power. The alcoholic's inability to stop drinking is the result of pathologically impaired decision making. The real alcoholic is severely dependent on alcohol and the parts of the brain responsible for the dependence are now thought to be substantially parts of the brain which govern unconscious thought. Drinking for the real alcoholic is mainly not under conscious control. Alcohol mainly affects the regions of the brain beyond conscious control. It affects the brain and mind and causes coercive drives to drink and reinforces them. In the alcoholic, alcohol changes the way the brain functions and the mind works: alcoholism is not just another bad habit.

The reinforcing effects of alcohol can cause the neuronal adaptations, the neuroadaptations, which result in dependence. The reinforcing mechanisms in the brain evolved to help maintain behaviours that are essential to survival such as eating, drinking and reproduction. In alcoholics, alcohol hijacks these reinforcing mechanisms and alters the function and communication between the liver, brain and other vital organ systems involved in hunger and the maintenance of nutrition. As a result hunger signals in alcoholics can motivate alcohol consumption in priority to food consumption. Further, periods of abstinence are marked by feelings of discomfort and craving, motivating continued alcohol consumption. Addressing recovery from real alcoholism accordingly involves more than addressing a bad habit: it involves addressing a chronic relapsing brain condition.

CHARACTERISTICS OF ALCOHOLICS IN RECOVERY

Recovery is a process of change. Before any change can take place the alcoholic needs to accept that change is necessary. His logical mind may well perceive and admit all the factors underlying his difficulties but he can continue to resist change. Recognising reasons for behavioural change, no matter how convincing, does not and cannot ensure acceptance of those reasons. Acceptance is a step beyond recognition and until the alcoholic accepts the need to change recovery will not start.

The recovery process is one with distinct stages of change. The process of change needs to be distinguished from the strategies and techniques deployed from time to time in the process. Certain strategies and techniques can be effective at certain times and in certain stages and when one ceases to bear another can be brought into play. What keeps an alcoholic sober one day may not keep him sober the next.

The resolution of drinking problems does not happen all at once but rather takes place over time. The way an alcoholic keeps sober changes.

Each stage in recovery needs to be addressed before moving on to the next and it is possible to become stuck at one stage or another. There is a progression of change relevant to change in general and to recovery in particular. The Transtheoretical Model identifies six well-defined stages of change pre-contemplation, contemplation, preparation, action, maintenance and termination, with the key to fostering successful change being the understanding as to what stage an individual is at and then deciding what strategies and techniques he should use to move forward.

However, whether the termination stage in the model is applicable in the case of the real alcoholic's recovery is questionable. The Transtheoretical Model's criterion for termination is "one hundred per cent self-efficacy and zero temptation across all high-risk situations". To reach the termination stage would mean that the alcoholic will not only ever drink again but also that he will not ever have a temptation to drink again. It would have to be the case that, no matter what the situation, he will never again turn to, or be tempted to turn to, alcohol as a way of coping, that is to say, as a way of dealing with a crisis and with the emotional distress caused by a crisis.

Many alcoholics in long term recovery in AA still feel that they cannot necessarily maintain their sobriety without AA. While they have had little, if any, temptation to drink for some considerable time, they cannot say that a temptation to drink might not arise in the future. Some traumatic event might occur which might trigger in them a wish to pick up a drink. Something might happen resulting in their experiencing a craving to drink again. It is common for thoughts of having a drink to arise from time to time in alcoholics: I have certainly thought of having a drink occasionally. I have heard AA members with well over twenty years sobriety say in meetings that they still occasionally experience a craving to drink. Many know how to resist such desires and cravings and they can soon pass, but some alcoholics with decades of abstinence drink again.

It is perhaps sensible to say that for many real alcoholics there is no real termination stage; they remain significantly in the maintenance stage. After all the brain circuitry relating to the cues which trigger drinking in alcoholics does not entirely atrophy. Accordingly, it is likely that most real alcoholics never leave the maintenance stage and very few, if any, reach the termination stage of being without any temptation to drink and without the need to continue any sort of personal relapse prevention activity.

A simple linear progression through the stages of recovery is possible but is relatively rare. A nonlinear pattern is the better illustration of how people change because most of those who initiate change, relapse a number of times returning to a previous stage.

During the process resulting in dependence, the real alcoholic's mind learns to ignore many natural stimuli and to respond primarily to his need for alcohol. This learning becomes embedded in the brain's procedural memory circuits and the mind's declarative memory circuits and amounts to the pre-contemplation stage.

To leave the pre-contemplation stage and move towards recovery, the alcoholic needs to bring the true nature of his alcoholism into consciousness. He needs to contemplate it and to reorganise it and to change his mindset. The transition from a drinking alcoholic to a recovering one can be arduous at least initially. The recovering alcoholic has to get used to a substantially different way of life. His drinking lifestyle has provided much of the meaning, structure and content of his life for years, often decades.

He needs to prepare himself for abstinence. He needs to be prepared for the result of his action in stopping drinking when suddenly his *raison d'être* has gone and something has to take its place if he is not to relapse. He needs to act by ceasing to drink. Living sober can be far from easy particularly at first. To begin with, the alcoholic feels strange, incompetent and lacking in important practical and social skills. He finds it difficult to function without a drink because he has done so much for so long under the influence of alcohol. He needs to learn how to maintain his sobriety and to take steps to guard against relapse.

Another challenge in managing the transition from a drinking to an abstinent lifestyle is the unrelenting nature of the task that the alcoholic has in remaining abstinent. He usually needs to distance himself from aspects of his past life and from his drinking networks in particular. He needs to avoid the cues and reminders that for him trigger the desire to drink or manage to resist them. At the same time he needs to develop a range of new activities and relationships both to replace those given up and to reinforce and sustain his new sober lifestyle. A further difficulty is that as a consequence of the alcoholic's coping with so much by drinking, without alcohol he will face coping with many situations and many emotions for the first time without his instant solution. He needs to experience that which is sufficient to alter his mindset and attendant belief system.

Environmental, social, cultural and psychological forces and influences are very important in determining who does and who does not develop dependent behaviours and, once dependent behaviour has developed, who does and who does not start and maintain the recovery process. The reasons why one person, and not another, becomes a real alcoholic involve the varied contributions of myriad experiences caused by myriad factors, interacting over time. Likewise, the reasons why one real alcoholic, and not another, recovers from alcoholism also involve the varied contributions of myriad experiences caused by myriad factors, interacting over time.

But one vital factor is different between the individual progressing towards and becoming alcoholic and the alcoholic progressing towards sobriety. The effort required from the individual to maintain the progression into alcoholism is comparatively small and is essentially logistical. All the individual has to do is acquire alcohol and drink it. The effort required from the individual to maintain the progression towards sobriety is profound, arduous and on many levels.

Another crucial factor is that because recovery, like all change, is a staged process, only strategies and techniques for effecting change appropriate for the particular stage at which an individual is, will really work. If an alcoholic is in the pre-contemplation stage no treatment technique will have much, if any, effect unless it triggers the contemplation stage. Unless he has completed his preparation it is improbable that he will actually stop drinking for very long. Unless the individual has reached the action stage he is unlikely to heed advice to stay away from bars or to attend AA. Unless he is at the maintenance stage he may well not continue to attend AA meetings or practise his personal relapse prevention programme.

EMOTION AND COMMUNICATION

In the real alcoholic there lurks the tyrant alcohol described by alcoholics in AA as "cunning, baffling and powerful". The abject and utter misery generated by alcoholic intake in the drinking alcoholic can, before insanity, a wet brain or death intervenes, finally beat the alcoholic into surrender. It stands, even in the recovering real alcoholic, more or less manifest, ready to plunge him back into misery, insanity and death. In my case, the loss, pain and misery involved in my struggle to stop drinking and my continuing relapses over the thirty odd years before my conversion played their part in the surrender involved in that experience. To relate Harry Tiebout's summing up of the conversion experience to mine, the effect on me was that after trying to run my own affairs to my own ruination, I finally gave up the battle and surrendered to the need for help; I entered a new state of mind that enabled me to remain sober for the time being.

The mental and physical traumas and emotional shocks which abusing alcohol can bring about can be a great persuader. If the resultant disruptive emotions increase suggestibility sufficiently, it can in some alcoholics trigger conversion which can enable them to start taking the steps which can instigate the recovery process. Other alcoholics display a defiance and tenacity which keeps them drinking to the bitter end whatever happens. Some commit suicide. Between sixteen and forty one per cent of suicides are thought to be attributable to alcohol. Thankfully, in my case, my misery and desperation eventually triggered what I hope was my final conversion from a drinking to a recovering alcoholic.

The purpose of emotion is to ensure that the individual engages with the real world which is essential for survival. Emotion is inextricably involved in alcoholism because of alcohol's affect on the brain in distorting the real world by hijacking the natural positive emotions relating to survival and diverting them to alcohol consumption. Emotion is also inextricably involved in initiating recovery. Conditioned behaviour can change during a state of strong emotion. In a strong emotional state the human brain and mind can reconfigure dramatically usually only to revert back to the state where the individual's previously conditioned lifestyle dominates.

However, an emotionally caused reconfiguration of an alcoholic's brain can amount to conversion to an abstinent state. If sufficient action is taken to prevent reversion back to the drinking state recovery can result. Paradoxically, notwithstanding the action necessary to prevent relapse, the recovery process seems to me to be more one of allowing change to happen rather than one of actively seeking change. This has been my experience.

Emotion can also affect communication with alcoholics relating to recovery. Those closest to the alcoholic often find him unapproachable because of the strength of the emotions involved. Doctors, clergymen and others often throw up their hands in despair when after exhaustive treatment or exhortation, the alcoholic still insists that he is not understood. After all, the non-alcoholic does not share the alcoholic's experience of dependence. Even the best psychiatrists proceeding on an intellectual level can fail to achieve in the alcoholic an emotional willingness to discuss his situation without reserve or substantially at all. I find that it is only with other alcoholics that I can truly communicate with regard to my and their alcoholism and with regard to recovery from alcoholism.

Usually only another alcoholic sharing the same experience particularly one who is in recovery can win the suffering alcoholic's entire confidence often in a remarkably short time. Until the emotions are engaged and an understanding reached little or nothing can be accomplished as regards recovery. The suffering alcoholic can realize, when he meets a recovering one, that they share a common experience. Further, the recovering one cannot easily be deceived: he knows the tricks of the trade. Barriers dissolve and mutual confidence, indispensable in effective treatment, can develop. If this essential rapport does not occur between the suffering alcoholic and the first recovering alcoholic he meets it will occur sooner or later when he meets others.

It is now known that the cognitive and emotional aspects of human cognitive functioning are much more closely interwoven than was formerly thought to be the case. Behaviour is driven far more by emotion than many would like to think. AA experience suggests that the best time to try and communicate with the drinking alcoholic is when he has recently come round from a drunken state, is substantially sober and is feeling extremely emotional with feelings of guilt and remorse. This reflects some classic advice to the revivalist preacher that he should find the point at which "the mind is tremblingly alive" as Charles Finney put it in his frank and detailed handbook *Lectures on Revivals of Religion* (1835).

In AA meetings continuing communication is maintained by the uninterrupted and unchallenged oral sharing by members of their individual experience, strength and hope. Hope can transcend the past and present by looking towards the future. Hope does not escape the present reality, but relates the momentary to a better future. Sharing in AA is essentially an emotional exercise and not any form of intellectual discourse, discussion, debate or argument. The members' sharing is often in narrative form. This, in accordance with known cognitive functioning, not only supports AA's structural beliefs regarding the maintenance of sobriety, but also purveys values, either explicitly or by presenting models of behaviour, and can also engender or enhance hope for the future.

One of the paradoxes of recovery from alcoholism is that the factor which makes the difference is a change in attitude towards the use of alcohol based on the individual's own experience which in the great majority of cases takes place outside any clinical interaction. Unless the real alcoholic's brain circuitry, mindset and attendant belief system change, in particular but not limited to his mindset as regards alcohol, he will drink again. Abstinence as such, the precondition of recovery from alcoholism for the real alcoholic, is only the beginning of recovery. As some put it "abstinence is only the ticket to the show, it is not the show".

Recovery for the real alcoholic is overcoming his dependence induced insanity, addressing his resentments, his bitter indignation (whether justified or not) at having been treated badly or unfairly and changing into a kind of person who no longer needs to drink (and does not want to) and never again does. Recovery involves a change of mindset through re-evaluation and self-education; it involves a new mindset. A new established and extensive neuronal circuitry needs to be built up in the brain which is more flexible in interactions with the senses, that is to say, with the outside world.

My conversion, my emotionally charged profound change of attitude took place when I was alone, tired, emotional and drunk. It did not seem at the time to be and it still does not seem to have been anything of my doing; it just happened. It definitely seemed to have nothing to do with my intellect. But then Albert Einstein (1879-1955) said that "the intellect has little to do on the road to discovery. There comes a leap in consciousness, call it intuition or what you will, and the solution comes to you and you do not know how or why."

WHY ONLY SOME

Real alcoholics suffer a build up of crises caused by their drinking in many areas of their lives which, eventually for some, forces them into recognition of their condition or precipitates such recognition. This recognition is vital if conversion is to take place whether with a distinct turning point or whether preceded by small incremental learning steps which result one day in the start of the recovery process, that day only being identifiable in hindsight as the day the alcoholic had his last drink.

It can be said that these real alcoholics are the lucky minority because their crises were so fortuitously configured as to somehow break through their almost impenetrable defences embodied in their denial system so characteristic of alcoholism. The unlucky majority are those whose circumstances have not forced or precipitated a recognition of their condition resulting in conversion developing into sustained recovery and who go on drinking.

Some alcoholics recognise their condition early in their drinking careers while others carry on drinking progressing further down the dependence path as illustrated by *the Jellinek Chart of Alcoholism and Recovery* until their crises fortuitously effect, sometimes quickly (even spontaneously) sometimes slowly, conversion resulting in sustained recovery. Most real alcoholics never start the recovery process at all.

There appear to be no clear antecedent differences between the small minority of real alcoholics who have progressed substantially down the dependence path who achieve sobriety and the majority of them who continue to drink alcoholically. Further, once alcoholism has taken on a life of its own, all real alcoholics, generally speaking, suffer similar traumas and emotional shocks following distressful events. Most suffer these traumas and shocks to the bitter end of insanity or death yet for some recovery is eventually initiated.

A factor militating against conversion developing into sustained recovery is the considerable effort and discipline required to engage effectively in the recovery process. Through his prolonged drinking the real alcoholic has developed the automatic, unconscious behavioural patterns of chronic alcoholism. His drinking is the product of deeply conditioned unconscious cues developed from childhood of which he is totally unaware unless they are pointed out to him and he is prepared to recognise them.

The cues operate directly causing the alcoholic behaviour without reference to the brain's rational thought and decision making processes which are by-passed. The brain's executive function is taken over by conditioned, learned responses. Usually, only with the real alcoholic's conscious effort informed by awareness and knowledge of dependence and its cues can alcoholism be countered. For the chronic real alcoholic this requires learning new skills and sustained effort. In stark contrast, a return to drinking requires no skill and minimal, or no, effort.

The definitive way to address the alcoholic's problems is for him to stop drinking. This can be simply stated but it can be profoundly difficult for alcoholics, for some apparently impossible. The drinking alcoholic's situation can commonly be likened to that of a skier with an avalanche behind him. He must stop skiing but, if he does, the avalanche will catch up with him. The alcoholic will be extremely vulnerable having just stopped using the one thing, alcohol, which had kept him going. No wonder most alcoholics drink again after a period of abstinence. All his problems, real and perceived, inevitably generated by his drinking will catch up with him and they will have to be faced. His habitual way to face problems is to drink alcohol.

A complete change of personality and lifestyle is intrinsically difficult and arduous for anybody in any event. There are also many ancillary reasons why a real alcoholic does not put in the effort required for recovery. He may be homeless, jobless, deeply in debt and experiencing problems with personal relationships. He may have a history of criminal activity and he may have a concurrent mental illness or disorder. He may be suffering from a chronic nutritional deficiency disease or from cirrhosis of the liver or other liver damage. He may have kidney damage, cancer or other physical injuries or ailments. Such issues can pre-occupy him leaving little time or energy to concentrate on change.

The real alcoholic usually has feelings of profound low self-worth. He may be so bound up with concerns relating to money, property, prestige or business or professional matters that recovery is afforded little attention and little, if any, priority. Some start abusing alcohol before certain full personality developments have taken place and before they have developed skills to interact meaningfully as adults in the community. All these factors make it less likely that the individual will give his recovery his full and undivided attention for so long as it takes. Even if a few, never mind a number, of them are present it is hardly surprising that the alcoholic does not recover.

There are some alcoholics who on the face of it have no pressing problems or issues who spend considerable time and effort on their admitted alcoholism with the firm intention of not drinking again. They may over time attend a number of treatment centres. They may attend one, or even two, AA meetings a day on a regular basis only breaking off from time to time to drink. This for some goes on for years. Although they protest their recognition of their alcoholism and take action to address it, no effective conversion occurs. The consequences of their drinking fail to initiate a sustained recovery process.

Most alcoholics look for easier or different ways to address their drinking problems rather than espouse any approach which might involve the effort of learning new attitudes and skills and which might require considerable discipline. It is usually a very difficult matter to persuade the alcoholic that he is the victim of a fatal and progressive condition. Innumerable alcoholics cling to the rationalization that their troubles are due to their personal circumstances and that their troubles are accordingly other peoples' fault. Countless alcoholics cannot see that they need any help at all let alone that they need substantially to change and that this is an inside piece of work and responsibility, that, essentially, they need to help themselves (albeit usually with the assistance of others). Even if an alcoholic recognises that he needs help it is likely that he thinks that only others can afford it him.

Drinking alcohol misleads the alcoholic into believing that his problems originate in other people and in situations and factors outside himself. However the only lasting solution to his problems is to confront them within himself, not by demanding solutions from others or by attacking others and blaming them and factors outside himself for all his difficulties. Drinking alcohol is a very effective way of stopping the vital process of learning about oneself. Recovery requires a capacity in the alcoholic to know himself.

Drinking and the alcoholic's self-centred pursuit of what alcohol offers also substantially diminishes his capacity for, and interest in, real human intimacy. This compromises and can prevent the effective change from an adolescent independence to a mature interdependence. Instead the alcoholic moves into an inwardly focused dependence on alcohol and the resources it is perceived to offer. As some in AA put it, alcohol becomes the alcoholic's God. Alcohol moves the alcoholic away even from the social opportunities it seems to offer in terms of camaraderie, friendship and intimacy. The apparent camaraderie, friendship and intimacy built on a foundation of shared drinking evaporate quickly.

Even if a significant conversion is experienced by an alcoholic, the window of opportunity to take matters further does not usually stay open for very long before the individual's denial system sets in again. If an individual has asked for help, appropriate help appropriately presented, often needs to be proffered quite quickly, sometimes immediately or almost immediately. Another crucial factor can be that lack of funds or funding can mean that treatment is unavailable, inaccessible or restricted, eliminating appropriate and speedy treatment options.

Nevertheless, there are what Robin Touquet calls "teachable moments" of which advantage can be taken. In the Department of Emergency Medicine at St. Mary's Hospital, London, Touquet and his colleagues have developed an alcohol test taking a minute and which is given to all patients with one or more of the main complaints considered to have alcohol abuse or alcoholism as their root cause. The test enables patients at risk to be identified and for them to be referred to a specially trained health care professional. Indications are that some sixty per cent of patients receiving a brief intervention as a result reduce their alcohol intake. There are many teachable moments at which drinkers might be persuaded to change their drinking behaviour such as may occur at doctors' surgeries, fracture clinics or gastroenterological outpatient departments.

The recovery process does not start if the individual refuses to recognise, or to face, his problems caused by drinking or if he is indifferent to them or detached from them. Nor does the process start if he constantly takes evasive action from the consequences of his drinking or if others cushion him from them. Even if it starts, the process is not maintained if the individual fails substantially to co-operate. The degree of effort and dedication which he puts into his recovery is critical as is the amount of discipline which he can muster to maintain his recovery regime.

The individual needs to be in an environment conducive to recovery whereby his brain can do the rest by a learning process involving re-evaluation, self-education and counter-conditioning. Persistent exposure in the right context and environment to the right messages and influences can create an increasing number of associations to be set up in the brain and mind. This can facilitate the development of a new neuronal infrastructure and working memory enabling the larger neural constellations that are at work in the adult brain and mind to be pressed into service for living soberly. However, having regard to the relatively permanent and substantial changes in mindset learnt during a long drinking career, this is no mean task. It is a relatively rare achievement for the real alcoholic who has progressed far down the path of alcohol dependence to relearn how to live without alcohol or other psychoactive substance on an ongoing, hopefully permanent basis.

For an individual to be successful in his recovery it would seem that he needs to live the belief system which is conducive to his recovery. This may be described as "intrinsic" belief. His emotions need to drive his recovery as well as his mind. The real alcoholic needs to be committed to his new belief system as regards alcohol and his sober way of life. This involves self discipline. He must feel responsible for his actions. This intrinsic belief can be contrasted with what may be described as an "extrinsic" orientation to the new belief system relating to alcohol where adherence is more to do with authority and peer pressure than self control and social responsibility. Extrinsic belief may not be enough to maintain and sustain recovery but it can precede intrinsic belief and intrinsic belief can develop from extrinsic belief.

In addition to the personal reasons why only some alcoholics recover are the reasons resulting from failure properly to treat alcoholism. Scientific treatment of alcoholism is relatively new and much is based on faith rather than empirical evidence. Health care professionals, researchers and policy makers can hang on to outmoded beliefs. They do not have all the answers. Health care professionals and researchers spend time arguing amongst themselves. They can appear not to know what they are doing especially to policy makers who accordingly fail to provide funds for research and to improve the treatment system.

Generally, there is persistent failure in providing the right sort of treatment at the right time. Far from all alcoholics, even far from all those who seek help, are treated effectively. In the public sector in the UK treatment is underfunded and uncoordinated. Vital treatment components are often not available or deployed when needed. Critical components of successful recovery include not only those relating to treatment as such but also include those relating to personal relationships, housing, debt, education, employment and mental health.

DICTATOR IDEOLOGY

The political psychology of the dictator is observed in alcoholism and needs to be countered in recovery from it. In order to take the focus off the real enemy within, the dictator, the enemy without is created and then enlarged. This technique has seduced whole populations into relinquishing their freedom. Powerful propaganda concerning the enemy without makes them willing slaves to the dictator within. In the alcoholic, alcohol is the dictator. An enemy without is created and becomes part of the rationalizing process of alcoholism. The alcoholic tells himself that, for example, he drinks because his wife nags him, or because he does not get the promotion he thinks he deserves, or because his friends avoid him or let him down. Each aspect of reality can, in effect, become the threatening enemy without. The alcoholic loses his freedom to alcohol in order to protect himself from his own misconception of a hostile reality. The rationalising system in those who suffer from alcoholism appears not unlike that in those who suffer from paranoia. But people who really drink for a reason often remain in control of their drinking; the real alcoholic does not.

   Research suggests that, once severe alcoholism is established, depression, psychopathic deviancy and paranoia can reach pathological levels. Once severely dependent on alcohol, the individual reveals the neurotic patterns consistent with self-centred, immature, dependent, resentful and irresponsible people who are unable to face reality. This suggests that individuals develop alcoholism first and then conform to the hypothetical alcoholic personality afterwards.

   Rationalization is a necessary support for the alcoholism that has taken over the alcoholic's personality. Apart from *delirium tremens* and alcoholic psychosis, rationalization does not necessarily reveal itself overtly, but it is there nonetheless, and it is important for the alcoholic to gain insight into its abnormal mechanisms. Psychotherapy, counselling, and self-help groups can guide the alcoholic towards gaining insight into resentment and feelings of rejection and guilt. If he is successful, he learns to cope with these feelings instead of running away from them or acting out on them. If acquired, his insight into the sources of his rationalizations may help to allay a great deal of his personality discomfort. In some cases the alcoholic's personality problems, as well as his problem with alcohol *per se*, need specifically to be addressed. Personality problems presented by alcoholics vary enormously. They have, however, an extraordinarily similar system of irrational thought.

MEN AND WOMEN

Alcoholism specifically relating to women has only been substantially addressed in the last twenty years or so. Men and women may have different treatment needs and may respond differently to different styles of treatment. More research is needed. Nevertheless, the similarities of alcoholism in men and women are, without doubt, far greater than the differences, although men are almost three times more likely than women to become alcoholics. Men and women are equally capable of recovery and the various treatment approaches are generally applicable to both sexes.

One major sex difference makes the course of alcoholism in women somewhat different. Women are metabolically less tolerant of alcohol and end up with higher concentrations of alcohol in the blood stream than men drinking the same amount. Further women are more susceptible to alcohol-related liver disease, cardiovascular disease, degenerative diseases and brain damage than men. Two recent US studies indicate that women who drink to excess experience more brain damage more quickly than men who drink the same amount. Women may experience even more severe long term effects than men. These studies are the first to show sex differences in the effect alcohol has on the brain shrinkage which is common in alcoholics.

According to a recent exhaustive ten year analysis in the US, women begin abusing alcohol for different reasons than men. Young women are more likely than young men to abuse substances in order to lose weight, relieve stress or boredom, improve their mood, reduce sexual inhibitions, self-medicate depression and increase confidence. Women in treatment are more than five times more likely than men to have been sexually abused as children and women are more likely to suffer eating disorders, both of which are major risk factors for alcohol abuse and alcoholism.

Crises, such as divorce, unemployment or recent departure of a child from the home are more likely to trigger alcohol abuse and alcoholism in women and a miscarriage is an additional potential trigger. Older women are more likely than older men to self-medicate with alcohol in order to deal with loneliness, financial insecurity or loss of a partner.

A SPIRITUAL ASPECT

Alcoholism and recovery from it involves complex biological, psychological, social, cognitive and emotional aspects. Some go further and assert that alcoholism and recovery from it also involves a spiritual aspect. Indeed, I have already referred to the possibility of a spiritual component in recovery, to process spirituality and spiritual awakening. I have mentioned spirituality a number of times. Some further assert that the spiritual aspect defies medical terminology or classification. A full description or explanation of alcoholism and recovery from it in purely scientific terms is accordingly impossible. Some, especially those who espouse AA tenets, would say that there is a spiritual dimension with which science cannot deal, in medical, psychological or any other scientific terms.

Many questions arise as to the spiritual aspect in alcoholism and recovery from it including what is meant by spirituality and whether spirituality is inextricably linked with religion and what part does spirituality and religion play in the aetiology of alcoholism and in recovery from it. Again some would say that it is impossible to define spirituality because it is an intangible, ineffable reality. However, if an understanding of alcoholism and recovery from it is being attempted in the context of which the word is so often used, even bandied about, I think it important at least to try to define and address spirituality, or at least some aspects of it, for such purposes and to address other related matters. These matters are seen by many to be central to alcoholism and recovery from it.

SPIRITUALITY AND HIGHER POWER

SPIRITUALITY AND RECOVERY

Despite many in the field of recovery maintaining that spirituality is not only important but central to the understanding of dependence in general and of alcoholism in particular it is little studied by scientists. This is hardly surprising because many scientists would not consider spirituality as the proper subject matter of scientific enquiry. At any rate, they might say, empirical measurement fails to capture the essence of spirituality. Scientific method is usually seen as irrelevant, even antithetical, to the realm of spirituality as it is commonly understood.

Further, although spirituality is referred to in the field of recovery beyond the traditional AA twelve-step approach, it is usually unclear in what sense the speaker or writer is using the word. The word is rarely defined and many maintain that spirituality is ineffable. Spirituality, they say, cannot be described or defined; it can only be experienced. Beauty and the scent of a rose both resemble spirituality in that they are intangible realities which may be known but never adequately expressed in words. In *The Spirituality of Imperfection* (1992), Ernest Kurtz and Katherine Ketcham state that to have the answer to what is meant by spirituality is to have misunderstood the question. When a definition of spirituality is attempted they say what is discovered is "not its limitations, but our own".

However there are many elusive phenomena that psychologists seek to understand, where their essence may be thought invisible to quantitative eyes like quality of life, character and psychotherapy itself. Such complex phenomena can only be measured in part, imperfectly. A major problem is to identify something which the scientist can effectively study. Clearly the current lack of a universally accepted definition of spirituality and the general lack of reliable and valid measurement devices will hamper progress. A useful approach as regards spirituality might be to treat it, not as a variable, but as what has been called a "latent construct", an abstract psychological concept such as intelligence or personality.

Intelligence and personality have been the proper subject matter of myriad scientific studies and other latent constructs like learning difficulties, for example, have been effectively studied for remedial purposes. It may be possible scientifically to study spirituality usefully for recovery purposes. There are some interesting findings already in the literature but scientific knowledge about the role of spirituality in alcoholism is tiny compared with what is known about neuroadaptation, genetics, conditioning, personality disorder and social modelling.

One report (David Larson *et al., Scientific Research on Spirituality and Health*, US National Institute for Healthcare Research, 1998) provides a working definition of spirituality to include feelings, thoughts, experiences and behaviours that arise from a search for a divine being and ultimate truth. The definition encompasses a number of domains including religious affiliation and history, social and private participation in activities, support and coping, beliefs and values, commitment, motivation and specific spiritual experiences.

Assessment instruments (questionnaires, inventories, scales, forms, tests, semi-structured interviews and so on) for these domains are available but vary markedly in quality and stage of development. The report summarizes the work of more than seventy researchers in the fields of mental health, physical health, neuroscience and psychoactive substance dependence and reviews their findings. It asserts that "the data from many of the studies conducted to date are both sufficiently robust and tantalizing to warrant continued and expanded clinical investigations".

No matter whether or not spirituality is ineffable or whether it can properly be defined and scientifically studied, there is much in life which can properly be described as "spiritual" if for no better reason than it is certainly not material or physical. Further, a great deal which is neither material nor physical pertains and goes on in the context of alcoholism and recovery from it.

Kurtz in *Not-God* (1979, 1991), a history of AA, suggests that the fundamental ancient spiritual insight reiterated in AA is that man is not God. The relevant concept of God is that he is the perfect, omnipotent, omniscient originator and ruler of the universe. Certainly the realization that I was not God (even in my own very limited intensely personal sphere of influence) was an essential realization in my early recovery and remains so. Kurtz describes "spirituality" as some "intangible, ineffable reality". But, for me, spirituality is more helpfully described in terms of the consequences in thought and action of that realistic realization that I am not God. If I am not God, I should not imitate or play God because rather obviously (when stated so boldly) I am not perfect, omnipotent or omniscient (let alone originator and ruler of the universe).

Spirituality can be seen, in the context of recovery, as the quality of any belief, thought attitude, activity or inactivity which drives the individual forward towards or facilitates some form of beneficial physical, emotional, intuitional, intellectual or social development, particularly, for the alcoholic, towards sobriety. It can be seen in a content sense, in terms of belief in God, or in a process sense in terms of factors, characteristics, attitudes, coping mechanisms, cognitive gadgets, actions and inactions, enabling an individual better to cope with life.

Depending on the individual and his concept of spirituality, spirituality can play many parts or no part in his recovery. It can be its very essence for one and in another's any suggestion of spirituality is rejected out of hand and each may or may not be referring to the same concept. In between are the other recovering alcoholics with a myriad variety of views on and concepts of spirituality. Most would probably say that there is in recovery some aspect which can properly be called spiritual, if only because the aspect in question is not material, physical or intellectual. If the spiritual element involved is not ineffable, as some would maintain, perhaps it is best addressed in general terms as the spirituality of limitation along the lines set out by Ernest Kurtz and Katherine Ketcham in *The Spirituality of Imperfection* rather than any form of conventional religious spirituality.

The question remains to some as to whether any scientific model can extend to and explain and address all aspects of alcoholism and real alcoholism in particular and recovery from them. Even all the ramifications of neuronal circuitry, reinforcement and neuroadaptation and the other discoveries of neuroscience yet to be made in the future course of research may not, it is suggested, be able fully to explain everything.

Some suggest that there may still remain, in a complete picture, some spiritual element or elements incapable of being effectively addressed within the confines of any purely scientific model. For example, Charles Bishop, co-author of *To Be Continued: The Alcoholics Anonymous World Bibliography 1935-1994* (1994) argues that those who try to categorize AA as a form of psychotherapy do it a disservice. According to Bishop, AA can be properly taken only on its own terms as a spiritual fellowship, not merely a treatment strategy or way to modify behaviour that can be couched in terms of modern neuroscience.

That any spiritual element may remain incapable of inclusion in a scientifically based model of alcoholism and recovery from it would, however, be disappointing to the scientist if not to the theologian. Many scientists believe that science is capable of addressing all aspects of a condition such as alcoholism. These scientists do not see the construction of medical and other scientific models as reducing their subject matter to the mere ebb and flow of chemicals and neuroadaptations. Rather they see the creation of useful and effective models of the relevant processes and mechanisms – and barring miracles, there have to be processes and mechanisms – as advancing understanding and furthering the efficiency of treatment. Models support and implement understanding, treatment and recovery and can support and implement human reason, judgment and insight.

Spirituality can be seen in a content sense and in a process sense. The content sense refers to what an individual perceives or believes applies or exists beyond the realm of the purely physical or material, such as codes of morality, ethics or justice or the soul or God. The process sense refers to the behavioural consequences and actions resulting from such perception or belief. The perception might be some system of morality, ethics or justice or the belief might be in the soul or God as supernatural entities, or in something else which is not supernatural but neither is it material or physical, perhaps some concept of soul or God distinct from the brain or mind or an emergent property of the brain or, indeed, some other belief.

In the context of alcoholism and recovery from it spirituality can, in my view, best be considered in terms not of content but in terms of process. This means that what the individual believes or does not believe in the content sense of spirituality can be kept distinct, distinct in particular from the recovery process. It also means that any therapist, counsellor or sponsor need not agree with what the alcoholic believes or disbelieves.

In its process sense spirituality can be seen as essentially pragmatic and practical albeit often having religious connotations for some individuals. The process sense can be seen to refer to the behavioural consequences and actions resulting from adopting certain attitudes, practising certain skills or following a certain programme as well as the behavioural consequences and actions resulting from the belief in the concepts, constructs and entities the subject matter of spirituality or religion in the content sense.

Spirituality can and often does involve a search for meaning and purpose greater than the individual and it plays an integral role in the lives of many people. As a result of their dependence, alcoholics lose much purpose, value and meaning in life and many have in recovery found succour in a larger search for purpose, value and meaning beyond their dependence which the pursuit of spirituality can generate. Spirituality is a prevalent, even pervasive, component of treatment programmes for alcoholism in AA and in Minnesota AA Model treatment centres. On the other hand, any concept of spirituality plays little, if any, part in Community Reinforcement Approach treatment centres and many therapy and counselling sessions.

Longitudinal studies indicate that many attribute their success in their efforts to change to spiritual aspects of their lives or spiritual features of their treatment. Research suggests that adults with spiritual commitment and involvement have more personal satisfaction than adults without such involvement. Process spirituality can encompass essentially secular goals such as self-esteem, comfort, intimacy and meaning. It can involve a sense of caring for others, a sense of acceptance and forgiveness and the adoption of basic human values and acts which refrain from causing harm to others or compromising their peace of mind.

Spirituality, in its process sense, can reverse the tendency of the human mind to experience private scenarios that have not actually occurred or to conjure up personalized events from the past without any external cues. Even when the individual is not locked into his own inner world, he is interpreting the world around him in the context of his idiosyncratic experiences and consequent values. The self-centred alcoholic needs substantially to compromise this tendency by becoming aware of other people and their effect on him. The practice of spiritual principles can help to address the adverse neuroadaptation in the alcoholic's brain caused by drinking. Such practice can compromise the self-centred fear felt and can counter the innate dysphoria experienced by so many alcoholics.

However, regarding the practice of spiritual principles compromising self-centred fear the dichotomy between the moral and medical notions of alcoholism can again be seen. Depending on the individual interpretation of spirituality, either faith can be seen as the counter to fear or information and assistance can. If the individual believes in content spirituality to the extent that God is looking after him, then faith can dispel fear. If the individual does not believe in God, then faith cannot dispel fear as it can for the believer. Rather the individual can substantially dispel his fear by accepting his perception that his own resources are insufficient for coping with the fear and asking for help, thus acquiring the information and obtaining the assistance needed to give him peace of mind.

For the non-believer, addressing his self-centred fear may involve more mental effort than for the believer whose fear can essentially be dispelled by virtue of his belief that his loving God will ensure that no harm will come to him if he does God's will. The non-believer, on the other hand, perceives of no God looking after him, and needs to take action to dispel his fear. In practice, though, there may not be that much difference between the activities of the believer and the non-believer because the believer's action in seeking to do God's will, can equate to the action pursued by the non-believer in addressing his fear. Addressing the fear and its concomitant emotional pain by avoiding the instant antidote in favour of the long term solution can for both be the road to self-knowledge and to self-esteem.

A very important component of what can be described as spirituality, in whatsoever sense, in recovery, is humility not in any pejorative or negative sense but in the positive sense of maturity, perspective and balance in the individual's relationship with himself, with others and generally with the world about him, of being grounded. It amounts to a clear recognition of what and who he really is. It includes an accurate (not underestimated) appraisal of his abilities and achievements, an ability to acknowledge his imperfections and limitations, an accepting and liberal attitude towards novel ideas and an honest and non-defensive examination of his personal attributes. It involves a well balanced analysis of strengths and weaknesses resulting in an even handed realistic view of himself. It amounts to a shift from self-centredness to self-acceptance. It also involves giving proper weight to the moment, recognising that nothing lasts and that it is that which gives the moment its deep significance. It involves recognising the significance, often the importance, of other people and the crucial importance of the alcoholic's relationships with other people.

This process sort of spirituality offers a basic, matter-of-fact set of practical guidelines drawn from the individual's inner abilities and resources. Once learnt and practised it can eventually emanate from within the individual giving him awareness, acceptance and guidelines for action or inaction. I am, I think, essentially a pragmatist. If a belief, an attitude or an action helps to make me less anxious and more content and thus sustains or maintains my sobriety, I try to adopt it or take it. The spirituality I have learnt in AA from other alcoholics seems to work; it certainly works for me. I am profoundly happier, more joyous and free than I ever was before.

SPIRITUALITY IN AA

AA's success in practice suggests that the two notions of alcoholism, moral and medical, can in some practical way be reconciled at least in the context of a programme of recovery from it which works. In the AA programme, the two approaches, the moral one and the medical one, can be seen as having been combined. The AA approach sees alcoholism in medical terms as a disease and recovery in moral terms as a spiritual awakening. One approach to reconciliation could be to focus on what spirituality means in the context of recovery with particular emphasis on AA.

Many regard purely materialist approaches to reality adopted by many medical practitioners as inadequate and have a genuine interest in recovering a spiritual dimension to life. Many seek a life-enhancing spirituality. They seek a deeply personal dynamic which provides meaning and purpose in life. While for many spirituality flows from and gives expression to their religious convictions, for many others spirituality is not grounded in traditional religious beliefs, but is, nevertheless, the expression of their core values and approach to life.

The AA approach to spirituality is more a reflection of a broader definition of it rather than one based on traditional religions, although many members use religion to bolster their spiritual experience. AA's approach can be seen as emancipating spirituality from its explicitly religious roots. The term spiritual awakening as used in AA can simply be seen as referring to the profound alteration in the alcoholics' attitude and life, triggered by a conversion, which occurs when they stop drinking and their recovery continues. Such a change, according to classic AA tenets, could not have been brought about by the individual alone. For many alcoholics in AA what takes place in a few months had not been accomplished in years of trying to stop drinking on their own. In many cases alcoholics recovering in AA find that they have tapped an unsuspected resource which they presently identify with their own conception of God.

To the Christian, practising the Twelve Steps of AA can be like, as one clergyman has put it, a walk through the Bible as it relates to redemption from error. The acknowledgement of powerlessness, the surrender to

God, the admission of wrongs and the desire to rebuild lives and rela-tionships are all in the Bible. However, to the irreligious the practice of the Twelve Steps can be seen as the following of an effective pragmatic programme exclusively based on the scientific tenets of good psychiatry and therapy (albeit expressed in spiritual terms but set free from religious ideology) in order to overcome a mental condition.

Both the moral and medical notions can see the source of the help requisite for recovery as being outside the alcoholic. The moral notion sees the outside help as being spiritually based and the medical as being scientifically based. However, if recovery is seen as the effective use of the outside help, be it spiritual or scientific, in developing the inner re-source of the particular individual requisite for recovery, then a degree of reconciliation can be accomplished. In the recovery context, it does not matter what the nature of the outside help is, provided that it facilitates recovery.

The issue as to whether or not alcoholism is a chronic relapsing men-tal condition should not be a stumbling block for those who believe in the moral approach to alcoholism. Further the spiritual element in recovery should not be a stumbling block for those who believe in the medical ap-proach provided that the nature of the relevant spirituality is understood. Both the doctor and the clergyman should embrace the same recovery process with its moral and medical elements.

THE MEANING OF SPIRITUALITY

Recovery from alcoholism involves coping with life without drinking. The drinking alcoholic fails to cope with life without drinking while the recovering alcoholic succeeds. Coping involves not only dealing effec-tively with difficulties and problems but also responding to life's strains, problems and vicissitudes in ways that serve to prevent, avoid or control emotional distress. Coping is a process involving an event experienced by an individual, his appraisal of it, an appraisal by him of the resources to hand to deal with it, activity to attempt to deal with it and the result or outcome of the activity in terms of success or failure in dealing with it. Recovery from alcoholism and coping cannot be investigated in terms of the individual or his situation alone, they need to be studied in terms of their interaction.

The spirituality relevant to recovery from alcoholism can be taken to mean that which is necessary for his recovery and which the alcoholic did not practise sufficiently before recovery and which by sufficient practise in recovery works in maintaining and furthering stable and contented sobriety. The relevant spirituality can be seen in content terms. in terms of God, or in process terms, in terms of factors which enable a person to cope contentedly with life.

This definition of spirituality seems to me to be the most helpful. It reflects the outside help requisite for recovery for the individual concerned howsoever sourced. It is not static but dynamic like coping. The relevant spirituality can, accordingly, also usefully be seen as a process involving the beliefs, attitudes, experiences and responses which the individual has and the social context in which he finds himself from time to time. The spirituality in my recovery comprised the coping factors which I learned in AA by listening and talking to other alcoholics.

An aspect of AA spirituality can be characterized as enhancing hope. Hope can transcend the past and present by relating the momentary to a better future. From contemplating suicide as my only solution, AA gave me hope for a tolerable future. The effective spirituality for others may well be AA spirituality too but it could be the coping mechanisms learned otherwise howsoever.

Although espousing spirituality often provides support to individuals in crisis, so doing does not provide direct solutions. Only appropriate action or inaction can bring about solutions. Considering spirituality and spiritual experience in terms of process means that what the individual believes or does not believe in religious or in any other terms can be kept distinct from the recovery process. In particular, effective spirituality and spiritual experience does not require belief in anything traditionally understood as supernatural. The spirituality of recovery can be secular or sacred or a mixture of both.

Spiritual interpretation can influence the appraisal process in crisis and coping, because a crisis pointedly questions meaning and identity.

Consequently coping with contingencies is a crucial function of spirituality. Spirituality can provide a set of meanings with a clear message about the conceivable interpretations of events and situations.

The dynamic nature of spiritual interpretation is important. Each individual over his life time has made myriad interpretations concerning life and self. In recovery from real alcoholism, where in general terms there has been a continuing decline followed by a turn around and continuing improvement (as illustrated by *the Jellinek Chart of Alcoholism and Recovery*), the individual's story can provide information about the recovery process and all the other processes involved in it. A biographical, narrative approach is helpful and an alcoholic's individual story plays a vital role in his recovery in the context both of psychotherapy and counselling and even more so in the context of AA.

HIGHER POWER

Spirituality traditionally goes hand in hand with some concept of a higher power. William Silkworth, who wrote the "Doctor's Opinion" in *Alcoholics Anonymous*, writing in 1939 asserted, with regard to alcoholics, that "in nearly all cases their ideals must be grounded in a power greater than themselves, if they are to re-create their lives". William James, also addressing profound lifestyle changes, wrote as follows. "Practice may change our theoretical horizon and this in a twofold way; it may lead into new worlds and secure new powers. Knowledge we could never attain, remaining what we are, may be attainable in consequence of higher powers and a higher life, which we may morally achieve."

Certainly in AA, while alcoholism was seen as a medical disease, great emphasis was and is placed on a power greater than the alcoholic which can restore him to sanity, that is to say, which can bring about his recovery. Bill Wilson described AA as a synthetic gadget drawing upon the resources of medicine, psychiatry and religion. Change, and recovery is change, is now seen as an integration of physiological and psychological processes and these processes embody certain change mechanisms. One such change mechanism is the conversion mechanism prevalent particularly in religious conversion.

This mechanism, it seems to me, is substantially the same as that which for some brings about his conversion from a drinking alcoholic to a recovering one. It seems to me that the power greater than the alcoholic in AA is the mechanism, the cognitive gadget, to use the term Pascal Boyer uses in *Religion Explained* (2001), which plays an important part in the recovery of many alcoholics who attend AA. There are, of course, other relevant mechanisms which can bear on recovery like the others embodied in the AA programme and those embodied in cognitive behavioural therapy, motivational enhancement therapy and other treatment approaches like the Community Reinforcement Approach.

The concept of a power greater than the alcoholic as a force in the recovery process can be problematic. Many alcoholics, particularly those who have been exposed to AA, are loath to attribute their recovery to themselves. They prefer to attribute their success to another or others, to God, to a group of drunks or to AA. Although this should not present any problem to the extent that the power greater than the alcoholic is perceived as affording the help required by him to help himself or as an effective personal cognitive gadget, it can have its dangers.

Not accepting responsibility or credit for recovery can compromise self-confidence, self-esteem, motivation, discipline and commitment and the ability to recover. If an individual thinks that others or some external higher power are responsible for his sobriety, it may prove difficult for him to stop drinking and to stay stopped. Recovery is an individual, inside piece of work and responsibility which ultimately only the individual can achieve. Nothing else, God, therapy group, AA or health care professional, can achieve it. Concentrating on seeking to master the skills of recovery, very much in the hands of the individual, is surely far more worthwhile than sitting back and expecting a miracle. Remembering his own efforts to change can reinforce the individual's motivation and commitment. Waiting for some sort of Damascene conversion as the only chance of recovery or just praying for it or just attending AA, a treatment centre or therapy or counselling sessions, is unlikely to be successful.

In the final analysis, it seems to me, William Silkworth's assertion simply amounts to recognition that the alcoholic must address reality, in particular that he cannot control his drinking – that he is powerless over alcohol as it is put in AA's First Step. He needs to accept that he is accordingly not omnipotent, that not only is he powerless over the affect that drinking alcohol has on him, he is also powerless over much else besides. He needs to accept that he is not God and that there are powers greater than himself, before he can start to rebuild his life on a firm footing. It is suggested in *Alcoholics Anonymous* that, first of all, the alcoholic must "quit playing God" accordingly. For me the coming to believe in a higher power to the extent that I have was not to do with coming to believe in some sort of specific entity, some God, which was omnipotent or whatever, but in coming to believe that I was not omnipotent, that there were powers relevant to me greater than me or mine. I had to stop playing or imitating God and I needed to espouse substantial humility.

A realistic humility needs to be adopted which does not compromise the limited power which the individual has. Humility is not disdain for oneself, or if it is, it is informed distain, deriving not from ignorance of what the alcoholic is, but from the knowledge, or rather the acknowledgement, of what he is not. By practising a realistic humility, in the positive sense of maturity, perspective and balance in the individual's relations with himself and others, profound change can be achieved which can "lead into new worlds and secure new powers" as William James put it.

The understanding of the nature of the higher power, in the recovery context, has developed considerably and there are those who would argue against the need for any higher power in the sense understood by Silkworth or at all. The Community Reinforcement Approach, in particular, takes no explicit cognisance of any power greater than the alcoholic but concentrates on reinforcement directly, eliminating positive reinforcement for drinking and enhancing positive reinforcement for recovery. So-called rational recovery groups have formed based on AA twelve-step groups but without adopting AA's concept of a power greater than the alcoholic.

Some, who see the higher power concept as relevant, see it in terms of content that is in terms of God, a self-help group, an individual therapist, counsellor or sponsor, or an inner resource. Others see it in terms of pro-

cess, that is, in terms of the behavioural consequences and actions resulting from the adoption and practice of something. The something might
be a programme like the AA programme, religious tenets or the teaching
of and learning from a psychotherapist, counsellor or sponsor. It might be
the receiving of and acting upon an inspirational message or the following of another's example. The process could be seen as one successfully
managed by those who have found out how recovery works by experience
gleaned by study, self-help manuals, trial and error, experimentation, im-
provisation, by following someone's example or howsoever.

The higher power believed in could be the individual's own so-called
higher self, an inner resource. It could perhaps be a power within yet
perceived as coming from without the individual. Some speak of their
guardian angel. Some individuals have such negative reactions to traditional religious ideas and concepts that they think of "GOD" as "Good
Orderly Direction", from wherever it derives. Some speak of "Group Of
Drunks" or the power that appears to flow through a meeting of a group
of alcoholics. Certainly there are myriad ways in which the requisite
power, process or entity, real or imagined, can effectively be brought into
play.

Of those who do espouse the power greater than the alcoholic idea,
many think it far better to make even an inanimate object, like a double-
decker bus, the higher power rather than to have no power greater than
the alcoholic at all. It is argued, however, that, if recovery is seriously
to be pursued with a substantial outcome, a more sophisticated concept
of the power greater than the alcoholic is desirable. The connotations of
the words "greater than the alcoholic" alone suggest that, say, a group
of recovering alcoholics would have more relevant inherent power than
any inanimate object. But many do not espouse the power greater than
the alcoholic idea and they would argue that if a real alcoholic takes appropriate and adequate action he can recover by virtue of the efficacy of
that action alone.

Although the power greater than the alcoholic aspect of the twelve-
step approach has established a broad appeal there are many other approaches to recovery which have been successful in many cases. It is

entirely possible for a real alcoholic to recover without him having, let alone utilizing, a concept of any sort of power greater than himself. An approach involving a higher power different from a classical AA power greater than the alcoholic is also entirely possible which avoids "turning over" problems stemming from AA's Third Step. Any question of the alcoholic turning his will and life over to God, which Step Three requires, can be excluded.

The higher power can be seen simply in terms of reality, as a cognitive gadget resulting in the adoption of a realistic humility in the face of all the powers and potencies bearing on the individual. The higher power, especially if it is seen in spiritual terms, can have enormous attention grabbing power and high relevance for human minds as a side effect of those minds' being organised as they are. A great deal of human culture embodies salient cognitive gadgets.

Humility is the virtue of the man who knows he is not God. The higher power can be perceived in the process sense as the practice of some sort of unselfishness or selflessness or process spirituality which can eventually emanate from within giving the individual awareness, acceptance and guidelines for action and inaction. Whatever the case, God, as conceived by the Jews, the Christians or the Muslims, whether believed in or not, offers all of us, in the difference between God as so conceived and man, an invaluable lesson in humility.

An individual's belief in a higher power can be seen, for many, as something in constant reformulation and in ongoing interaction with the recovery process. It might simply start as an open-mindedness to consider the possibility of a higher power. Some of those who assert the need for a higher power claim that the relevant power can be virtually anything, even an inanimate object.

A higher power, like spirituality, can be perceived in a content sense, for example, as an omnipotent personal God capable of resolving coping problems or in a process sense as a dynamic mechanism facilitating an individual's ability to cope with life. AA has its concept of a power greater than the alcoholic and asserts its essential role in recovery. The Community Reinforcement Approach sees the dynamic process facilitating an individual's ability to cope with life without alcohol essentially as the reinforcement mechanism.

In the US AA recovery context in the 1930s when it began, belief in a power greater than the alcoholic was thought essential for recovery and it was perceived essentially as the Judeo-Christian God. Nevertheless, it was acknowledged that some people were agnostic or atheist. Chapter 4 in the Big Book was headed *We Agnostics*. In that chapter it is asserted that a spiritual basis of life and belief in God in some sense is necessary if recovery is to be achieved. But, spirituality being in effect distinguished from formal religion, the power greater than the alcoholic which needs to be believed in is not necessarily the God of any particular religion. The individual did not need to consider another's conception of God, only his own.

Even so, in the religious climate of the time, for the great majority, the recovery process would have been seen as eschewing sin and seeking righteousness in biblical terms. In the early AA context "sin" would no doubt have been defined as "that which blocks one from God and from others". That was the definition adopted by Oxford Group founder Frank Buchman and Oxford Group leader Samuel Shoemaker, who had such a profound influence on Bill Wilson, the author of the Big Book's main text.

Some in the West would still maintain that the only true higher power is the Christian God; those who assert other higher powers "err, not knowing the scriptures, nor the power of God". Many familiar with recovery from alcoholism will still say that coming to believe in a power greater than the alcoholic, in a God of the individual's understanding, is vital for the real alcoholic if he is to attain and maintain sobriety. But, given that the dire consequences of drinking alcohol suffered by alcoholics bring great misfortune, this may not reflect any necessary causal connection with a higher power in the content sense but simply the fact that the connection between misfortune and religion is salient the world over. My recovery, certainly, has not been predicated on a belief in a Christian God, but I know of many whose recovery has been.

In England, a Christian God is still a popular higher power. However, the influence of formal religion on people's lives in some Western cultures is lessening and for some the tenets of the Christian church, in particular, have become more distant from modern thought, with the concomitant social changes. This does not necessarily mean that belief in God or in religion has declined proportionally. The tenets of Christianity are espoused by such organisations as the Alpha Course (a course addressing key issues relating to the Christian faith) which is growing worldwide. With England becoming increasingly multi-cultural, religions other than Christianity are increasingly practised. Many new movements seek to fill the human need for explanation and assurance, for belief in God and in a religion.

Where a higher power is asserted as necessary for recovery nowadays, it can be conceived in many guises apart from the God of traditional religion. However, more often little if any reference is made to any higher power, the recovery process being expressed in purely practical terms, that is, in terms of what the individual needs to do in order to achieve sobriety reflecting modern models of change, especially the Transtheoretical Model. Numerous health care professionals now recognise self-efficacy, the ability of individuals to recover by themselves.

RECOVERY APPROACHES WITHOUT SPIRITUALITY

In contrast to AA self-help groups there are self-help groups which offer a recovery approach with no talk of a higher power or of spirituality. A purely scientific approach is adopted. Recovery is pursued in terms of effective action in bringing about a conversion of the alcoholic's mindset and lifestyle from a drinking one into a secure and contented abstinent one by natural processes of change – essentially by the alcoholic's own efforts albeit usually with the help of others. This scientific approach is shared by numerous psychotherapists and those involved in the Community Reinforcement Approach (CRA). The recovery process is seen as being brought about by the alcoholic's own efforts facilitated by the psychotherapy treatment given by the therapists and by the treatment given in the CRA treatment centre, not by some power greater than him.

Advocates of the CRA do not accept AA principles. Powerlessness, for example, is not emphasised and such phrases as "loss of control whilst in active addiction" are used instead. Further, there is no talk of the need for a higher power. CRA practitioners seek to empower clients to take full responsibility for themselves and their recovery. However, CRA practitioners do not usually object to their clients attending AA, recognising that attendance can help achieve the CRA's two major goals, the elimination of positive reinforcement for drinking and the enhancement of positive reinforcement for sobriety.

In addition to community reinforcement approaches, some with their own self-help groups, like US based Save Our Selves or Secular Organisations for Sobriety (SOS), while following the AA model to some extent, offer an alternative recovery approach for those alcoholics who are uncomfortable with the spiritual content, and the power greater than the alcoholic aspect, of traditional twelve-step based programmes. SMART Recovery, which is also US based, is another science based organization of self-help groups. There are a number of other recovery resources offering various treatments as alternatives to the twelve-step approach including those using the latest medications designed to treat alcoholism.

Founded by an alcoholic who had initially attended AA, SOS began in 1985 and has a database of over 20,000 members worldwide. It takes a self-empowerment approach to recovery and credits the individual, rather than God, for achieving and maintaining his own sobriety. SOS supports healthy scepticism and encourages the use of the scientific method in seeking to understand alcoholism. In SOS members share their experiences, understandings, thoughts and feelings in friendly, honest, anonymous and supportive group meetings. In November 1987 the Californian courts recognised SOS as an alternative to AA in sentencing offenders to mandatory participation in a rehabilitation programme.

SMART (Self-Management and Recovery Training) sponsors over three hundred free face to face meetings around the world and over sixteen meetings online each week. It offers a Four-Point programme with a scientific rather than a spiritual foundation. The programme is based on Rational Behaviour Therapy developed in the 1950s and much of the information imparted by SMART is drawn from the field of cognitive behavioural therapy.

SMART teaches self-reliance rather than powerlessness. It views alcoholism as a maladaptive habit rather than as a disease. Its Four-Point programme involves enhancing and maintaining motivation, coping with urges, solving other problems and balancing momentary and enduring satisfactions. SMART teaches many cognitive-behavioural, motivational coping and problem solving techniques which are likely to be useful regardless of the particular spiritual orientation of the participant. It takes the view that each individual finds his own path to recovery. For some that may include traditional twelve-step based programmes like AA and although the SMART approach differs from AA, it does not exclude it. Some SMART participants choose to attend AA meetings when they cannot attend a SMART meeting. SMART acknowledges that some find that what they hear at AA meetings helps them on their path to sobriety.

MY AND AA'S HIGHER POWER

My own understanding of higher power in the recovery context is the *de facto* source of help to which the real alcoholic in recovery turns and on which he relies in addressing his alcoholism and his recovery from it. It is the help that helps him help himself. I see my higher power not in any content sense but in a process sense, as a useful cognitive gadget which can help me cope with life. The higher power in which I have become grounded and which has brought about the re-creation of my life (to use Silkworth's phraseology) happens to be the process which has taken hold of me by virtue of my attending AA, becoming involved in AA and my efforts to practise its twelve-step based programme. I do not see the need to posit anything supernatural in describing my recovery or in connection with its explanation.

I am also aware of that human facility which supports so many hypotheses, theories and beliefs that, once they are entertained, evidence is soon apparently found to support them. Once an individual entertains the possibility of a higher power, he will tend to detect and recall positive instances that seem to confirm a higher power. But he will tend to be far less good at detecting possible refutations. Positive instances remind him of the hypothesis and he can readily count them as evidence: negative instances do not remind him of it and he does not therefore count them at all. The concept of a higher power may well only be the product of such a facility but it can nonetheless be helpful and useful.

Numerous alcoholics, including myself, have or have had great difficulty and considerable reservation about accepting any concept of a higher power. Before joining AA, I had rejected any such concept as being irrelevant to an intellectually self-sufficient scientific and rational modern man. AA makes a great deal of a power greater than the individual and I had to rethink my attitude with regard to the concept. In the event, it is my experience, and it has been the experience of many other AA members, that if an individual maintains an open mind and continues regularly to attend AA meetings, in time, he will find an answer to, or at least some accommodation with, this distinctly personal higher power dilemma.

Silkworth's assertion was, inevitably, made against the background of the traditional western concept of self which has traditionally been ex-pressed as the rational, indivisible, morally autonomous individual who is sovereign of his own consciousness and having the right to communicate directly with God. The higher power which Silkworth would have had uppermost in mind when he wrote the *Doctor's Opinion* would, no doubt, have been the Christian God. Alcoholics from individualistic cultures, such as in the western world, who see themselves in terms of what they do, accomplish or possess and who are familiar with Christianity may well relate to the content higher power approach to recovery identified by Silkworth. However, some modern academic Christian theologians are now inclined to dispense with the concept of a personal God, tending to see God in more abstract terms. On that view, God may be sought in the mind rather than in the outside world – a view expressed by St. Augustine of Hippo (354-430) and by non-theistic Buddhists and Hindus.

AA has its roots in the US evangelical Christian Oxford Group of the 1930s and in the temperance and total abstinence movements which grew up in the US in the nineteenth century and the first half of the twentieth century. The US had been at the forefront of the temperance and total abstinence movements the ideas of which spread to the English speaking countries and to the Nordic countries. With some of the basic elements of nineteenth century total abstinence thought and organization, combined with elements of evangelical Christianity and themes from twentieth century psychology and psychoanalysis, AA has been a major US export particularly to countries with temperance cultures. AA (like nineteenth century temperance) has a strong missionary element which it carries over from its evangelical Christian roots.

However, AA does not have universal appeal. Its penetration is far higher in countries with a strong temperance tradition like the UK, Canada, New Zealand, Australia, Finland and Iceland. Countries without a temperance tradition like France, Spain, Portugal, Austria, Italy, Hungary, Czechoslovakia and Russia show substantially less AA activity. Further AA does not enjoy popularity on the scale it enjoys in the US in other countries, not even with English speaking countries with strong temperance cultures. Even in the UK, the number of AA groups *per capita* remains much lower than in the US. The number of treatment centres offering 12-step based treatment in the UK is significantly less than the number offering other forms of treatment.

In the US, AA's twelve-step approach dominates in-patient and out-patient treatment, therapeutic communities and most of the psychoactive substance dependence self-help groups. In countries outside the US, AA is only one of several available forms of treatment. In Finland, for example, most individuals with drinking problems turn to the national health-care system, to the network of A-clinics (which use a variety of psychotherapeutic approaches) and to the indigenous Finnish self-help movement called A-Guilds being local associations of former clients of A-clinics.

Be all that as it may, the essence of the higher power in the context of alcoholism is that it is not the individual himself. Provided that the individual accepts a "higher", "greater" or "other" power other than his own mind or self it appears not to matter much, if at all, what it is. The real alcoholic needs to accept that he is powerless over alcohol, in the sense that he cannot control his drinking were he to drink alcohol, and that he most likely needs help to overcome his alcoholism. For me this is the context in which the phrase "higher power" in the context of recovery from alcoholism has some meaning.

The core of initial recovery for many involves the real alcoholic's conversion, amounting to his stopping his resistance to his alcoholism and accepting it in the sense of recognising its power and submitting to it by stopping drinking alcohol. He needs the humility to capitulate, to surrender and to admit that he is powerless over the affect that drinking alcohol has on him: he needs to accept that he cannot drink asymptomatically. He needs to be converted away from a belief in his own power over drinking alcohol. Great strength can come from the mind having adequate knowledge of itself, from its knowing that there exists something greater than itself. Humility is the means through which the self, the mind, can free itself of its illusions about itself.

For me surrender and conversion, in simple practical terms, means my acceptance that I cannot control my drinking of alcohol and sincerely and unreservedly asking for, and accepting, help accordingly. There remain those, though, whose refusal to surrender or compromise, to seek or accept help or to experiment, is so powerful that they appear to prefer to pursue on their own a hellish life of drinking rather than an open-minded and experimental quest for something better.

Accepting some sort of inchoate, flexable higher power idea, as a helpful cognitive gadget at least, seems reasonable to me not only in the context of alcoholism but also generally. Perhaps all that this amounts to is that experience has at last taught me that I am not omnipotent and that accordingly there must be a power (or powers) greater than me. As David Hume (1712-1776) wrote "a wise man proportions his belief in the evidence". The higher power simply equates to the potencies I have ample evidence of which are not me or mine. Knowing that I am not God, I try not to act as if I were.

THE IDENTITY OF HIGHER POWER

For some time in early recovery, I sought a belief in a substantial higher power, in a God of my understanding, and I acted as if there was one. I still go along with the idea to some extent as a helpful cognitive gadget. I have constantly experienced things working out for the best without any help from me or indeed with my active resistance which could be perceived as attributable to a higher power. I am for ever hearing personal stories asserting apparent evidence of the work of a higher power in the rooms of AA.

Accordingly there would appear to be some sort of circumstantial evidence for believing in some sort of personal higher power and apparent grounds for some confidence in it. I would, though, discount this evidence because, once such belief is entertained, the tendency would be that positive evidence of a higher power, and not negative evidence, would be recognised. Nevertheless, the concept of a higher power idea can be helpful; it has been to me. It would appear essential that the real alcoholic must find enough humility to face the fact that he cannot control his drinking and that alcoholism is a potentially fatal condition. In finding the necessary humility and in the consequent realization that he needs help in strengthening his inner coping resources by espousing external coping resources the alcoholic can come to belief, as AA's Second Step puts it, in a power greater than himself in some sense.

The coming to believe process can be outlined as follows. If an outcome is good, the individual will be reminded of his concept of the higher power and he will readily count each positive outcome as another one which confirms the effectiveness of the higher power. If the outcome is negative it is likely not to remind him of the higher power and the outcome will not be counted at all. If he does bring to mind the higher power in the context of a bad outcome, he may well put it down as good, if only he could see it, the higher power acting in mysterious ways, the benefit of a particular outcome being beyond his own understanding.

Like identity itself, the identity of any higher power, which an individual might believe in, can usefully be treated as a process. It can be seen as a dynamic process in constant reformulation. As he progresses in his recovery, an individual's concept of a higher power can develop. He might believe in God or a higher power already or belief in a higher power might start as an open-mindedness to consider the possibility of one. The individual might progress to a concept of his higher power being another human being like a therapist, counsellor, priest, sponsor or mentor or a group of recovering alcoholics such as an AA group or AA itself or being something insentient like a style of treatment or a programme of recovery. Some concept of a supernatural power, perhaps a personal, loving and caring entity with whom communication is possible and which the individual chooses to call "God" might develop. Belief in any such concept of God, having so developed, might in time dissipate and pare down to letting "God" stand for the ultimate mystery of life and the universe or that which is not understood.

Some find that the God in which they believed and in which they still believe is not an effective higher power for the purposes of recovery. Some even find that belief in the God they have always believed in is unhelpful in their pursuit of recovery and that they cannot rely on him to maintain their sobriety. Some find a distinct higher power to serve that purpose.

For some any thought of a higher power is never entertained, for others the thought of a higher power once entertained may eventually be eschewed as being misconceived or irrelevant. For some the higher power idea may be approached not in terms of belief in something as being the higher power but rather that the individual is not the higher power. The individual's belief may be not in God, but in his not being God.

SPIRITUAL AWAKENING

In addition to speaking of a power greater than the alcoholic many speak of a spiritual awakening in the context of the recovery process especially in AA. As with the power greater than the alcoholic concept, the spiritual awakening concept holds more sway in the rooms of fellowships based on AA's Twelve Steps and in Minnesota AA Model treatment contexts. But many recover from alcoholism without having any sort awakening that they would describe as spiritual. They would say that they had brought about their own recovery by means of successfully bringing to bear and effecting their individual mechanisms and processes of change.

The nature of the spiritual awakening asserted by some of those who speak of it would seem to be that, or akin to that, described by William James as "mystical". The psychiatrist Richard Bucke described spiritual experience as "cosmic consciousness". Some would say that the subject matter of these descriptions defies definition, even expression and that no adequate report of their contents can be given in words. Its quality, it is asserted, must be directly experienced; it cannot be imparted or transferred to others. In this peculiarity the states are more like states of feeling than like states of mind. No one can make clear to another who has never had a certain feeling, in what the quality or worth of it consists.

Although so similar to states of feeling, the spiritual experience seems to some of those who experience it to be also a state of knowledge. It seems to be a state of insight into depths of truth unplumbed by the discursive intellect. It is, for some, illumination, revelation, full of significance and importance, all inarticulate though it may be; and, as a rule, it carries with it a curious sense of authority which remains. Bucke, whose own experience led him to investigate it in others, wrote of it as follows. "I had attained to a point of view from which I saw that it must be true. That view, that conviction, I may say that consciousness, has never, even during periods of the deepest depression, been lost." No scientific approach can disprove the reality of the transcendent or supernatural experiences of the believer to that believer.

But difficulties arise in seeking understanding (as contrasted with just experiencing or witnessing) and explaining recovery from alcoholism if reliance is to be placed on propositions which defy definition, even expression and in respect of which no adequate report of the contents thereof can be given in words. Those who have mystical spiritual experiences often make a positive virtue of their belief being strong and unshakeable, in spite of not being based upon evidence. They assert that mystery in itself is a good thing. Mysteries are not meant to be solved, they are meant to strike awe and the very mysteriousness of the belief moves the believer to perpetuate the mystery. Such thinking, that mysteries are better not solved, others would say, is a symptom of a mind afflicted with what has been called the mental virus of faith. Operating in like manner to a computer virus subverting the proper actions of legitimate programs in a computer, a mental virus, it is contended, can act on the circuitry of the brain.

Whatever the truth of the matter, there is no doubt that, apparently regardless of culture, some human beings report having profoundly awe-inspiring experiences involving direct perception of the sacred. Bill Wilson reported his white or hot flash. Some describe a unifying vision of the world, bound together by a living presence, in which nothing really dies. Some have feelings of blessedness, peace, joy, and happiness. Many have a sense of paradox. Some of these experiences are life-changing; a few are world-changing, resulting in the foundation of religious traditions or of organizations ranging from the Jesuits (the Society of Jesus) to AA.

Awe-inspiring experiences share some characteristics with less extreme religious, aesthetic, and emotional experiences, but they have enormously greater power. The question of the nature and value of these awe-inspiring experiences, and the insights that come out of them, needs to be addressed. To assume away the possibility of religious or spiritual factors, as so much of the scientific study of religion has done, would be as unscientific as accepting without investigation the sincerity of mystics' reports as conclusive evidence about the structure of the cosmos.

Because so many alcoholics in recovery speak about God and spirituality when they talk about their alcoholism and their recovery from it, both within and without the rooms of AA, I think they need to be fully addressed in a book about recovery from alcoholism. For so many, spirituality and a higher power, in some sense, are a vital component of their recovery and the power felt during meetings of alcoholics, in particular, and in other recovery settings generally can be palpable. It is easy to feel that there must surely be some spiritual higher power in these settings.

A believing AA member can speak in terms of a "loving God as He may express Himself in our group conscious" (to quote from Tradition Two of AA's Twelve Traditions) while a non-believer can speak in terms of the power of the experience and process in AA contexts leaving open the source of that power. I would suggest that the source of power is simply that generated by the other people in the room or other recovery setting and that there is no need to posit any supernatural power. Many would not agree with me, but many would.

In any event, however, there is much in life which can properly be described as spiritual if for no other reason than it is certainly not material, physical or intellectual and a lot which is neither material, physical nor intellectual goes on in the rooms of AA and in the recovery process generally. Much benefit can be obtained from being awakened accordingly. For many recovering alcoholics, the spiritual path as they understand it provides a source of energy and sustenance that enables them to cope, without drinking, with the myriad tasks associated with living life on life's terms.

GOD

As I understand it, according to the best efforts of linguists and researchers, the root of the present word "God", which is Old English, of Germanic origin, related to Dutch "god" and German "Gott", is the Sanskrit word "hu" which means "to call upon, invoke, implore". This conjecture is fairly plausible as it yields a sense practically coincident with the most obvious definition deducible from the actual use of the word, "an object of worship".

Many people believe in God and see him as an entity which is related to, but is outside, the world in which humans live, which has at least some improbable and counter-intuitive (contrary to common-sense expectation) characteristics and which are usually independent of time. The word "God", in particular, usually refers to a deity in a religion, especially in monotheisms, being a deity considered to be the creator of everything that exists – in effect the subject matter of Aldous Huxley's *The Perennial Philosophy* (1946), which is an anthology and an interpretation of the supreme mystics, eastern and western. For my part, for general purposes as contrasted to uses referring to individuals' specific belief, I favour the use of the word, if pressed on the matter, in the manner described by Richard Dawkins in his piece *The Great Convergence* in *A Devil's Chaplain* (2003) as the Einstein/Hawking trick of letting the word stand for "that which we do not understand" or for the "ultimate mystery of life and the universe".

Faith in God can be inspirational; it has inspired great architecture, art and music. People who believe in God usually feel that they have a purpose in life: they often achieve things in life which they would not have achieved without their faith. The Protestant work ethic played a profound part in the

Industrial Revolution in the UK. The drivers of modern Western capitalism have their origins in Protestant belief.

If an individual believes that life is meaningless and random he is less likely to lead a purposeful life. If he believes that there is a purpose in life, he will tend to fulfil that purpose. If an individual believes that it is God's will that he should recover and be happy, joyous and free then this belief could well assist the recovery process.

Not all religions have a God in the Christian sense; religions may be divided into two groups. One group, including Judaism, Christianity, Islam, and some ancient Indian traditions, can be called "God religions"; their fundamental faith is in a creator. The other group of religious tradition, including Buddhism and Jainism, one of the great classical religions of India, can be called "godless religions"; followers do not believe in a creator.

PRAYER

Bill Wilson advocated prayer and so do many in recovery. Wilson would have taken, as many would today take, prayer to involve God. They would take prayer to mean a solemn request for help or expression of thanks addressed to God or other deity. I prefer to use the word, if useful at all, in a broader sense in the context of recovery. It has been defined, for example, as "a habit of interior attentiveness, an activity that creates a formerly unknown self". I do not think that prayer need necessarily involve God or other deity. It can take many forms. It can take the form of a fervent wish. It can take the form of a request, linguistic discourse, worship, supplication or a search for comfort. Much prayer can be seen as an internal dialogue within the mind, within the self system, in which problems are aired, anxieties allayed and responsibility for action placed elsewhere.

If a definition of prayer involving God or other deity is accepted, then, because of the combination of supernatural and everyday characteristics in a deity, prayer is almost inevitably paradoxical. Characteristically the deity is seen as omniscient yet the supplicant's needs must be formulated and communicated. But as with belief in God and other religious ideas, whether or not the efficacy of prayer has any foundation in objective reality can be seen as irrelevant. If belief in it and its practice are conducive to the recovery process in a particular individual, that can be more than enough for the believing individual alcoholic seeking sobriety. Prayer has been described as a placebo, as a robust neurological phenomenon which can work whether or not any God or deity addressed exists because of expectation alone.

Praying can perhaps have an effect similar to meditation, endorsed in many secular as well as spiritual theories of healing. The answers that come from prayer can comfort and inform the individual. They can improve his sense of well-being which in itself can be beneficial. Prayer can help recovery by focusing the mind on things to be grateful for in life. It can also induce a relaxed state of mind which is thought to be good for health generally. Prayer can give the experience of solidarity and dedication with a ritualistic meaning. Faith in God and praying to him can *de facto* confer benefits.

It could be said that, if regular prayer composes the mind and confers health benefits, the person who prays is following the intelligent course, regardless of the veracity of the tenets of any religion. But if it is taken that prayer by definition or otherwise involves a request for or expression of thanks addressed to God or other deity it is difficult to see how an intelligent atheist (or agnostic for that matter) can pray: he could nevertheless perhaps meditate to advantage. However if the definition of prayer as a habit of interior attentiveness, an activity that creates a formerly unknown self, is accepted, then prayer could well be the intelligent course if a new self results which is more contented.

Discerning the exact influence of prayer is difficult, not least because it is embedded in the total lifestyle, the spiritual attitude and the social context of those who practise it.

ETHICAL WAY OF LIFE

The positive effects of a spiritual mindset and lifestyle derive from self-discipline, an emphasis on responsibility, a limiting of options and the espousal of an ethical way of life. Innate in human beings is an evolved axiom that their own welfare is in essential ways affected by the welfare of others. Ethical behaviour, including altruism, where individuals give appropriate, or even primary consideration, to the interests and welfare of other individuals, members of groups or the community as a whole, has its evolutionary roots in self-interest, the unconscious desire to protect individuals' genetic heritage. It evolved in the context of small family groups but, with population increase, has become extended to individuals and social situations where the individuals are completely unrelated genetically.

With some instruction, human beings can readily learn that the well-being of others can be improved by modest sacrifices in their own well-being which in turn increases their own happiness. Individuals can learn to behave accordingly. Spiritual behaviour has an important social component.

Spiritual behaviour can involve a degree of ritual which can play a vital role in the alcoholic's conversion from a drinking mindset and lifestyle to a sober one. The ritual might be attendance at AA meetings or at church services with their common formats. The function of the ritual in these cases is to direct emotions and allow individuals to be included in a larger framework shared socially. In this manner the experience of the conversion from a drinking to a recovering alcoholic can be reinforced and can become long lasting.

Spiritual behaviour can become the source of change experiences by which individuals can discover a new future after experiencing a lack of purpose and meaning. It also plays a role in coping with crisis and thus in maintaining sobriety. In AA meetings and in church attendance there can be a release of emotions which can act as a protection factor.

CRISIS AND COPING

A crisis can be seen as a period of particular significance. Most alcoholics, like most human beings, are essentially lazy in that they tend not to contemplate action or take action beyond that which they assess to be needed immediately. During a crisis this minimal approach is often not appropriate and the individual can be forced to contemplate more substantial action which can bring about significant change that can be beneficial to the individual.

Recovery involves coping with life without drinking. Coping is a process involving experiencing events, appraising them and the resources to hand to deal with them and consequent action or inaction which has an outcome in respect of them. Commonplace life events are more likely to cause the alcoholic difficulty early in recovery rather than later. The same goes for the alcoholic's ability to appraise them and behave appropriately with regard to them. Outcomes in early recovery are likely to be less successful on the face of them but more is often learnt from mistakes made than from successes achieved. As spiritual principles, particularly those principles necessary for recovery and which the alcoholic did not practise sufficiently before recovery, are adopted and recovery matures, life events are likely to cause less difficulty. Appraisal becomes more efficient, behaviour becomes more appropriate and outcomes become more satisfactory, if not in the short term then in the longer term.

The appraisal of an event as beneficial may lead to a spiritual interpretation of gratitude and (particularly for the religious) providential care. The appraisal of a challenge, threat or loss may lead to an interpretation which recognizes the need for self-discipline, the need to practise the individual's personal relapse prevention programme or to engage in his personal relapse prevention activity. For members of AA an appraisal of an event or situation causing or potentially causing emotional disturbance (those caused by anger, jealousy, envy, self-pity and hurt pride in particular) often indicates that it would be helpful if he were to speak to his sponsor or another alcoholic or attend an AA meeting.

The appraisal of resources subjectively determines the gravity of a situation. The individual has available two types of resource, internal comprising his own coping skills and external comprising outside support. A crisis is perceived if the internal resources are appraised as insufficient for coping with the event. As regards internal coping resources the attitude of the individual is important. Positive and negative thoughts can influence outcomes. Negative thought patterns can become self-fulfilling prophecies of difficulty and disaster while positive patterns can increase chances of success.

If an individual feels that his internal resources are insufficient in a particular situation then the sensible thing for him to do is to seek outside support. The outside support could take the form of another person (for example his doctor, lawyer or therapist) or persons (his AA group), or set of principles (the AA Twelve Steps), or God, or whatever else to guide his actions, as opposed to his grandiosely assuming that he is the final authority on all matters generally and on the situation or event in question in particular. External coping resources can be found on several levels of social relations once the alcoholic breaks free from his isolation and he engages with others in the community.

The practice of AA spirituality can generate positive attitudes. This in turn can greatly enhance the individual's ability to cope with life. By living a programme of recovery as advocated in AA, the individual can take the view that, whatever happens, all is or will be well. All outcomes can be perceived as good even if they appear to be bad. If the outcome of seeking to cope with an event is bad then, in a sense and paradoxically, that too is good because he can learn from the experience how better to cope next time.

LIVING AS NARRATIVE

Whether or not involving spirituality or God, personal identity processes can be understood in a narrative way as the constant shaping and reshaping of life stories that hold together the experiences of life. Recovery is a personal identity process, the change in the identity of the individual from a drinking to a recovering alcoholic. In constant interaction with the context, the individual is presenting and reconstructing his story for the purposes of finding identity and acceptance.

In AA, by virtue of its oral tradition of sharing life stories and experience, the alcoholic can not only establish his own identity but can also find acceptance of his identity. A subjectively composed and construed life story that integrates the individual's past and present is to some extent the individual's identity. The two processes of identity and acceptance are mutually dependent. A lack of acceptance in social identity will be a negative complication in finding a meaningful personal identity. Lack of personal identity will make it difficult to find acceptance. Both social and personal identity is needed. Finding a stable social identity and stable personal identity can form a sound basis for recovery and secure, contented sobriety.

Coping processes are an essential part of the development of personal identity, and crisis can be critical in the transition between developmental stages. The concept of development through crises and coping suits a narrative view well. Coping and identity shape one another. Identity stories tell the individual who he is and where he stands in the world. They define, interpret, and direct the individual's relationship with his fellow human beings and with any God of which he may conceive. By continuing to tell his story, particularly in AA, the alcoholic can maintain his sobriety and lead a contented life without drinking alcohol.

For an alcoholic to attain, sustain and maintain his recovery it can be helpful for him to withdraw from a confusing world from time to time and to participate in a relatively small group of other alcoholics who share the same essential story and whose purpose is to remain sober and help others to achieve sobriety. The advantage of this is that it can reduce confusion and can offer a coherence of meaning. However, AA has an approach which the individual may find unacceptable for any number or reasons. Each alcoholic in recovery finds his own solutions to his problems.

Central to viewing recovery from alcoholism as a process, and to a narrative perspective of it, is seeing any conversion not simply as a starting point. A narrative approach presupposes a historical perspective. A crisis does not occur in a narrative vacuum, but at a specific point of an already existing personal story, a frame of reference, that has evolved over many experiences and interpretations. This personal story leads to a certain way of living, preventing some events from happening and making the individual prone to other eventualities. The current personal narrative is the product of previous crises, assessments, coping measures and outcomes.

Acceptance and courage play crucial roles in coping and recovery from alcoholism is a matter of coping with life without alcohol or other relevant psychoactive substance. Effective coping involves problem focused and emotion focused approaches depending on whether the facts of the matter can be changed by the individual or not. Problem focused coping tries to alter the situation and it is effective if the facts can be changed. Emotion focused coping tries to change the meaning of the situation, which can be effective if the facts are inalterable. One spiritual coping strategy is summed up in the so called "Serenity Prayer" which is chorused at the end of many AA meetings: "God grant me the serenity to accept the things we cannot change, courage to change the things we can, and the wisdom to know the difference".

10

BELIEF

RELIGION

Many recovering alcoholics sustain and maintain their recovery by virtue of their religious beliefs. Metaphysical speculation is as inevitable for mankind as breathing. It is, as Immanuel Kant (1724-1804) wrote, part of the human condition that "reason has this particular fate that in one species of its knowledge it is burdened by questions which, as prescribed by the very nature of reason itself, it is not able to ignore, but which, as transcending all its powers, it is also not able to answer".

Mankind is very curious and has a great desire for connection and explanation. Religion usually concerns the belief in and worship of a superhuman controlling power, especially a personal God involving a particular system of faith and worship. Religion is ubiquitous and a major phenomenon inherent in innumerable cultures. One of the main reasons why religion is so universal is because it aspires to provide human beings with connection and explanation. Every man and woman comes to his or her individual consciousness in a mysterious universe and longs to understand it.

William James in *The Varieties of Religious Experience,* gives an individualistic definition of religion as "the feelings, acts, and experiences of individual men in their solitude, so far as they apprehend themselves to stand in relation to whatever they may consider the divine". James hoped to escape controversy by this, as he puts it, "arbitrary definition of our field". He appreciated that the use of the word "divine" could engender controversy but stressed how broad his definition of divine (and hence his definition of religion) was. There are, after all, systems of thought which would commonly be held to be religious which are agnostic or atheistic.

There are also transcendent idealistic views that see God evaporate into some abstract ideal which is not a superhuman person or supernatural being but rather some immanent divinity in things, some essentially spiritual structure of the universe. As regards Christianity, there are those who see Christ's divinity not as an added ingredient to his human person, but an integral emergent property of it. They go on to argue that, Christians having no *a priori* knowledge of God but only that known through Christ, it follows that God is not a supernatural agent external to humanity, but an emergent property of human life itself. The divine aspect of Christ was not the result of any supernatural intervention and accordingly it is open to all. God, they argue, is not a supernatural agency separate from and prior to the created order, including the human race. Rather God is seen as living in the human mind as the sum of all values and ideals guiding and inspiring the lives of human beings.

Distinguishing religion from spirituality in the recovery context is useful. Religion usually involves a unified system of beliefs and practices relating to one particular superhuman controlling power or, in godless religions, concept, which unite into a single community, often called a church, all those who adhere to them. This characterization reflects the functional orientation of religion. Religion has a purpose – to unite a human group into a single religious community.

Many people dislike, even detest, such a purpose. Different understandings of spirituality particularly those equating spirituality with, or with aspects of, religion may account for the objections to AA based twelve-step programmes as being essentially unacceptable, inappropriate or misconceived in a modern secular society. Further, the use of the word "God" in the Twelve Steps does not encourage those of an irreligious disposition seeking recovery and considering AA as an option, to pursue what AA might offer.

Despite this distinction between religion and spirituality, those who practise religion would be right to say that spiritual qualities can be the fruit of genuine religious endeavour and that religion accordingly can have a great deal to do with developing them and with what may be called spiritual practice. The distinction between religion and spirituality is, nonetheless, helpful in attempting to understand the recovery process.

No belief in any religion is required for the process but, arguably, the adoption of spiritual practice, in some sense, is. Indeed in some individuals, religious belief can militate against recovery while in others it can facilitate it. Often the religious recovering alcoholic distinguishes the spirituality which brought about his recovery from his religion and the spirituality encompassed by, or embodied in, his religion.

Dependent on the basic human need to understand and explain events some believers simply assert their faith in God while others would give as the dominant reason for their faith an essentially scientific one. Most religions offer a theory of life, its origins and reasons for existence. In doing so, they demonstrate that religion can serve the same purpose as science, that is, the provision of explanations involving the identification of causes and agency. The vital difference between the two, some say, is that science is restricted to secondary causes while religion aspires to address primary causes.

Some take the view that science will be able to explain everything. Others say that it cannot because it cannot explain that there is something, when there could have been nothing, the so-called "first cause". While science can explain a flashing light at sea in terms of a bright lamp going on and off at specific timed intervals (the secondary cause) it cannot go behind this to the mind of the mariner signalling SOS (the primary cause). However, a scientist with knowledge of Morse code could.

Peter Atkins in *Creation Revisited* (1994) seeks to explain how each step in the history of the universe followed from its predecessor by simple physical law. Once the building blocks of nature, such as quarks, electrons and the forces that hold them all together, are understood it will be possible, he argues, to reconstruct, in principle, the processes which resulted in elements, in more complex organisms and finally in conscious human beings. He concludes that, accordingly, there is no need for God.

However, it is tempting to argue that, although God may not be needed to explain the evolving universe once it had begun, he is needed to explain its beginning. Stephen Barr in *Modern Physics and Ancient Faith*

(2003) argues that the Big Bang theory of the beginning of the universe is essentially where materialists find their assumptions confounded and theists are vindicated. Having a beginning, Barr argues, there must be something that caused the beginning, a "first cause", which he sees as God not just as a cause within time but as the creator of space and time.

For many, it may be difficult to accept that the universe came from nothing, that there is no "first cause". Mankind comes to his individual consciousness in a mysterious universe and longs to understand and explain it. Mankind's longing for substantial explanation has created metaphysical constructs better to satisfy his need to understand and his need for assurance and peace of mind. He commonly believes in God. He has been shaped by evolution to soak up the culture of his people and religion is ubiquitous. That everything came from nothing may, accordingly, be an unacceptable explanation to many.

It does not follow, however, that the metaphysical constructs are valid or the consequent explanations true. Brian Greene in *The Fabric of the Cosmos* (2004), for example, manages a very credible explanation of the mysteries of time and space without any need to involve a "first cause". In any event, the phrase "first cause", has, to use Einstein's phraseology, "a far reaching uncertainty of interpretation" which renders it incapable of useful meaning and thus it is impossible to gather any evidence for it.

In the context of recovery from alcoholism, these matters may largely be held to be irrelevant. Perhaps it is best for the purposes of understanding and explanation to adopt William James's pragmatism, that is to say (roughly), that a proposition is true if it is useful to believe. Perhaps the dimension of utility is the essential mark in the recovery context, rather than that of truth in any absolute sense. Beliefs, be they scientific or religious, are true for the individual if they support the attainment of his recovery and its maintenance. It may be that science is the be all and end all and any further questions beyond its scope are meaningless and *a fortiori* any answers to them meaningless. Nevertheless, it may be useful to an individual for him to believe that the universe cannot be explained by science; it needs to be explained by the existence of God.

In any event, religion is concerned with faith, in the claims to salvation of one faith or tradition over another, an aspect of which is commonly acceptance of some form of metaphysical or supernatural reality, in perhaps a concept of heaven, paradise or nirvana (a transcendent state, the final goal of Buddhism, in which there is neither suffering nor desire, nor sense of self) based on faith rather than proof. It is often concerned with a hypothetical being that answers prayers and can perform miracles.

Religions like Christianity, Judaism and Islam are concerned with the nature of God and with religious beliefs and theory and their systematic development. They are concerned not so much with the individual as with community, with rules and regulations, with compliance, with asserting the only true God, and with teaching the true word. Religion is not so much concerned with the individual's personal understanding of God but with the God he must believe in and understand as dictated by his priest, mentor, rabbi, guru or religious leader.

Connected with religious concepts are religious teachings, dogma, rituals and prayer. While dogma, ritual and prayer, along with the questions of heaven and salvation, are directly connected to religious faith, they need not be to spirituality, to the qualities of the human spirit such as love, compassion, patience, tolerance and forgiveness. Individuals can develop these inner qualities to a high degree, even the highest degree, without recourse to any religious or metaphysical belief system. While mankind could possibly do without religion (and some, like Richard Dawkins, argue that mankind would do far better without religion), it would seem to be indispensable for many. It has been the cause of much bloodshed and conflict as well as much good. In contrast, spirituality can be said to be the antithesis of conflict.

Many seem to need spirituality in a content sense and this is what religion can offer. Religion offers a response to what many see as the problem of human insufficiency. Try as individuals might to maximize significance through their own insights and experiences or through those of others, many feel that they remain finite and limited. At any time an individual can be pushed beyond his immediate resources, exposing his basic vulnerability. To this most basic of existential crises, religion can hold solutions. The solutions may come in the form of religious support when other forms of social support are lacking, of explanations when no other explanations seem convincing, and of a sense of ultimate control through God when life seems out of control. Reverence for some higher purpose can comfort an individual in ways that no medication or technology ever can, regardless of whether the higher purpose exists. Religion can enhance self-worth by emphasising personal qualities rather than material possessions or social achievement. The belief that God loves the individual for himself can be comforting and supportive.

William James and Aldous Huxley (1894-1963), in particular, have argued that religious belief is special and that what is special about it is the experience of it. Thus exceptional people have a purer version of that experience and common religion is just a blander, diluted form. The idea that religious tenets can be shown to be empirically valid by virtue of experience rather than argument has been addressed by some cognitive neuroscientists. No scientific basis for the idea has been found. In particular, no basis for the proposition that there may be some religious centre in the brain, some special cortical area, some special neural network that handles God related ideas, has been found.

It is possible to measure brain activity during extreme experiential episodes. These episodes where the individual experiencing them interprets them in religious terms are indistinguishable from those where the individual experiencing them has no religious interpretation. Further, neuroscientists have discovered evidence that, where normal communication between cortical and other brain areas is impaired, people can experience subjective sensations indistinguishable from the religious sensations described by mystics. For example, fasting for extended periods can impair normal communication between cortical and other brain areas and mystics who fast for extended periods experience special feelings and states of mind which they describe as religious exaltation. The truth of the matter is that such religious experiences are more likely to be the product of abnormal brain function rather than communication with the divine.

Concepts, and religious concepts are no exception, require all sorts of specific human capacities. These capacities include an intuitive psychology, a tendency to attend to some counterintuitive ideas, as well as various social mind adaptations. By describing how these various capacities are recruited and how they contribute to the features of religion found in many different cultures, religion can be explained without any need to distinguish religious concepts from any other concept. There is no evidence that religious concepts are qualitatively different.

However, in a very limited sense it can be said that God exists but only as a human concept with high survival value, or infective power, in the environment provided by human culture. God is a concept transmitted by the spoken and written word, aided by great architecture, art and music. Rudiments may be found among the lore of primitive peoples throughout the world and ideas of God become increasingly developed in the higher religions. The survival of the God idea is a consequence of its great survival appeal. Belief in God offers a way of looking at the world which satisfies the human need for explanation and assurance. It provides answers to deep and troubling questions about existence and much more.

Power to intervene in the world is often ascribed not only to the principal supernatural being but also to figures of intermediate status like saints. The Christian saints have been supposed to act as intermediaries with God in order to ensure fertility of humans and animals and to provide protection against diverse forms of adversity including sickness, pests, storms and enemies. Deities who control events are helpful in many other related ways. They might point the way between alternative courses of action or indicate when the time was auspicious for particular undertakings.

They can be used to reduce uncertainty in many different ways. If hardship is inevitable, it can give some relief to know that it was decreed from above. Struggle and hardship in this world can be justified, even encouraged, for the rewards in the next. So much can be suffered in the expectation of comfort in the everlasting arms of a loving God in Heaven. Religion offers a way of justifying the way the individual copes with adversity by seeing it as acceptable to, and guided by, God.

FAITH, HOPE AND PEACE OF MIND

An element of the religious mindset is faith. It is far easier, and more natural with humans' cognitive disposition, simply to believe rather than to analyse, test and verify. Faith can secure its own perpetuation by the simple unconscious expedient of discouraging scientific inquiry. But this does not mean that for many believers religious faith is not the product of conviction based on adequate evidence as far as he is concerned. Theologians can apply as much thought and analyses to their beliefs as scientists do to their theories. Faith and belief seem to be by-products of the way concepts and inferences are doing their work for religion in much the same way as for other domains including science.

As Friedrich Nietzsche (1844-1900) wrote, there is something about human nature which makes individuals capable of being inspired by what they believe to be right to do. The action taken can be both wonderful and appalling. The tendency seems to stem from mankind's evolved cognitive systems. Faith can be very powerful; it can drive people to free slaves and to suicide bomb. It can also drive alcoholics to recover. As William James noted "the sentiment of reality can indeed attach itself so strongly to our object of belief that our whole life is polarized through and through, so to speak, by its sense of the existence of the thing believed in, and yet that thing, for the purpose of definite description, can hardly be said to be present to our mind at all".

In the treatment context, the aphorism of Karl Marx (1818-1883) "[religion] is the opium of the people" masks a very important therapeutic principle. For many, religion may actually provide the relief that abuse of alcohol only promises. Real alcoholics before recovery feel defeated, mentally ill and helpless. They suffer impaired morale and low self-esteem. If they are to recover, powerful new sources of self-esteem and hope need to be discovered. Religion can be characterized as enhancing hope.

Religion is one such source: it provides fresh impetus for both hope and enhanced self-care. For the real alcoholic to achieve sobriety, profound personality changes need to take place. It is not just a coincidence that such dramatic change is associated with religious conversion.

Religion also protests forgiveness of sins and relief of guilt. Absolution, in some sense, is an important part of the healing process and thus of the recovery process. The AA programme appears to mobilise the ingredients present in substantial religious involvement without necessarily imposing any of religion's impedimenta like virgin birth, resurrection from the dead, whether or not the Sabbath begins at five or six o'clock in the afternoon, or whether a veil should be worn, let alone the Mystery of the Transubstantiation.

Pascal Boyer in *Religion Explained* argues that human beings' evolution as a species of cooperation is sufficient to explain the benefits of spirituality and the psychology of moral reasoning, that is to say, the way humans (as children and as adults) represent moral dimensions of action. This requires no special concept of religious agency, no special code and no models to follow. Religious concepts are to an extent parasitic upon the evolved natural moral intuitions of humanity. Religious concepts are parasitic in the sense that their successful transmission is greatly enhanced by mental capacities that are there anyway, God or no God.

As a species of cooperation, human beings cannot survive as single persons without the company of others. Each individual needs others to survive. Although individuals quarrel and disagree with each other and complain about each other and so on, the fundamental fact of human existence is that each individual needs other individuals who are the objects of the quarrels, disagreements and complaints. Relationships between individuals are necessary for human being; they are indispensable.

An essential part of an alcoholic's recovery is the need to move away from his isolation and self-centred attitude and towards consideration of others. A compassionate and affectionate attitude and a sense of caring is not only of benefit to society, but also of great benefit to the individual. On the other hand, arrogance, hatred and ill-feeling not only create distress for others, but also suffering in the individual. Ill-feeling, hatred or jealousy causes great discomfort to the individual harbouring them. If the individual has not learnt the ability to sustain substantial peace of mind and contentment, he can easily seek refuge in alcohol or other psychoactive substances.

NEED FOR BELIEF

There is something about human nature, as Friedrich Nietzsche noted, which makes individuals capable of being profoundly inspired by that in which they believe. Further, belief and expectation are the key elements in the mind-over-matter placebo effect, the phenomenon that an individual's symptoms can be alleviated by an otherwise ineffective treatment by virtue of the individual's belief and expectation that it will work. Belief by the alcoholic in the efficacy of the treatment he is undergoing or in the actions which he is taking in order to initiate, sustain and maintain his recovery is crucial. Thus the individual's belief in his treatment may be more important than its nature, even whether it is objectively effective. For the purposes of instilling the requisite belief in the individual undergoing formal treatment, the attitude of the health care professional providing it can be critically important. The rapport between the health care professional and the alcoholic can be far more important than the nature of the treatment being provided.

In any event, it is essential for recovery that the real alcoholic believes that he is a real alcoholic and that he cannot and never will be able to control his drinking. He needs to believe that it is the first drink that counts and that he will only be able to recover by maintaining abstinence from alcohol. He needs also to believe that abstinence is possible and that he can stop drinking himself and can recover accordingly. Then as previously discussed, there is the matter of believing in a "Power greater than ourselves" or "God as we understood Him", upon which AA puts so much emphasis and which can, it is asserted, bring about the recovery process.

Many are reluctant to believe in anything without proof or without some experience which justifies an opinion. The *Oxford Dictionary of English,* (second edition 2003) notes two core senses of "believe" (1) accept that (something) is true, especially without proof and (2) hold (something) as an opinion; think. As regards the need for the alcoholic to believe that he is one, that recovery is possible and that he can recover the second core sense seems to me to have more application; some sort of proof or experience is likely to be needed. For example, AA attendance can demonstrate that alcoholics can recover and suggest that, if they can, he can. As regards believe in God then the first core sense would have more application.

The core of initial recovery appears to be a need for the individual to believe either in his own ability to stop drinking by himself or, if he accepts that he cannot stop by himself and that he is powerless over the affect that drinking alcohol has on him, to a belief in a higher power to his own that can stop him drinking. Unless he somehow manages to stop drinking by himself, he needs to come to believe that at least as regards drinking alcohol he cannot rely on his own power. Usually, he needs to find sufficient humility or willingness to accept that, accordingly, he needs to move away from the entrenched belief in his own control and to come to believe in something, someone, some group of people, some source of help, some process, some concept, some programme or some higher power, which can enable him to stop.

Belief in the possibility of recovery in general, and in a recovery pro-gramme in particular, may persuade an alcoholic to start preparing for and taking steps towards recovery. If he comes to believe that maybe something will work there is likely to be more motivation with more time spent thinking and trying various possibilities, increasing chances of success. Two of the great difficulties facing individuals with alcohol problems involve mistaken belief. The first mistaken belief is that they do not have a problem: the second is that, if they admit that they have a problem, they can never get better. Alcoholics can believe that they are not alcoholics. They can also believe that they are hopelessly enmeshed in irrevocably damaged and damaging lives. If, though, an individual can have instilled in him the belief that he is an alcoholic together with a belief that change is possible then recovery can become possible.

Belief involves mental assent to, or acceptance of, a proposition, state-ment or fact, as true on the ground of authority or evidence. This covers everyday usage but the nature and degree of the authority or evidence is left open. In the religious use of the word the authority is absolute and ev-idence can be eschewed. In everyday use it implies an opinion or thought based on some evidence or experience. In scientific use it requires testing and a high degree of empirical evidence. An understanding of the concept of belief is, perhaps, particularly apposite in matters the subject of debate with strong argument on both sides as is often the case in religion or politics – and in the recovery field.

In the context of recovery from alcoholism what are important are the individual's mindset and attendant belief system as regards life in general and alcohol in particular and whether it is or is not conducive to the recovery process. It is the reality and effectiveness of the acceptance, attitude or thinking and the consequent action of the individual stemming from the belief which matters and not the degree or nature of the authority or evidence from which the belief stems or upon which it is based.

The phenomenon of belief is the result of successful activation of a whole variety of mental systems. The recovery process and the beliefs surrounding it are to do with the need to change the alcoholic's mindset and attendant belief system and with a practical programme of activity the purpose of which is to develop the skills and attitudes which the individual needs to initiate, sustain and maintain his recovery. These skills and attitudes are essentially pragmatic, practical ones which enable the individual effectively to cope with life and its realities on a daily basis without drinking alcohol. The exercise of appropriate skills and attitudes can bring about recovery and increasing contentment to the individual and to his fellows.

The requisite beliefs in himself and in the recovery process should be distinguished from any other beliefs which he might have. In particular any religious beliefs should be distinguished. The extent to which any religious belief before recovery bears on his recovery may lie in the extent to which the individual feels himself in a personal relationship with God. An impersonal God who merely rewards and punishes may change the believer's perspective on the world but a relationship with a personal God can change the core of his being. Belief in a personal God before recovery can continue into recovery giving the individual a feeling of addressing recovery together with that God.

The individual alcoholic might be theist, atheist, agnostic or indifferent. The challenges of recovery for each are different. The original

God of the theist often ceases to be the higher power which facilitates recovery although frequently remaining complementary. There is the individual, once a theist, who has rejected God absolutely because he has failed to fulfil his demands. The atheist can claim that, in the absence of any evidence for him, God should for all practical purposes be discarded. Some atheists claim proof that God does not exist. The agnostic does not know; some do not care. There are intellectually self-sufficient men and women where the God of their intellect has replaced all others. In a sense, everybody has a higher power or God; for the atheist it might be the forces posited by science in which he believes and it might be scientific method which is the central principle, the central value, the central drive in his life. For the agnostic it might be the power of reason and logic; for the codependent his partner, for the compulsive overeater, food, for the drinking alcoholic, alcohol.

The primary basis for belief is to be found in experience, in the experience of the subjection to authority or the evaluation of the evidence by the individual that has resulted in his mindset and attendant belief system. There are many experiences in which people have become aware of a higher power impinging on their lives. Some are mystical experiences, some are conversion experiences and some involve a sense of presence. Sometimes visions are involved which may come with the force of a revelation. Some only involve awareness of everyday matters. For some alcoholics it can be their recognition that alcohol itself had become their higher power. This recognition can show them that the concept of a higher power is tenable, even that the God idea might be helpful. It makes little, if any, practical difference whether or not the higher power or God which the individual conceives really exists or whether it is a mental exercise or a cognitive gadget.

REVELATION AND SCIENTIFIC ACTIVITY

Some alcoholics in recovery, as in Bill Wilson's case, have some sort of Damascene revelation. Wilson said of his own revelation that it was not essentially different from those conversions since experienced by countless members of AA; it was only more sudden. My conversion involved some sort of revelation. Unlike Wilson's experience, though, my experience was in no sense religious and many like experiences should not be categorised as religious. Some revelations fit into Karl Jaspers' description of the limit situation, one that is about as bad as could be and which requires a radical change of attitude if it is to be effectively addressed: they may or may not have a religious element.

Those who do experience a profound Damascene revelation appear to strike against the limits of their own being. They say that they become aware of a being that transcends their own, yet with which they sense both difference and affinity. The German Protestant theologian Rudolf Otto (1869-1937) analysed such experience which, in his view, underlies all religion. Otto, one of the most influential thinkers about religion in the first half of the twentieth century, called the experience "numinous". He said it has three components. These are often designated with the Latin phrase: *mysterium tremendum et fascinans.* As *mysterium*, the numinous is "wholly other" – entirely different from anything experienced in ordinary life. It evokes a reaction of silence. But the numinous is also *tremendum*. It provokes terror because it presents itself as overwhelming power. Finally, the numinous presents itself as *fascinans*, as merciful and gracious. However, it may well be qualitatively the same sort of feeling as the feeling of awe and fascination that modern science can provide and science does so, some would say, beyond the wildest dreams of theologians.

Douglas Adams (1952-2001), author of *The Hitchhiker's Guide to the Galaxy*, in an interview, asserted that he would "take the awe of understanding over the awe of ignorance any day". Such would tend to be the assertion of those in whom the scientific mindset dominates. For many (particularly in Western Europe) the human need for explanation and assurance is now satisfied much more by science than by religion. Claims by religions that supernatural beings can intervene in the world are often viewed with much more scepticism. Those in whom the religious mindset dominates, though, would tend to assert that they would take the awe of religion over the facts of science any day. In the context of recovery from alcoholism it matters not which mindset is espoused; what matters is whether or not the belief system in the individual and his mindset is conducive to recovery. Whether or not the scientific approach gives a better explanation or description than the religious one is irrelevant.

Religious belief systems are important to many people. At the individual level many people gain a great deal of comfort from their religious beliefs and activities. Science does not easily offer emotional comfort. Religious faith can buttress people's sense of control and self-esteem, can offer meanings that oppose anxiety and can provide hope. Religion sanctions socially facilitating behaviour: it can enhance personal well-being and it can promote social integration.

In a sense scientific activity and method are quite unnatural given humans' cognitive dispositions. Many human intuitive inference systems are based on assumptions that scientific research has shown to be less than compelling. It is more difficult and harder work to acquire scientific data than religious dogma. The former require much effort in their verification, the latter none. Scientific activity is both cognitively and socially unlikely; it has only been developed by a small number of people, in a small number of places, for what is only a minuscule fraction of mankind's evolutionary history.

Science may be every bit as unnatural to the human brain and mind as religion is natural. Susan Blackmore suggests that human beings may be naturally religious by virtue of mankind's cultural evolution. This may even be so notwithstanding that recent research supports the general rule that modernization undermines religion worldwide and that supernatural explanations are in substantial decline in many advanced industrial societies. That supernatural explanations are being eschewed does not mean that scientific ones are taking their place. Unscientific or irrational secular explanations may replace supernatural ones: in which case the human brain and mind may properly be described as being naturally unscientific or irrational rather than naturally religious *per se*.

Much belief, including religious and unscientific or irrational belief, is not so much detached from reality as connected with it by beneficially adaptive and motivating behaviour. Where individuals enjoy their religion, seeing it as something life-enhancing and identity-giving, they are going to find atheism unattractive. The recent surge of evidence-based studies demonstrating the positive impact of religion on human wellbeing has yet to be fully assimilated by atheist writers. While religious beliefs can be false as literal descriptions of the real world, they can reflect effective behavioural adaptation. Some contrast a factual realism, based on literal correspondence, with a practical realism based on behavioural adaptation. Rationality may not always be the appropriate standard, it is suggested; adaptation may sometimes be a more appropriate one.

Whatever the truth of the matter, alcoholics, in order to recover, certainly do not have to acquire an immediate and overwhelming God-consciousness followed at once by a vast change in feeling and outlook, although the Pauline symbolism of the death of the old, drinking individual and the resurrection of the new, abstinent individual is apt. While many recovering alcoholics speak of an identifiable conversion, in many others the change takes place slowly over a period of time with the individual kicking against the pricks but experiencing incremental changes of an educational variety initiating, maintaining and strengthening their recovery.

SCIENCE AND RELIGION IN RECOVERY

Some seek to distinguish factual reality from practical reality. Unlike religion, it is argued, science is committed to so-called factual realism, to objective, empirically verified, reality. Most other approaches to a general understanding of the human condition include factual realism as an important even essential element but subordinate it to so-called practical realism, to behavioural adaptation, when necessary or appropriate. Such approaches may not reflect the objective truth accurately but adherence to them can result in behaviour more adapted to the human condition. Religion is committed to practical realism, the subjective reality of the biologically and culturally well adapted human mind. Some argue that the factual reality of science needs to be tempered by the practical realism of religion if the human condition is to be comprehensively addressed. Adaptive reality can facilitate the brain's ability to cope with the practicalities of life despite the fact that adaptive reality cannot be empirically proven to be factual reality.

There have recently been a number of proposals which seek to unite religion and science (particularly medicine) in the context of recovery. Most, in my view, are facile and ill defined. The notion that physicians, *qua* physicians, have the time or training to make assessments or recommendations about religious matters is misguided. Recent proposals to extend the physician's task to include assessing religion and directing the patient towards approved forms of religious activity are inappropriate. Religious views are often intellectually inconsistent with scientific ones. Religious statements are commonly based on faith not evidence. Scientific statements are based on evidence and proof. The languages of religion and science can be radically different. Physicians should be encouraged to rely on clinically trained clergy or religious advisers for any appropriate assistance in understanding the patient's religious beliefs and activities and any possible effects of them on his medical condition.

While some accept the possibility of scientific explanations for every mystery of the natural world, some do not, particularly for the mystery they see as the greatest one of all; that there is something, when there could have been nothing. It may be that religion will thrive as long as there are human beings alive to reflect on the mystery of the "first cause".

Religious views can be intellectually inconsistent with scientific ones. Religious statements are often based on conviction *per se* rather than evidence, let alone proof. Scientific statements are essentially based on evidence and proof. If God could and did intervene in nature and contravene the laws of nature at will as many theologians maintain, then the attempts of scientists to understand the world in terms of natural causes and empirically tested scientific theories would be profoundly compromised if not made ultimately impossible. Man's ability to understand the world, and his not inconsiderable success so far in understanding it, relies on it being orderly and subject to consistent and verifiable natural laws without any supernatural intervention by God or any other supernatural being.

J. B. S. Haldane (1892-1964) contrasts the scientific and religious approaches as follows. "The main objection to religious myths is that, once made, they are so difficult to destroy. Chemistry is not haunted by the phlogiston [a substance supposed by eighteenth century chemists to exist in all combustible bodies and to be released in combustion] theory as Christianity is haunted by the theory of a God with a craving for bloody sacrifices. But it is also a fact that, while serious attempts are constantly being made to verify scientific myths, religious myths, at least under Christianity and Islam, have become matters of faith which it is more or less impious to doubt, and which we must not attempt to verify by empirical means. Chemists believe that when a chemical reaction occurs, the weights of the reactants are unchanged. If this is not very nearly true, most of chemical theory is nonsense. But experiments are constantly being made to disprove it… Chemists welcome such experiments and do not regard them as impious or even futile."

Religion and science are often held to be opposed to one another but perhaps religion (or, at least, the process spirituality involved in religion) and science, at least for the purposes of recovery from alcoholism, can operate in the same dimension in practice. After all, in most societies, religious and secular systems are closely interwoven. Being a Christian can mean not so much church attendance or holding specific Christian beliefs, but rather attempting to live up to the moral code which Jesus Christ advocated. While belief in dogma can underpin one individual's entire life, another's religious dogma is not necessarily central to his religious belief. What counts in recovery is the effectiveness of the individual's beliefs in keeping him sober and it matters not whether those beliefs are true, verifiable, dogmatic, illogical, without foundation or anything else provided that they work for the purposes of keeping him sober.

In recovery science and religion can be seen to drive two distinct approaches, already referred to as the medical and moral approaches. The scientific, medical approach to recovery can be characterised as numerous styles of professionally guided group therapy, focusing on push forces, described in terms of drive, and conditioning. The emphasis is on what the individual alcoholic can do to bring about change. In Jungian psychological terms, the psychological approach can be likened to Logos, the principle of reason and judgement, traditionally identified with men and masculinity. Logos seeks out meaning, analysis and definition; it seeks knowledge. On the other hand the religious, moral approach to recovery is resolutely non-professional and eschews definition and analysis. It focuses on pull forces, described in terms of meaning and virtue. The emphasis is on willingness to be changed. In Jungian terms the approach could be likened to Eros, the principle of connection and relationship, traditionally identified with women and with femininity. Eros seeks out attachment, relationship and amalgamation; it seeks inspiration.

Many practitioners in the field of the treatment of alcoholism would acknowledge that the two approaches can be complementary and that both are to some extent needed. While science informs treatment and recovery in terms of knowledge, structure, technique, measurement, assessment and replication, treatment and recovery also requires art in terms of talent, creativity, meaning, communication and spirituality. Logos's reason and judgement needs to work with Eros's connection and relationship. But the different emphases can lead to diverse approaches and, at times, to styles that can be difficult, if not impossible, to harmonize. The mindsets of scientists and those of artists and theologians are very different reflecting an ancient tension between those who seek knowledge by empirical means and those who believe that they are inspired.

Science and religion both address the same fundamental questions that flow from the human condition. Certainly the question of recovery from alcoholism is the proper subject matter of science but for some there are religious aspects. Science offers an explanation of how things are and how they arise and work based on evidence. Classic Western religion offers an explanation of how things are and how they arise and work with little if any evidence in a scientific sense. Some explanations and answers are predicated simply on belief in the existence of God, on faith in him alone. Many would assert that the hypothesis of God offers no worthwhile explanation for anything, for it simply postulates what is sought to be explained and leaves it at that. Many would assert that science can better explain our origins than can the book of Genesis. However, Genesis may well not have been intended as a scientific account of creation but rather it should be read as a symbolic story. An individual may believe in creation according to the Bible but the evidence for evolution is so strong that to reject it the individual would have to be ignorant, stupid or insane.

Susan Blackmore maintains that human beings are designed by natural selection to look for cause and effect. Human perceptual systems have evolved to build adequate models of the world and to predict as accurately as possible what will happen next. While there may be no ultimate truth, there are more or less truthful theories and better or worse predictions. On this basis science can be seen as more truthful than religion but it does not necessarily follow that scientific beliefs are more successful or more effective for the purposes of recovery.

Blackmore would call the God idea a meme, that is, an element of a culture or system of behaviour passed from one individual to another by imitation or other non-genetic means, with an infective power in human society. Belief in God and in the other ideas and concepts in the religious mindset can facilitate the recovery process in one individual as much as the practice of a programme of recovery based on scientific evidence of effectiveness can facilitate the recovery process in another. A particular individual may, in the course of recovery, change from a scientific mindset to a religious one or vice versa or may vacillate between them or aspects of them.

Richard Dawkins, for one, would argue that science is a far better approach to understanding and explanation than religion. Dawkins has suggested that the beliefs of religion, the strong belief in doctrines based on religious conviction rather than evidence, particularly its mysteries, are symptomatic of a mind afflicted with mental viruses, particularly the virus of faith. But, as Alister McGrath points out in *Dawkins' God* (2005), Dawkins does not give any evidence-based arguments for this. Atheism may just as well be a mental virus.

However, many would accept Dawkins' conclusions about religious beliefs. But there is much more to religion than simply belief in dogma. Dawkins uses an evolutionary approach to explain the ubiquity of religion, arguing that human children are shaped by evolution to soak up culture and using computer viruses as a model for the spread of religious beliefs. But merely to dismiss the literal interpretation of religious dogma does not go far enough for many purposes.

Religious systems often deserve a more subtle and a fuller approach by way of analysis than Dawkins affords them. Religious systems involve far more than structural beliefs like the Trinity in Christianity. They usually involve narratives like the story of Jesus Christ's life, rituals, prayers, sacrifice and other practices. A code of personal and group conduct is involved, associated with an explicit or implied system of values. Religious experience and social aspects are involved.

Religious concepts have arisen by virtue of an evolutionary process involving Darwinian natural selection. Advocates of meme theory would say together with memetic cultural evolution. Culture, such advocates would say, has a selection dynamic of its own due to historical and other information transmission distinguishable from purely genetic selection and transmission. Successful religion is a practical matter; it is useful to its believers. Implicitly, Gods are presented as having minds, as generic forms of agency.

The nature of being and the reason for events can be described and explained in terms of God satisfying the believers' needs for certainty and comfort. This is all part of the psychological functioning which has evolved in humans. The human agency-detection system tends to jump to conclusions. There are evolutionary reasons for having a hyperactive system for the detection of agency. As both predators and prey it is better to over detect than under detect. The disadvantage of over detection is minimal while under detection could result in starvation or being killed.

It is not so much that individuals try to visualise what God is like but that individuals readily believe that they detect traces of God's agency in many of their daily experiences. A bus arrives at the bus stop just after it was reached or a parking place suddenly becomes available, therefore God was ensuring that the believer would not be late for his important appointment. None of this, of course, proves anything as to God or his agency on earth but such experiences can strengthen the believer in his belief and can confirm again to the believer that God is looking after him and will continue to do so. This is very comforting; nothing happens in God's world by mistake. Such feelings and thoughts and actions predicated on them are part of a believer's mindset. Several distinct brain systems below consciousness are delivering intuitions all of which are compatible with a general interpretation: questions as to whether God exists, or that the individual's beliefs are true, do not arise.

Many alcoholics assert that belief in God and faith in him has played a vital part in initiating and maintaining their recovery. It is equally true that many alcoholics assert that belief in God and faith in him has played no part whatsoever in initiating and maintaining their recovery. In the context of recovery from alcohol it matters not what the beliefs of the individual are or from whence they came. It matters not whether they are based on science or religion. What matters is that they amount to a mindset and attendant belief system conducive to the alcoholic's personal recovery.

Perhaps above all, the alcoholic seeking sobriety must be mindful of the intellectual vice of contempt prior to investigation. Many alcoholics see themselves upon some intellectual eminence. They often look down with distain on the follies of others. This habit of thought, however comfortable to the mind which entertains it, is more apt than almost any other disposition to produce hasty and contemptuous, and consequentially erroneous, judgments both of persons and opinions. The higher power or God and other spiritual expressions in the recovery process are those in accordance with the individual alcoholic's own conception. Prejudice should not be allowed to deter the individual from asking what they mean to him.

In any attempt to understand and explain something like recovery from alcoholism where religion, spirituality and faith have been very much involved historically and are still explicitly and implicitly much involved currently, it is important not to approach the religious, spiritual and faith aspects in the purely destructive manner adopted by some scientists. This purely destructive approach is unsatisfactory. It dismisses out of hand and without empirical study something that is of great value to many seeking to achieve and to maintain sobriety. This is why I have addressed spirituality, belief, religion, God and higher power at such length.

TOWARDS SOLUTIONS

Characteristic of the real alcoholic is a narcissistic self-centred core, dominated by feelings of omnipotence, intent on maintaining at all costs its inner integrity. Inwardly the alcoholic brooks no control from man or God. He, the alcoholic, is and must be the master of his destiny. He will fight to the end to preserve that position. No power greater than the alcoholic plays any part in this fight.

Nevertheless, the real alcoholic can move away from reliance on his own perceived omnipotence. The individual can begin to doubt his own ability to carry on and to realise that something has to change. Struggle, doubt and perplexity can be creative and can play a positive role in recovery. Personal experience can overcome powerful intellectual dissent or other profound resistance to spiritual principles. Belief in a higher power can arise from his own experience of ceasing to drink alcohol, something which he often had been incapable of doing before for any significant period in adulthood. The real alcoholic can come to believe that someone or something has been looking after him all along and might well continue to do so. At the very least the alcoholic can come to admit that he is not God.

For many real alcoholics there comes a time when he does not want to live but baulks at suicide. He feels that he cannot live with or without alcohol. He will feel utterly alone. He will be at his wits end. This emotional turmoil can eventually trigger conversion instigating the recovery process. Instead of contemplating suicide that day in October 1994, I rang AA and I attended an AA meeting. Looking back, I had come to believe that I could stop drinking. Before then I believed that even if abstinent for a considerable period, I would inevitably drink again sooner or later.

The first effective help, as the founders of AA discovered, can come from people who have suffered or are suffering in a similar way. To find that other people have been or are in the same situation can immediately lift some of the shame, guilt, remorse and other negative feelings which hamper or prevent recovery. From contact with other alcoholics, the alcoholic can come to believe that recovery is possible and he can see in others that which he desires himself. For those who enter group therapy or attend AA, the first relevant higher power may well be the power of the group. It can be the collective energy and help available from that group of people. Like morality, recovery appears to stem from feeling, not from reason, from the heart rather than from the head, so to speak. The real alcoholic must desire recovery to achieve it. Reason commands morality or serves it only to the extent that it is desired.

At present the remaining questions regarding alcoholism and recovery from it far outweigh what is known. I suspect, nonetheless, that scientists may one day, despite all the difficulties involved and with more adequately funded research, establish generally agreed constructs, definitions, models, measurement devices, assessment instruments and so on, which will enable them to discover substantially all, if not absolutely all, the numerous causes of, and factors relating to, alcoholism and recovery from it.

Causal theories of alcoholism and recovery from it have been linear yet nonlinear aspects have been identified. Psychology and the social sciences need better models for understanding complex human behaviour than traditional linear models provide. Chaos theory may help in providing such models. Chaos theory may well be applicable to alcoholism and recovery from it because it can help in understanding sudden changes in behaviour, irregular behaviour and unpredictability, all of which occur in the development of alcoholism and recovery.

Linking chaos theory with existing psychological theories and cognitive therapies may provide more flexible and useful models for the complexities of alcoholism and recovery from it. Researchers may then be able to identify, policy makers to promulgate and health care professionals to put into place efficient treatment approaches, methods and techniques successfully to bring about recovery from alcoholism. Effective preventative measures may also be developed. Even so the scientific explanations and approaches may not satisfy everyone; some will no doubt still be looking to non-scientific, spiritual constructs and values for the ultimate truth of the matter.

11

ABSTINENCE AND RELAPSE

ABSTINENCE AND THE DRY DRUNK

Some have questioned the value of abstinence arguing that the correlation of abstinence with overall emotional adjustment cannot be assured and the potentially adverse consequences of abstinence cannot be ignored. I have effectively ignored any adverse consequences of abstinence because abstinence is a prerequisite of my recovery and recovery for all other real alcoholics. I would, in any event, find it difficult to compile a list of substantial adverse consequences of abstinence.

A major consequence of abstinence is the denial to the abstinent of the quick fix use of alcohol to dull emotional pain or discomfort caused by stress, crisis or trauma. The abstinent individual cannot use alcohol as a form of self-medication to help him to cope with life. Drinking alcohol to gain confidence or to counter boredom or dysphoria is also denied. The individual would be deprived too of the perceived ability of alcohol consumption to release inhibition, to facilitate more intimate personal relationships, to assert status (particularly masculine status) and to "have a good time". However, the extent to which these consequences are indeed adverse is debateable.

Nevertheless, overbearing attempts to enforce abstinence can have serious unintended negative results. The alcoholic, as a consequence, can, for example, determine never to attempt to stop drinking again. Harm reduction approaches often appreciate the importance and value of incremental steps towards abstinence which can be built on over time and, in the meantime, can reduce harm.

It may well be that the real alcoholic's brain circuitry has been so changed by the effects of alcohol that the circuitry is no longer capable of sufficient re-configuration to allow the individual to drink asymptomatically. It may even be that the brain of a real alcoholic is so configured in the first place that he could not drink much alcohol for long without displaying symptoms of alcoholism anyway. In any event, given adequate time to rebuild their lives, abstinent alcoholics resemble the general population far more than actively drinking alcoholics or non-alcoholics with personality disorders. In every category of life adjustment, abstinent alcoholics do best and the heaviest drinkers do worst.

Yet, since relapses and remissions are common, the parameters of abstinence need to be addressed. This book is primarily concerned with real alcoholics and for them the desired goal is lifelong comfortable abstinence if they are not to return to symptomatic drinking, with the very real risk of another recovery not being achieved and death or insanity resulting. Accordingly, for real alcoholics, the classification of abstinence into categories, such as occasionally, currently or securely abstinent, is not as relevant or important as it may be for alcohol abusers. Perhaps it is worth noting, though, that it appears that the longer abstinence is maintained the lower the risk of relapse becomes.

Abstinence for the real alcoholic is a means, not an end. Real alcoholics cannot return to asymptomatic drinking, let alone social or carefree drinking and abstinence is necessary to achieve their essential goal of emotional and social rehabilitation. Sobriety for me involves more than abstinence as such; it means far more, it encompasses emotional sobriety, maturity and contentment. The pejorative term "dry" is reserved for those who, while abstinent, otherwise remain essentially unchanged from their alcohol dependent selves. Their mindset does not substantially change, neither does their lifestyle. Drinking alcohol is certainly bad for the alcoholic and those around him and abstinence from alcohol is usually better, it can be argued, even where the alcoholic retains his dependent personality.

Alcoholism is characterised by relapses and remissions as my own drinking history reflects. It is often the case that a real alcoholic has a number of questionable starts. Attempts at control usually precede abstinence.

Some relapse frequently and some go for long periods of time between relapses without drinking alcohol before they can properly be said to have started the recovery process in any real sense. The quality which determines true recovery, as contrasted with mere abstinence, is the change in the alcoholic which not only promises long term continuous and contented abstinence but also amounts to substantial emotional sobriety.

The process of recovery, once initiated, involves a struggle away from dependence and a striving towards self-discipline, particularly at first. The degree of struggle depends on the individual; some seem hardly to struggle at all, others to struggle a great deal. No matter what, recovery involves a move away from dependence towards self-control. It is also the process of substituting for alcohol something positive. It is difficult to abandon dependence without putting something in its place. The importance of substitute dependencies may explain why Antabuse, for example, which puts nothing in the place of alcohol, has not lived up to its early promise.

Recovery should be distinguished from the state which has been described as "dry drunk" where the alcoholic although not drinking alcohol exhibits many of the negative and destructive symptoms of the drinking alcoholic. The dry drunk may not be drinking but he has not substantially changed. Typically substitute dependences, like those on other psychoactive substances, work, food, gambling, shopping or sexual intercourse or any number of them will be driving the dry drunk. Codependence can also be an issue. Alcoholic drinking takes up a great deal of time and the dry drunk usually fills the vacuum with all manner of unhealthy substitutes. Nothing healthy has taken the place of alcohol and the dry drunk remains in conflict and disunity without any material change of personality.

My years of abstinence before 1994 were years when, although I was not drinking alcohol, were filled with compulsions and obsessions and unhealthy activity. Those years were characterised particularly by dependence on my work, pursuing it obsessively, shopping compulsively, particularly for expensive consumer durables, and, for the last ten years or so, substantial codependency as regards my wife. In a sense I could have been described as insanely sober. My years as a dry drunk became increasingly miserable. Running constantly in the background towards the end was the thought of suicide.

If all that the real alcoholic does is just to stop drinking he may be more acceptable to society, but otherwise nothing much has been accomplished towards the achievement of sobriety. If the stream of alcohol is simply dammed and nothing else is done, then a condition merely of suppressed alcoholism is produced. The partially repressed but imperative alcoholic urge becomes endowed with powerful redirection.

Over time before recovery, whether drinking or not, I developed substantial collections of resentments, real and imagined. These old resentments led to futility and unhappiness squandering hours that might have been worthwhile. They highlighted those aspects of my life where I saw myself as a victim. Dwelling on resentment, I made my life miserable. Becoming increasingly anxious, I was more and more driven by self-centred fear.

The dry drunk state is precarious whether as one insecurely maintaining abstinence, an intermediary stage between drinking and recovery or a falling away from reasonably contented sobriety. The dry drunk suffers much, if not all, of the torment of the drinking alcoholic without the temporary respite afforded by drinking. Further the fact that the alcohol is abstinent, and thereby *ipso facto* has usually reduced the harm caused by his drinking at least to some extent, can militate against conversion resulting in recovery. The state of dry drunkenness has been described by one alcoholic as "a purgatory worse than hell, for one suffered the torment under the illusion that this was heaven; further, from this alcoholic limbo one passed more usually to the hell of active alcoholism than to the heaven of true sobriety".

A RELAPSING CONDITION

It is becoming increasingly accepted that real alcoholism is a chronic relapsing condition stemming from underlying neuropathologies (to use the World Health Organisation phrase). Strictly speaking, an individual can only relapse if he is in recovery, that is, he has stopped drinking for a considerable period of time, has understood and accepted his alcoholism and is actively pursuing a recovery programme of some sort. Some distinguish relapse from a lapse.

A lapse is where the alcoholic drinks only a limited amount of alcohol before becoming abstinent again within a short period of time, a few days, a day or two, even an hour or two. A relapse is where the alcoholic resumes his alcoholic lifestyle for a substantial period.

According to a research report *Relapse & Recovery: Behavioral Strategies for Change* (2003) by the Caron Foundation, one of the oldest and largest addiction treatment centres in the US, relapse rates for alcoholism and other psychoactive substance dependence do not differ significantly from rates for chronic diseases. Relapse rates for alcoholism range from 50 percent for resumption of heavy drinking to 90 percent for a brief lapse. The potential for relapse is part of chronic disease. As is the case with alcoholism, patients with diseases such as hypertension (abnormally high blood pressure), diabetes and asthma frequently fail to comply with their treatment regimens. Just as individuals with chronic diseases must adjust their lifestyles and assume responsibility for managing their own care, so do those who are dependent on alcohol.

In many cases the alcoholic begins recovery following conversion as a result of heavy drinking and its profound adverse effects. His memories of the adverse consequences of his drinking are and remain acute for some considerable time after a heavy drinking episode. During such time he is more likely to comply with suggestions regarding the maintenance of his recovery. The fight, so to speak, has been knocked out of him. But, as time passes and the memory of his suffering weakens, the need for compliance lessens. He can readily stop any relapse prevention activity and drink again. It is accordingly important to sustain the alcoholic's acceptance of his alcoholism; his acceptance that he cannot drink asymptomatically. It may be, though, that, for a number of alcoholics in recovery after a considerable time, their conversion state can endure without the need for any specific relapse prevention activity.

Be that as it may, recovery requires effort and discipline while relapse requires none. Relapse for the real alcoholic involves drinking alcohol again. All real alcoholics are subject to relapse; real alcoholism is a relapsing condition. The condition for the real alcoholic, at least, is only capable of arrest, never cure. For many, if not all, real alcoholics, their natural or default status is a drinking one and there needs to be something active in place to prevent reversion to drinking once a period of abstinence starts. Numerous alcoholics drink again after receiving treatment, particularly after their first experience of it. Many alcoholics require a number of attempts before they start to recover and before they arrest their alcoholism for any substantial period of time. Relapses after a period of recovery can, however, contribute towards an alcoholic overcoming his alcoholism in the longer term. Most therapists will say that relapse is part of the learning process.

For those who have treatment, mounting evidence suggests that relapses generally occur soon after it if no effort is made to sustain its benefits. Usually the treatment has not lasted long enough to stabilise the alcoholic's life and to teach him how to stay sober. In any event no amount of sober experience, no amount of modified brain circuitry can definitively turn the real alcoholic brain into a non-alcoholic one. The alcoholic brain and mind has formed strong motivational associations and they have become extremely susceptible to the motivational and rewarding effects surrounding alcohol and its consumption. This susceptibility, although it can substantially diminish over time, is remarkably persistent.

In recovery the alcoholic's conditioned denial, defiance and resistance can return. In early recovery, the alcoholic's thinking can become dominated by doubts about being alcoholic, by recall of the good drinking times or by concentration on the difficulties of abstinence. This thinking and much more, including conditioned cues, can trigger and be part of the process of relapse. In later recovery, the alcoholic can become confused and he can overreact. He can manage his life situations poorly and as a consequence face progressive life problems and stress cycles leading to relapse.

Relapse can occur unless appropriate help and support is on hand when it matters and such help and support is asked for and accepted. After years of recovery, painful memories or new challenges can present themselves with which the alcoholic can fail effectively to deal whether by failing to ask for help, failing to accept them or otherwise. Self-defeating behavioural patterns and lifestyle can return resulting in overwhelming pain and problems which can result in emotional crisis and eventual relapse. A sober and reasonably self-disciplined, balanced lifestyle needs constantly to be maintained to sustain sobriety. Each individual has a lifestyle, aspects of which can support recovery and aspects of which can potentially cause relapse.

CUES

By virtue of alcohol's effect on the autonomic nervous and limbic systems relapse can be triggered by cues previously associated with drinking or by the presence of alcohol. The cues can be very subtle. A place, a person, a thing, a situation, an emotion or other cue can bring back an intense desire to drink. Multiple memory systems in the brain are involved together with automatic subconscious changes in organ systems and behavioural sensations. Habitual, profoundly learned sequences of behaviour are elicited involuntarily by certain stimuli. Conditioning also occurs in relation to withdrawal effects. The emergence of withdrawal symptoms can result from exposure to conditioned cues. The effects of environmental cues can be similar to the priming effects of actually taking a drink. The conditioned cues, once established, are difficult to extinguish and the original learning from which they are derived is never erased.

In alcoholics there can also be a series of linked conditioned cues. In the absence of alternative forms of release, the alcoholic can forget, deny or ignore the strongest caveats and become more and more focused, consciously or unconsciously, towards and on that first drink. Relapse can reflect conditioned behaviour, not capricious desire or a simple response to psychological conflict. The drinking habit can become embedded in the memory circuits of the brain and this aberrant form of learning can explain why alcoholics relapse after long periods of abstinence. Certain cues can reawaken memories deeply processed by the brain and cravings for alcohol can recur.

RELAPSE OVER TIME

Relapse after a substantial period of abstinence does not usually come on suddenly and without warning although it can, for example, upon the occurrence of a traumatic event. It is usually a process occurring over time. First indications that the process of relapse may have started could be a decrease in personal confidence in maintaining sobriety, becoming defensive when talking about recovery, seeking to impose recovery on others, reappearance of compulsive behaviour and loss of a structured lifestyle.

The process can start with resentment, real or imagined, and can progress to feelings of irritation, anger or depression. The process can increasingly generate an attitude of indifference and self-pity and the individual can drink again. Relapse can be a complicated process. It can have numerous warning signs and can be insidious in its progress. But relapse can be avoided if the alcoholic is honest, open and willing and able to recognise and deal directly with each symptom as it appears and if he seeks and accepts appropriate help and support.

There are warning signs distinctive to each alcoholic that depend on his personality and lifestyle. For some the relapse warning signs relate to the exaggeration of strength and the denial of weakness. The alcoholic can become preoccupied with self, power and control, driving others away. He can become angry and isolated. For others the signs relate to the exaggeration of weakness and the denial of strength. The alcoholic can focus increasingly on others and he can assume the victim role. Others reject him accordingly and he can become depressed and isolated.

In many cases the individual's conversion fails to mature into stable sobriety and remains insecure. Even if the surrender does mature the alcoholic can revert to his former attitudes and ways of feeling, sometimes quickly, sometimes slowly. Many alcoholics need to rely on, or choose to engage in, some relapse prevention programme or activity to maintain sobriety. This may involve, on a regular basis, participation in AA or a peer support project, therapy, counselling or religious activity. Mature and stable sobriety can be subject to erosion. However, erosion can be countered by teaching alcoholics how to recognise and manage the relevant relapse warning signs and programmes can be practised, plans put in place and action taken to minimise the risk of relapse.

HUMAN BEHAVIOUR

It may seem odd that an alcoholic, who has restored himself to society and has not drunk alcohol for years, should suddenly, by drinking again, put himself once more into mortal danger. William Silkworth, writing in the AA *Grapevine* in 1947, suggested that the reason is often simple. He asserted that the real alcoholic was and remains essentially a sick person. While he may get better, even well, his disease is only arrested. There is nothing odd about a person who has arrested atherosclerosis, for example, relapsing. Atherosclerosis is a major form of heart disease in Western countries where fatty deposits build up on the inner wall of the coronary arteries. No one is startled by the fact that he has another heart attack. There is always the risk of recurrence. Alcoholism shares a number of features with at least some chronic diseases.

Alcoholism may have similarities with chronic diseases like hypertension, diabetes and asthma which require continuing care throughout the individual's life. Treatment for these diseases is effective but heavily dependent on adherence to a medical regimen for that effectiveness. Many hypertension, diabetes and asthma patients fail to adhere to their regimens. Problems of poverty, lack of family support and concurrent disorder have been found to be major and approximately equal predictors of disengagement and relapse across the chronic diseases of hypertension, diabetes and asthma and across alcoholism.

When an atherosclerosis patient recovers sufficiently to be released from hospital he is given careful instructions for the way he is to live when he gets home. He must obey certain stringent rules. For the first few months, perhaps for several years, the individual follows directions. But as his strength increases he can become slack. When nothing untoward seems to result he can soon start disregarding more and more of the directions given to him when he left hospital. Eventually he can relapse. The behaviour which led to the relapse results from erroneous thinking. The individual can think himself out of a sense of his own perilous condition. He can, sometimes deliberately, turn away from his knowledge of the fact that he has a serious disease. He can grow overconfident and he can decide no longer to follow directions.

Alcoholic relapse appears to have essentially the same pattern with the arrested alcoholic as with the arrested atherosclerosis patient. The alcoholic usually decides to take a drink again some time before he actually takes one.

He starts thinking erroneously before he embarks on the course that leads to drinking again. There is no reason to ascribe the relapse to alcoholic behaviour as there is no reason to ascribe a second heart attack to atherosclerosis behaviour. The alcoholic relapse is not a symptom of a psychotic condition. There is nothing odd about it. The individual has simply failed intelligently to safeguard himself against relapse.

Alcoholics are human beings. They can safeguard themselves intelligently against relapse but they can also fail to do so. The alcoholic may think himself special and different; that he has unique tendencies and reactions. Some health care professionals carry the same idea to extremes in their analyses and treatment of alcoholics. There is sometimes a tendency to label everything that an alcoholic may do as alcoholic behaviour. The truth is that it is essentially human behaviour. It is misconceived to consider all the personality traits observed in alcoholics as peculiar to the alcoholic. Emotional and mental quirks are frequently classified as symptoms of alcoholism merely because alcoholics have them, yet those same quirks can be found among non-alcoholics too. They are symptoms of the human condition; they are qualitatively the same, even if they can be somewhat, even considerably, exaggerated in alcoholics.

Alcoholism does, though, manifest itself in some discrete ways. With other psychoactive substance dependence, it does have a number of baffling peculiarities which differ from those of all other diseases, disorders and conditions. Alcoholics, even though in long term recovery, are never very far away from the possibility of fresh personal disaster. Each real alcoholic in substantial recovery knows that he must observe a high degree of awareness, honesty, humility and tolerance, or else drink again. At the same time, many of the symptoms and much of the behavioural patterns of alcoholism are closely paralleled and even duplicated in other mental illnesses and disorders. Relapse is likewise paralleled.

The alcoholic who has learned some of the techniques or mechanics of recovery but misses the philosophy, or the spirit of it, may get tired of just following directions– not because he is alcoholic, but because he is human. Rules and regulations irk almost anyone, because they are restraining, prohibitive and appear negative. The individual can lack the discipline to maintain his recovery regime. Good recovery philosophy and practice, on the other hand, is positive and can provide ample sustained positive attitudes and a sustained desire to follow the path of recovery enthusiastically. As the alcoholic becomes more and more aware that the practice of his recovery programme makes him happy the happier he becomes to practice it.

ADDRESSING RELAPSE

Alcoholics can learn their own signs and symptoms of relapse. They should watch their thinking. Important enemies of maintaining recovery are rationalization, distortion and denial as the problems of drinking alcohol seem increasingly far away and less threatening. Being at an increasing distance the individual can come to minimise the dangers and risks of drinking and to maximise its appeal. The process of forgetting is involved.

Some alcoholics are better than others at seeing the signs of the beginning of a slide into a relapse. The signs will not change much, and they are very good indicators to the individual that he needs to take proactive steps to prevent a relapse. In particular female alcoholics need to understand how their menstrual cycle relates to risk of relapse. Men may also have hormonal factors relevant to relapse.

If the individual who has relapsed is able to be honest in recognising it as such, and if he has continuing motivation for abstinence, relapses can constitute valuable learning experiences. They can demonstrate to the individual the power of his dependence and they can help identify triggers and cues for relapse and how to cope with them. In severe cases, the individual may need again to be detoxified and to return to treatment in order to focus on a revised treatment plan. He may just return to AA or restart his recovery from an earlier stage in the process of change. Happily many who relapse do not give up on themselves and their ability to change. They return to the contemplation or preparation stage and get ready for action again. Some immediately return to the action stage picking up their recovery programme where they left off. Some, however, become so demoralised by a relapse, or a number of relapses, that they lose all energy for change and continue to drink to their dying day which can be quick in coming.

12

MY EXPERIENCE OF WHAT WORKS

MY EXPERIENCE OF RECOVERY

It is only with regard to my experience that I can speak with any authority regarding what works in initiating, sustaining and maintaining recovery. Each unique real alcoholic who achieves reasonably secure, stable and contented sobriety does so in his own way. But I have come across many alcoholics, a number of whom I know very well, for whom essentially the same factors as have worked for me have worked for them. Although it is always somewhat problematical to extrapolate from one's own experience and to make general statements about others based on it, I have in this concluding Chapter attempted to set out some of the factors relating to how recovery works which are reflected in the experience of many of the numerous alcoholics with whom I have come into contact over the years and which are consistent with my research.

Because I happen to have experienced my recovery in an AA context, I have inevitably approached recovery from alcoholism from an AA oriented point of view. I have found that Harry Tiebout, who studied the recovery of alcoholics in AA, has described the process in convincing terms. He explained the process in terms of a surrender and conversion followed by a conversion state being of short duration or of lasting duration. If the conversion state is of sufficient duration the alcoholic has time to learn new skills and to adopt altered attitudes which can result in recovery. It was his way of describing what AA members would call having "a spiritual awakening as the result of these steps", to quote Step Twelve, enabling them to stop drinking.

Although the AA twelve-step based programme has worked for me in some sense as a pragmatic programme of recovery, I have had difficulty to the present day with its tenets, particularly those relating to powerlessness, power greater than the alcoholic, God and spiritual awakening. While AA has to an extent combined the moral and the medical approaches, in truth only Step One really adopts the medical approach. Steps Two to Eleven inclusive adopt the moral approach closely following the evangelical Christian Oxford Group tenets of the 1930s and Step Twelve affirms William James's general assertion in *Varieties of Religious Experiences* that spiritual awakenings are real and should be acted on.

I have used Tiebout's language to describe my and other alcoholics' conversions but I have also used AA's language. In AA twelve-step terms, I am not sure exactly what can be said to be Tiebout's conversion. I would say that it is embodied in Step Two and is expressed in terms of "coming to believe in a Power greater that ourselves". This would make sense because all that Step One does is to state the alcoholic's problem in medical terms but offers no solution. Steps Two to Eleven inclusive offer the solution. By practising them the alcoholic can have a spiritual awakening. In Tiebout's terms, I would describe the spiritual awakening as the conversion state lasting long enough for the alcoholic effectively to learn the new skills and altered attitudes requisite for recovery. Step Twelve simply exhorts the recovering alcoholic to pass the AA message of recovery to other alcoholics and to practise the AA principles in all his affairs.

Despite the language of AA's Twelve Steps, they can, with careful interpretation, help anybody from the militant atheist to the ardent theist. I have seen it as an important part of my purpose in writing this book to suggest a way whereby the Twelve Steps can be construed and practised to enable the irreligious, including the militant atheist, happily to become an active member of AA and to benefit fully from membership. AA can be such an effective recovery resource and it is available on a twenty-four hour, seven days a week basis without any fee or subscription having to be paid. It is an efficient way to deliver talk therapy and, in the final analysis, talk therapy is the way to treat alcoholism.

MINDSET

It seems to me, and many other alcoholics with whom I have discussed the matter, that the root of our troubles is indeed selfish self-centredness as suggested in AA's Big Book, *Alcoholics Anonymous*. In my case, by the time I went up to Oxford I was, in my view, intellectually self-sufficient. I had specialised in the sciences at school and it seemed to me that the answer to all things lay in the proper application of scientific method. My intellect was my greatest asset and it was all I needed. I no longer believed in any God or anything supernatural. My study of philosophy, politics and economics at university and my later qualification and practice as a lawyer confirmed, beyond doubt in my mind at the time, that I was totally self-reliant. I was, so to speak, God in my own sphere of influence. Everything to do with me revolved around me. I saw myself as being in control and this perception of control included my consumption of alcohol. While I did not exactly rule the world, it did seem to me that I ruled my limited part of it.

However, after my conversion, my mindset changed and, at the very least, I entertained the notion that I might not really be wholly in control of my little world after all and that, in particular, I might not be in control of my drinking. I became aware of my desperate need for outside help with regard to my situation in general and with regard to my drinking in particular. Perhaps the solution to my problems did not entirely lie within me and the potency of my intellect after all. Perhaps I was not God even within my own sphere of influence.

There are some similarities between my conversion and that of Bill Wilson. Like me, Wilson was not prepared before his conversion to give up what he saw as his greatest asset, his inquiring, rational mind for what he originally saw as an illusion, God. But after his conversion he never doubted the existence of God again. Wilson was prepared to question his mind and to give up his dependence on his rational mindset. His mind, after all, had been but the witness to what to him had been his ineffable spiritual conversion.

Wilson began to see his mind as guilty of rationalisation. The process of recovery was to him something more to be witnessed as a spiritual awakening rather than as something capable of being understood by the mind through reasoning. While I, too, after my conversion, began to see that my mind was only too capable of rationalization and erroneous thought, unlike Wilson, I continued to disbelieve in the existence of God. Further, I later took the view that my mind did not witness an ineffable conversion followed by a spiritual awakening beyond the understanding of mere reason but rather that it became subject to a process which was capable of being understood in scientific rather than spiritual or religious terms. The process of recovery could even, at least to some extent, be understood by the mind of the individual who was experiencing it.

I have heard many alcoholics speak of their conversions some of which have similarities to mine and to Wilson's and some of which have been more of the slowly incremental, educational variety. What I have learned from my own experience, and my understanding of the experiences of others, suggests that the way to initiate recovery from dependence on alcohol is not to seek independence but to transfer the dependence onto something less damaging. The achievement of a healthy interdependence as a well balanced social being takes time and it is not immediately attainable. It is not dependence *per se* that is the issue. The issue is to stop the individual being morbidly dependent on alcohol. For this to happen, the alcoholic needs at first to become dependent on something else. Conversion is about looking for help outside the limitations of the alcoholic's dependent mindset perverted by alcohol.

Wilson maintained that the alcoholic needed to substitute his dependence on alcohol for dependence on God as he understood him. Many Christians would have no difficulty with this or with the idea that alcoholics are powerless over alcohol and much more. After all the Christian concept of God is that he is omnipotent so mankind's essential powerlessness is consistent with their belief. Thus real alcoholics being totally dependent on alcohol will need to become dependent on something totally powerful and the Christian God fits the bill.

However, this reasoning can, at the very least, cause difficulties for those who are not religious. To those with an irreligious mindset, the argument is erroneous. Alcoholics, like other human beings, are neither totally dependent nor totally powerful. Many would say that alcoholics are not totally dependent, even on alcohol. Moreover, alcoholics are surely not so dependent on alcohol that they have to believe in and become dependent upon God and must turn their will and their life over to God, in whom and only in whom total trust and faith can properly be placed leaving nothing, no residual power, in the individual. The something else upon which the alcoholic needs to depend in substitution for alcohol to maintain sobriety, does not have to be the Christian God or any other deity or supernatural entity. The something else, the higher power, can be many other things.

Accepting that the individual is not omnipotent does not mean that he is totally powerless, totally dependent. Many would argue that the need to abdicate all claims to power over alcohol while willingly and even enthusiastically embracing total dependence on an omnipotent ultimate reality is misconceived. Most believers would surely agree that "faith without works is dead" to quote the Bible. The requirement of works implies some power within the alcoholic or there would be no ability. Humanity as well as deity must surely be involved in recovery and some would argue that the deity element is superfluous although for some beneficial. After all, a few alcoholics recover all by themselves and numerous alcoholics recover without a belief in any sort of deity.

The AA members and those health care professionals who argue the need to abdicate all claims to any power over alcohol, differ from others in the recovery field as regards the part in recovery played by the individual. Many health care professionals seek to lead alcoholic clients to responsible personal autonomy. The only higher power needed in the recovery process is the practitioner who teaches the client how to cope without drinking by his own efforts. This approach is certainly viable for some alcoholics as is another very common therapeutic approach involving group therapy where the higher power can be variously the group, one or more of its members or its facilitator or any combination of them from time to time. Notwithstanding my flirtation with AA's power greater than the alcoholic and God of his understanding concepts, I would say that, in the final analysis, I have recovered by myself albeit with the help of others in AA and outside AA. The help from others in AA was mutual self-help, but self-help all the same.

The drinking alcoholic commonly has a penchant for identifying with omnipotence, particularly, in the West, with the omnipotence within the concept of the Christian God. The drinking alcoholic also tends to see himself as superior compared with other people. In his behaviour he happily plays and imitates God. On the other hand the recovering alcoholic increasingly tends to identify with the limitations of other people which limitations, he comes to recognise, he shares with them. He appreciates that he is not God and tries not to play or imitate God accordingly. This is the change of mindset usually at the heart of the recovery process and it need not involve a belief in any power greater than the individual save only to the extent that the individual needs to engage with other people to learn about and experience reality.

The God idea can be useful in helping the alcoholic to understand his behaviour before and after he comes into recovery but a belief in God is not necessary. By contemplating the Christian concept of God as omnipotent and omniscient and comparing it with the reality of man's powerlessness and ignorance, the alcoholic can begin to appreciate the absurdity of playing or imitating God. Human strength can increasingly be seen as being rooted in human weakness. As no one human experience is comprehensive each can benefit from the experience of others. This crucial change of attitude can be brought about in myriad ways some involving AA, some involving individual or group psychotherapy and some essentially involving the individual alone albeit usually in contact with others.

NO CURE BUT CONVERSION AND RECOVERY

There is currently no cure for alcoholism, perhaps there never will be. It can only be arrested. Alcoholics are always in danger of relapse albeit some more so than others. For some alcoholics, even real alcoholics, the process of personal change that is recovery can be achieved. Those who successfully arrest their alcoholism are said to be in recovery. Acceptance of abstinence, belief in the feasibility of change, readiness to change, effort, ability and self-discipline are all critically involved. The alcoholic needs to learn how to cope with life without drinking alcohol. This can be accomplished essentially by talking – by oral communication between the alcoholic and a therapist, a counsellor or another alcoholic or group of alcoholics. The talking can be supplemented by reading and written work.

While it can be simply stated that the way to address the alcoholics' problems is for them to stop drinking, this can be profoundly difficult for them, for some apparently impossible. Just to stop drinking is not in itself enough to enable a real alcoholic to achieve long lasting sobriety. The vacuum resulting from stopping drinking needs to be filled. Other personality and behavioural issues have to be addressed.

Most alcoholics relapse after their first treatment. Many alcoholics require a number of attempts before they finally overcome their dependence in the long term. There is evidence that even an apparently unsuccessful treatment episode can still contribute towards an alcoholic's eventual recovery.

The recovery process can be successfully managed by those with the requisite motivation who have found out how it works and who have the mental capacity to change substantially. Individuals can create or become part of an environment in which change can occur, in which motivation can be maintained, setbacks can be turned into progress and sobriety made a secure and stable reality. In my case, my conversion was brought about by trauma and my subsequent recovery involved a process of increasing awareness and acceptance of the realities of life brought about by attending AA meetings and communicating with other alcoholics.

Trauma and emotional shock can trigger conversion; it can cause individuals to behave in very different ways. Their personalities can break down and new ways of thinking can then be accepted and developed. Trauma can bring about changes in brain function and operation, in mental activity, and, consequently, in behaviour and experience. Trauma can open the way for the new mindset, belief system and behavioural structure requisite for recovery to take hold and a new, sober, way of life can be built.

Although for many, if not most, real alcoholics, trauma is what initiates conversion, for some nothing dramatic or traumatic needs to happen for the recovery process to start. Circumstances can conspire or can be manipulated to facilitate the conversion of an alcoholic from a drinking to an abstinent one. Most conversions take place outside any therapeutic setting. Rather than treatment bringing about conversion, treatment is usually entered into by virtue of it. I decided to attend AA again as a consequence of my conversion which took place at home.

For me and most alcoholics, abstinence, a prerequisite of sobriety, needs to be sustained by active steps and significant help from others. Sobriety is conditional on the individual's full participation in its continuation and his ability to sustain it and discipline to maintain it. The conversion involves the acceptance by the individual that his drinking of alcohol is beyond his control and his asking for help accordingly. Once the conversion occurs the new behaviour is at risk of reversal unless something is done to stop reversal happening. For many, recovery requires the continuous practice of some sort of personal programme to prevent relapse.

Recovery is for the real alcoholic to espouse and effect by action. In nearly all, if not all, cases it appears to involve the acceptance by the individual that he is an alcoholic, his desire to recover, his belief that sobriety is possible, his acknowledgement that he needs help to achieve sobriety and his taking of sufficient appropriate action to that end. Conversion amounts to the triggering of the desire for and acceptance of help. Any higher power concept involved, in the Twelve Steps of AA or otherwise, amounts to that which can be a useful mechanism in the process of change, an effective cognitive gadget in the recovery process and a source of help accordingly.

MUTUALITY

Although the alcoholic can obtain help and support from many sources, I have found the help and support of other alcoholics essential. Only other alcoholics fully understand the processes and factors involved in alcoholism and recovery from it. Accordingly other alcoholics can be crucial in helping and supporting alcoholics seeking to achieve and maintain sobriety. Often, only another alcoholic sharing the same experience particularly one who is in recovery, can win the drinking alcoholic's entire trust. Alcoholism is best treated by talk therapy and the effectiveness of talk therapy depends on trust.

The real alcoholic can increase his chances of recovery by joining a group of alcoholics which is intent on recovery and listening to members of the group tell of their experiences and taking in the received wisdom of the group. The more he immerses himself in the milieu of the group and the more he dedicates himself to recovery on an ongoing basis the greater the chances of success and the greater the quality of sobriety. The real alcoholic can find the group a facilitating environment in which he can learn his way to stay sober. Once sober he can find the group invaluable in helping him to maintain and sustain his sobriety. I do not think that I could have sustained my recovery without being part of such a group of alcoholics.

Recovery is a long term, for some a life time, enterprise. Numerous recovering alcoholics stay in touch with one another for the rest of their lives. My experience suggests that most of the alcoholics that I have come across need to maintain their sobriety by some sort of relapse prevention programme or activity but this activity need not be AA attendance.

An individual may need ongoing support for longer than formal treatment can be continued or, indeed, afforded. An individual cannot stay in a treatment centre indefinitely and the continuing cost of on-going professional therapy, counselling or other treatment may not be thought justified even if funds are available for the attendant fees. Consequently, involvement in AA can be said to afford the real alcoholic who needs an on-going relapse prevention programme the best chance of continuing sobriety if he is prepared to espouse it. AA is free. Its members are ready to help alcoholics on a twenty-four hour, seven days a week basis and AA groups meet every day in myriad venues all around the world. Alcoholics communicate with each other in ways they cannot with non-alcoholics.

There is no doubt that AA is an important and effective recovery resource. It is remarkable that, unlike other mutual self-help organisations, it has survived its founders' generation and continues to thrive. This is due in large part to Bill Wilson and his crucial work in establishing AA's Twelve Traditions and its organizational structure such as it is, which he played so vital a role in putting in place, in order to preserve AA's unity and effectiveness. Each AA group has but one primary purpose. It is to carry its message to the alcoholic who still suffers. Each group must be self-supporting by its own contributions. Learning from the failure of the Washingtonian Movement, an AA precursor, Wilson established the Tradition that AA should have no opinion on outside issues and that it should never be drawn into public controversy.

As Wilson appreciated, the crux of the matter is that, as John Donne (1572-1631) wrote, "no man is an Island, entire of it self; every man is a piece of the Continent, a part of the main". In isolation lie incapacity, weakness, and inability to cope; in mutuality, giving and receiving help, lie capacity, power, sanity and ability to cope. This, it seems to me, is what recovery is to a large extent about. It need have little or nothing to do with God or absolutes of power or dependence. It has much to do with just getting along together as one of many in the milieu of other essentially similar social beings all needing help, both in giving and in receiving. It amounts to joining the human race. Drinking alcohol for the alcoholic severely compromises, often prevents, his being part of any community. He is not minded to give and he feels no need to receive; he is effectively isolated from the human race. He thinks he is that which he is not, an island unto itself, and he behaves perversely accordingly.

The need to give it away to keep it, so often expressed in AA, simply reflects the essential give and take of mutual self-help and the effectiveness of sharing experience as a means of learning. In an AA or similar group, alcoholics can share the same incompleteness, the same weakness, insecurity and vulnerability by looking for the similarities and not the differences between them. Additionally, against the background of shared experience, the individual alcoholic can learn about the differences between himself and others. The recovering alcoholic's sobriety can become richer as more share in it; it can be progressive.

The core dynamic of AA in seeking to achieve sobriety is the shared honesty of mutual vulnerability openly acknowledged. Unlike the basis of most methods of seeking achievement in life, AA proceeds from a basis of weakness rather than strength. The basis of most methods of seeking to achieve most aims in life, by negotiation or otherwise, is strength (real, perceived or protested).

Some treatment approaches still proceed on the basis of strength, on the basis that the practitioner has the power to treat the alcoholic's condition over which the alcoholic is powerless. Such approaches leave little, if anything, to the individual's personal autonomy. The common religious approach also proceeds on the basis of power stressing human weakness while protesting the deity's strength. Particular religions commonly posit a deity to solve the problem of empowerment.

For many, though, subjecting themselves to a dictatorial regime is unacceptable and positing any sort of deity is objectionable and unnecessary: all that is necessary is self-help or, more likely, mutual self-help. While many individuals alone may not be able to bring about their recovery, with some help from others, many, even most, would indeed seem potentially to be able to recover from alcoholism, even severe alcoholism. No power greater than the individual needs to be involved. All that is required is self-help by acquiring knowledge, adopting new attitudes, acquiring new disciplines and by learning new skills often in the context of a mutual help situation of some sort. There is no need for anything supernatural; all that is required is essentially within the inner resources of the individual. They need to be tapped though and there is the rub, the central, most important difficulty.

There is, however, a danger in too much emphasis on self-help and the power of the individual. It can be redolent of the real alcoholic's "root of all his troubles", that is, his selfishness and his claim in effect to be God inherent in his extreme self-centeredness. Many alcoholics do imitate or play God, but they can learn not to, or, rather, not to so much. The alcoholic can learn to relate to others. He can learn to help and to be helped, to give and to receive.

HOPE FOR THE ALCOHOLIC

I often hear in AA meetings alcoholics in recovery say that "if I can recover anybody can". I am tempted to assert this myself. However, so to say would be misleading. Each individual in recovery needed to experience the unique set of circumstances which triggered his recovery. Whether he does or not seems essentially to be a matter of chance but alcoholics can take steps to make recovery more likely. Talk therapy, supplemented by pharmacotherapy if needed, seems to be the most effective way to treat alcoholics. Talk therapy can be delivered in many ways including the Community Reinforcement Approach, cognitive therapy and twelve-step programmes and medication is generally available.

While much still needs to be learned about alcoholism and recovery from it, the alcoholic, even one with the severest dependence and the most profound problems, has a chance of recovery if he is honest, open-minded and willing and sufficiently motivated. I have seen many, by their own account with chronic dependence and acute problems, recover in the rooms of AA. This does not mean that AA is the only way such an alcoholic can recover; it means that he can recover and it shows that AA can help.

I would say to the individual, who fears that he is an alcoholic and who realizes that, if indeed he is, he should stop drinking, that he has a good chance of achieving contented sobriety by exposing himself to talk therapy. AA might be the first port of call. Because AA is an efficient, readily available source of free talk therapy, I would urge him to persevere with it even though he is unhappy with much of its language, even much more besides. If he really cannot stomach AA then he might seek cognitive therapy or other treatment on a more scientific basis.

Contented sobriety is, for the real alcoholic, a goal worth making every effort to achieve. As *the Jellinek Chart of Alcoholism and Recovery* sets out, he can change from an individual obsessed with alcohol and plagued by irrational fear, to one with the hope of a new and useful life. He can achieve an enlightened and interesting way of living which opens up all sorts of novel and satisfying possibilities.

As to those who suffer the consequences of another's alcoholism, they might consider therapy or joining Al-Anon. In any event, they should try to make their own well-being a priority rather than that of the alcoholic.

As for alcoholics in recovery, health care professionals, policy makers and those interested in addiction in general and in alcoholism in particular, I hope that what I have written has been of interest, even informative.

The debate about alcohol, alcohol abuse, alcoholism, harm reduction, treatment and recovery continues. Some individuals just use alcohol, some abuse it and some become dependent on it. To study alcoholism and recovery from it is almost as broad a task as to study society itself. Addressing alcoholism and recovery from it is only part of a much greater issue to do with how society reduces the harm caused by a psychoactive substance available to all, enjoyed by most, dangerous to many and fatal to some.

REFERENCES, BIBLIOGRAPHY AND FURTHER READING

AA General Service Office; *Living Sober*, 1975.

AA Grapevine, Inc.; *The Language of the Heart*, 1988.

Abbott, Lyman; *The Life of Henry Ward Beecher*, 2002.

Academy of Medical Sciences; *Calling Time, The Nation's drinking as a major health issue*, 2004.

Al-Anon Family Group Headquarters, Inc.; *How Al-Anon Works for Families and Friends of Alcoholics*, 1995.

Alcohol Concern; *Primary Care Alcohol Information Service; Fact sheet, Alcohol Treatment options and outcomes*, 2003.

Alcohol Concern; *Research Forum Papers; How good is treatment?*, September, 2003.

Alcohol Concern; *Factsheet 6: Post-traumatic Stress Disorder & Alcohol*, 2004.

Alcoholics Anonymous Great Britain; *Thirty-Eighth General Service Conference Final Report*, 2003.

Alcoholics Anonymous World Services, Inc.; *Twelve Steps and Twelve Traditions*, 1953.

Alcoholics Anonymous World Services, Inc.; *Alcoholics Anonymous Comes of Age*, 1957.

Alcoholics Anonymous World Services, Inc.; *Dr Bob and the Good Old Timers*, 1980.

Alcoholics Anonymous World Services, Inc.; *Pass It On*, 1984.

Alcoholics Anonymous World Services, Inc.; *Alcoholics Anonymous*, 4th edition 2001.

American Psychological Association, Division 50; *The Addictions Newsletter, Special Issue: Spirituality in Addiction and Recovery*, 1998.

Atkins, Peter; *Creation Revisited*, 1994.

Austin, John; *How to Do Things with Words*, 1961.

Australian National Comorbidity Project; *Current practice in the management of clients with comorbid mental health and substance use disorders in tertiary care settings*, 2003.

Australian National Drug and Alcohol Research Centre; *The Treatment of Alcohol Problems – A Review of the Evidence*, 2003.

Ayer, Alfred; *Hume: A Very Short Introduction*; 2000.

B, Dick; *New Light on Alcoholism: God, Sam Shoemaker, and AA*, 1999.

Babor, Thomas *et al.*; *Alcohol: No Ordinary Commodity; Research and Public Policy*, 2003.

Barr, Stephen; *Modern Physics and Ancient Faith*, 2003.

Beck, Aaron; *Cognitive Therapy and the Emotional Disorders*, 1976.

Bishop, Charles; *To Be Continued: The Alcoholics Anonymous World Bibliography 1935-1994*, 1994.

Blackmore, Susan; *The Meme Machine*, 1999.

Boyer, Pascal; *Religion Explained*, 2001.

Brown, David; *A Biography of Mrs. Marty Mann: The First Lady of Alcoholics Anonymous*, 2005.

Bucke, Richard; *Cosmic Consciousness*, 1901.

Cahalan, Don; *Problem Drinkers: A National Survey*, 1970.

Caron Foundation; *Relapse & Recovery: Behavioral Strategies for Change*, 2003.

Carroll, Kathleen *et al.*; *Computer-Assisted Delivery of Cognitive-Behavioral Therapy for Addiction: A Randomised Trial of CBT4CBT*, American Journal of Psychiatry, May 2008.

Chamberlain, Linda and Butz, Michael; *Clinical Chaos: A Therapist's Guide to Nonlinear Dynamics and Therapeutic Change*, 1998.

Chambers, Francis; *Analysis and Comparison of Three Treatment Measures for Alcoholism*, British Journal of Addiction, 1953.

Chapman, P.L.H. and Huygens, I.; *An Evaluation of Three Treatment Programmes for Alcoholism*, British Journal of Addiction, 1988.

Clark, David and Davies, Sarah; *An Evaluation of the Structured Day Care (Community Rehabilitation) Programme of the Burton*

Addiction and O'Connor Centres, 2004.

Cloninger, Robert *et al.*; *Inheritance of Alcohol Abuse: Cross-fostering analysis of adopted men, Archives of General Psychiatry 38*, 1981.

Comte-Sponville, André; *A Short Treatise on the Great Virtues*, 2002.

Dalai Lama; *Ancient Wisdom, Modern World*, 1999.

Damasio, Antonio; *Descartes' Error, Emotion, Reason, and the Human Brain*, 1994.

Dawkins, Richard; *The Selfish Gene*, 1976, 1989.

Dawkins, Richard; *A Devil's Chaplain*, 2003.

Dawkins, Richard; *The God Delusion*, 2006.

de Botton, Alain; *Status Anxiety*, 2004.

Dennett, Daniel; *Darwin's Dangerous Idea*, 1995.

Dennett, Daniel; *Breaking the Spell*, 2006.

DuPont, Robert *et al.*; *Recent Research in Twelve Step Programs*, in *Principles of Addiction Medicine*, (ed. Norman Miller), 1994.

Edwards, Griffith; *Alcohol The Ambiguous Molecule*, 2000.

Elrath, Damian; *The Quiet Crusaders: The Untold Story Behind the Minnesota Model*, 2001.

European Association for the Treatment of Addiction (UK); *Rehab: What Works?*, 2004.

Finney, Charles; *Lectures on Revivals of Religion*, 1835.

Fiorentine, Robert and Hillhouse, Maureen; *Drug Treatment and 12-step Program Participation: The additive effects of Integrated Recovery Activities, Journal of Substance Abuse Treatment*, 2000.

Frank, Jerome; *Persuasion and Healing: A Comparative Study of Psychotherapy*, 1961.

Ganzevoort, R. Ruard; *Religious Coping Reconsidered, Journal of Psychology and Theology*, 1998.

Glatt, Max; *Jellinek Chart of Alcoholism and Recovery*, 1958.

Gold, Paul and Brady, Kathleen; *Evidence-Based Treatments for Substance Use Disorders*, 2003.

Gorski, Terence; *Understanding the Twelve Steps*, 1989.

Grant, Bridget *et al.*; *Prevalence and Co-occurrence of Substance Use Disorders and Independent Mood and Anxiety Disorders, Archives of General Psychiatry*, August 2004.

Grayling, Anthony; *Wittgenstein: A Very Short Introduction*, 2001.

Greene, Brian; *The Fabric of the Cosmos*, 2004.

Greene, Joshua *et al.*; *An fMRI Investigation of Emotional Engagement in Moral Judgement, Science*, 14 September 2001.

Greenfield, Susan; *The Private Life of the Brain*, 2001.

Greenfield, Susan; *i.d. The Quest for Identity in the 21st Century*, 2008.

Haldane, John; *Science and Theology as Art-Forms*, 1927.

Hasin, Deborah; *Classification of Alcohol Use Disorders*, 2003.

Hinde, Robert; *Why Gods Persist*, 1999.

Hinterkopf, Elfie; *Integrating Spirituality in Counselling: a Manual for Using the Experiential Method*, 1998.

Hoffman, Norman; *Assessment Is the Key, Addiction Today*, September/October 2002.

Hon, Jeffrey; *The Active Ingredients of Effective Treatment for Alcohol Problems*, 2003.

Hong, Howard and Hong, Edna; *The Essential Kierkegaard (Kierkegaard's Writings)*, 2000.

Hume, David; *An Enquiry Concerning Human Understanding*, 1748.

Humphries, Keith; *Circles of Recovery: Self-help Organisations for Addictions*, 2003.

Huss, Magnus; *Alcoholismus Chronicus*, 1849

Huxley, Aldous; *The Perennial Philosophy*, 1945.

Institute of Medicine, Washington; *Prevention and Treatment of Alcohol Problems: Opportunities for Research*, 1989.

James, William; *The Varieties of Religious Experience*, 1902.

James, William; *Pragmatism: And Other Writings, (Penguin Classics)*, 2000.

Jaspers, Karl; *Philosophy and Existence*, 1971.

Jellinek, Elvin; *The Disease Concept of Alcoholism*, 1960.

Jung, Karl; *Man and His Symbols*, 1964.

Kant, Immanuel; *Religion within the Limits of Reason Alone*, 1793.

Kant, Immanuel; *Critique of Practical Reason*, 1788.

Katz, Leonard (editor); *Evolutionary Origins of Morality, Cross-Disciplinary Perspectives*, 2000.

Kellermann, Joseph; *Alcoholism A Merry-go-round Named Denial*, *18th printing*, 1979.

Koenig, Harold; *Religion, Spirituality, and Medicine: Application to Clinical Practice, Journal of the American Medical Association*, 2000.

Kurtz, Ernest; *Not-God*, 1979, 1991.

Kurtz, Ernest and Ketcham, Katherine; *The Spirituality of Imperfection*, 1992.

Larson, DB, Sawyers, JP and McCullough, ME (editors); *Scientific Research on Spirituality and Health: A Consensus Report, Rockville, MD, United States National Institute for Healthcare Research*, 1998.

Lash, Steven; *Increasing Participation in Substance Abuse Aftercare Treatment, The American Journal of Drug and Alcohol Abuse*, 1998.

Laudet, Alexandra *et al.*; *Predictors of Retention in Dual-Focus Self-Help Groups, Community Mental Health Journal*, August 2003.

Lesch, Otto *et al.*; *Diagnosis of Chronic Alcoholism — Classificatory Problems. Psychopathology 23*, 1990.

Lesch, Otto *et al.*; *Subtypes of Alcoholism and Their Role in Therapy*, *Alcohol*, 1996.

Leshner, Alan; *Addiction Is a Brain Disease, and It Matters, Science*, 1997.

Lindström, Lars; *Managing Alcoholism*, 1992.

Linskey, Eunice; *Anonymously Yours*, 2003.

Longabaugh, Richard *et al.*; *Network Support for Drinking, Alcoholics Anonymous and Long-term Matching Effects. Addiction*, 1998.

Loper, Rodney *et al.*; *Minnesota Multiphasic Personality Inventories,*

Characteristics of College Freshman Males Who Later Became Alcoholics, Journal of Abnormal Psychology, 1973.

McGrath, Alister; Dawkins' God, 2005.

McGrath, Alister; The Dawkins Delusion?, 2007.

McLellan, David; Karl Marx: His Life and Thought, 1987.

McLellan, Thomas et al.; Supplemental Social Services Improve Outcomes in Public Addiction Treatment, Addiction, 1998.

McLellan, Thomas, et al.; Drug Dependence, A Chronic Medical Illness: Implications for Treatment, Insurance, and Outcome Evaluation, 2000.

Maxwell, Milton; The Washingtonian Movement, Quarterly Journal of Studies on Alcohol, Vol. 11, 1950.

Merton, Thomas; No Man Is an Island, 1955.

Mill, John Stuart; Principles of Political Economy, 1848.

Mill, John Stuart; Three Essays on Religion, 1874.

Miller, William et al.; Treating Addictive Behaviors: Processes of Change, 1998.

Miller, William et al.; The Community-Reinforcement Approach, 1999.

Meyers, Robert et al.; Community Reinforcement and Family Training (CRAFT): Engaging Unmotivated Drug Users in Treatment, Journal of Substance Abuse, 10(3), 1999.

Moos, Rudolf; Addictive Disorders in Context: Principles and Puzzles of Effective Treatment and Recovery, Psychology of Addictive Behaviors, Volume 17, number 1, 2003.

National Institute on Drug Abuse, The Science of Addiction, 2007.

Nace, Edgar; Alcoholics Anonymous, Substance Abuse; A Comprehensive Textbook, 1992.

Nelson, Candice; Natural Recovery from Alcohol Problems and its Implications on the Disease Model of Addiction and the DSM-IV Diagnostic Criteria for Alcohol Dependence, 2004.

Nietzsche, Friedrich; Beyond Good and Evil, 1886.

Nietzsche, Friedrich; Ecce Homo: How One Becomes What One Is, 1888.

Otto, Rudolf; *The Idea of the Holy*, 1923.

Paquette, Vincent; *"Change the Mind and You Change the Brain":
Effects of Cognitive-behavioral Therapy on the Neural Correlates
of Spider Phobia*, 2003.

Pargament, Kenneth; *The Psychology of Religion and Coping: Theory,
Research, Practice*, 1997.

Pargament, Kenneth *et al.*; *Religious Struggle as a Predictor of
Mortality among Medically Ill Elderly Patients, Archives of
Internal Medicine*, August 2001.

Pascal, Blaise; *Pensées*, 1670.

Perry, Bruce; *Childhood Experience and the Expression of Genetic
Potential: What Childhood Neglect Tells Us about Nature and
Nurture*, 2002.

Playfair, William; *The Useful Lie*, 1991.

Prochaska, James, Norcross, John and DiClemente, Carlo; *Changing
for Good*, 1994.

Room, Robin; *Alcoholics Anonymous as a Social Movement, Addiction
Research Foundation, Toronto*, 2003.

Room, Robin, Babor, Thomas and Rehm, Jürgen; *Alcohol and Public
Health, Lancet*, 5th February 2005.

Russell, Bernard; *Is There a God?*, 1952.

Ryan, Alan; *Philosophy of John Stuart Mill*, 1970.

Salter, Gemma, Davies, Sarah and Clark, David; *Recovery from
Addiction and the Role of Treatment Processes*, 2004.

Sargant, William; *Battle for the Mind*; 1957, 1997.

Schuckit, Marc *et al.*; *An analysis of the clinical relevance of type 1
and type 2 alcoholics. British Journal of Addiction*, 1989.

Schuckit, Marc; *A Clinical Model of Genetic Influences in Alcoholic
Dependence, American Journal of Psychiatry*, 1994.

Schuckit, Marc; *Science, Medicine and the Future: Substance Use
Disorders, British Medical Journal*, 1997.

Schuckit, Marc *et al.*; *Five-Year Clinical Course Associated with
DSM-IV Alcohol Abuse or Dependence in a Large Group of Men
and Women*, 2003.

Scottish Advisory Committees on Drug and Alcohol Misuse; *Report of the Joint Working Group; Meeting the Needs of People with Co-occurring Substance Misuse and Mental Health Problems, "mind the gaps"*, 2003.

Scruton, Roger; *Kant: A Very Short Introduction*, 2001.

Silkworth, William; *Slips, Do alcoholics suffer from "Alcoholic Behavior" or are they simply victims of human nature?*, AA *Grapevine*, January 1947.

Sloan, Richard and Bagiella, Emilia; *Claims about Religious Involvement and Health Outcomes, Annals of Behavioral Medicine*, March 2002.

Social Survey Division of the Office for National Statistics on behalf of the Department of Health, the Scottish Executive and the National Assembly for Wales; *Report; Psychiatric morbidity among adults living in private households*, 2000.

Stinchfield, Randy; *Hazelden's Model of Treatment and Its Outcome, Addictive Behaviors*, 1998.

Strecker, Edward and Chambers, Francis; *Alcohol: One Man's Meat*, 1938.

Storr, Anthony; *Freud: A Very Short Introduction*, 2001.

Tanner, Michael; *Nietzsche: A Very Short Introduction*, 2000.

Taylor, Andy *et al.*; *Alcohol problems and the family: Challenges and opportunities, Alcoholis*, 2002.

Tiebout, Harry; *The Act of Surrender in the Therapeutic Process*, 1949.

Tiebout, Harry; *Surrender versus Compliance in Therapy*, 1953.

Tiebout, Harry; *The Ego Factors in Surrender in Alcoholism*, 1954.

Trotter, Thomas; *An Essay, Medical, Philosophical, and Chemical, on Drunkenness, and its Effects on the Human Body*, 1804.

United Kingdom, Department of Health; *Dual Diagnosis Good Practice Guide*, 2002.

United Kingdom, Office of Science and Technology; *Report, Foresight: Drugs Future 2025?*, 2005.

United Kingdom Prime Minister's Strategy Unit; *Interim Analytical*

Report, 2003.

United Kingdom, Prime Minister's Strategy Unit; *Alcohol Harm Reduction Strategy for England*, 2004.

United States Congress, Office of Technology Assessment; *Components of Substance Abuse and Addiction*, 1993.

United States National Institute on Alcohol Abuse and Alcoholism; *National Epidemiologic Survey on Alcohol and Related Conditions*, 2001-2005.

Vaillant, George; *The Natural History of Alcoholism Revisited*, 1995.

Volkow, Nora and Fowler, Joanna; *Addiction, a Disease of Compulsion and Drive; Involvement of the Orbitofrontal Cortex*, 2000.

Volkow, Nora, Fowler, Joanna and Wang, Gene-Jack.; *The Addicted Human Brain: Insights from Imaging Studies*, 2003.

Wagner, Fernando and Anthony, James; *From First Drug Use to Drug Dependency: Development Periods of Risk for Dependence upon Marijuana, Cocaine and Alcohol*, 2002.

Walters, Nicholas; *Combating Social Exclusion Occasional Paper 3, University of Surrey*, 1999.

Wesley, John; *Journal*, 1735-1790.

White, William: *Slaying the Dragon*, 1998.

Wilson, David Sloan; *Darwin's Cathedral*, 2002.

Wilson, James; *The Moral Sense, American Political Science Review*, 1993.

Wilson, Bill; *Origin of the Twelve Steps*, 1953.

Wilson, Bill; *After Twenty-five Years*, 1960.

World Health Organization; *ICD-10, (The Tenth Revision of the International Statistical Classification of Mental and Behavioural Disorders)*, 2003.

World Health Organisation; *Report on Neuroscience of psychoactive substance use and dependence*, 2004.

www.alcoholconcern.org.uk.

www.alcohol-phaseivproject.co.uk.

www.alcoholics-anonymous.org.

www.alcoholism.about.com

www.americanatheist.org.
www.anaaddictions.co.uk.
www.ChildTrauma.org.
www.dailydose.net.
www.hazelden.org.
www.pm.gov.uk.
www.scotland.gov.uk.